Hungarians in exile

Reiner Dorati Szell

Discographies compiled
by John Hunt

CONTENTS

- 3   Acknowledgement
- 4   Introduction
- 7   Fritz Reiner discography
- 75   Antal Dorati discography
- 228   Antal Dorati: a postscript
- 231   George Szell discography
- 317   Credits

Hungarians in Exile
Published by John Hunt.
Designed by Richard Chluparty
© 1997 John Hunt
reprinted 2009
ISBN 9780952582-79-3

Published 1997 by John Hunt
Designed by Richard Chlupaty, London

Copyright 1997   John Hunt

Sole distributors:
Travis & Emery,
17 Cecil Court,
London, WC2N 4EZ,
United Kingdom.
(+44) 20 7 459 2129.
sales@travis-and-emery.com

ACKNOWLEDGEMENT

This publication has been made possible by contributions and advance subscriptions from the following

Richard Ames, New Barnet
Stefano Angeloni, Frasso Sabino
Yoshihiro Asada, Osaka
Jack Atkinson, Tasmania
Bruno Barthelmé, Le Creusot
E.C. Blake, York
J. Camps-Ros, Barcelona
J. Charrington, Cardiff
Eduardo Chibas, Caracas
Robert Christoforides, Fordingbridge
A. Copeman, Cambridge
F. De Vilder, Bussum
Richard Dennis, Greenhithe
John Derry, Newcastle-upon-Tyne
Hans-Peter Ebner, Milan
Bill Flowers, London
Henry Fogel, Chicago
T. Foley, Cork
Peter Fu, Hong Kong
Nobuo Fukumoto, Hamamatsu
Peter Fulop, Toronto
James Giles, Sidcup
Philip Goodman, London
Jean-Pierre Goossens, Luxembourg
Johann Gratz, Vienna
Peter Hammann, Bochum
Michael Harris, London
Tadashi Hasegawa, Nagoya
Naoya Hirabayashi, Tokyo
Martin Holland, Sale
John Hughes, Brisbane
Bodo Igesz, New York
Richard Igler, Vienna
Eugene Kaskey, New York
Shiro Kawai, Tokyo

Rodney Kempster, Basingstoke
Detlef Kissmann, Solingen
Eric Kobe, Lucerne
Elisabeth Legge-Schwarzkopf DBE, Zürich
John Mallinson, Hurst Green
Carlo Marinelli, Rome
Finn Moeller Larsen, Virum
Philip Moores, Stafford
Bruce Morrison, Gillingham
W. Moyle, Ombersley
Alan Newcombe, Hamburg
Hugh Palmer, Chelmsford
Jim Parsons, Sutton Coldfield
Laurence Pateman, London
James Pearson, Vienna
Tully Potter, Billericay
Peter Pugson, Buxton
Phil Rees, Pewsey
Patrick Russell, Calstock
Yves Saillard, Mollie-Margot
T. Scanes, Ashford
Neville Sumpter, Northolt
Yoshihiko Suzuki, Tokyo
H.A. Van Dijk, Apeldoorn
Mario Vicentini, Cassano Magnano
Hiromitsu Wada, Chiba
Urs Weber, St Gallen
G. Wright, Romford
Ken Wyman, Brentwood
Masakasu Abe, Chiba City
Helger Steinhauff, Stemwede
John Larsen, Mariager
Valery Ryvkin, New York

Hungarians in exile

Hungary's gift to the musical world, like that of several other Central European countries dominated this century by Fascism and Communism in turn, has been a brace of musical executants whose contribution to the classical music business cannot be overestimated.

The three eminent conductors whose recordings are the subject of this volume yielded to the power of the New World and its vast opportunities well before World War II, enriching and elevating some of America's most accomplished orchestras with their talent. Before this, Fritz Reiner, Antal Dorati and George Szell had served their apprenticeships in the great European centres as true Kapellmeisters of the old school (in Budapest - where apparently all three came under the tutorship, directly or indirectly, of masters like Bartok and Kodaly - as well as in Vienna, Berlin and Dresden). Szell and Dorati were fêted guests when they returned to work with European orchestras, whilst Reiner restricted his European activities more and more in favour of his ties to Chicago. All three can be broadly described as disciples of the Toscanini school, with that much-vaunted credo of fidelity to the musical score as uppermost in their philosophies.

Fritz Reiner's legacy to record collectors is the fruit of his commitment to RCA Victor and the Chicago Symphony Orchestra. In the space of a mere decade there emerged a series of epoch-making recordings. To quote a single fine example I would mention the RCA/BMG CD 09026 612502 with works by Ravel, Liszt, Weber/Berlioz and Rachmaninov - a faithful reflection both of Reiner's eclectic tastes and the undeniable skill of RCA's engineers in the 1950s in presenting a natural instrumental palette. If only Toscanini could have enjoyed such treatment! According to Reiner's biographer Philip Hart, earlier sessions which Reiner undertook with the Pittsburgh Symphony Orchestra in the 1940s were beset with technical difficulties. Now, some of this material is emerging in carefully transferred Sony CDs, revealing the skill of both maestro and orchestra in adapting to studio conditions.

An even more comprehensive survey of standard repertory was captured by Columbia and Epic engineers in the LP era with **George Szell** and his Cleveland Orchestra. On their visits to Europe this combination always struck me as the most European-sounding of the big American ensembles. However, mellowness was a quality which often eluded the engineers of the sessions in Severance Hall, a loss fully made up for when Szell recorded back in Europe (in Amsterdam's Concertgebouw and Vienna's Musikvereinssaal in particular). His finest recorded testimonials are, in my view, the group of recordings made in Amsterdam and conveniently grouped together in a Philips CD set (442 7272) and Decca's Vienna recording of the incidental music to Beethoven's Egmont (448 5932).

The compilation of **Antal Dorati**'s discography is the brainchild of my colleague Richard Chlupaty, and I would refer you immediately to his own postscript at the end of the Dorati discography. I would simply add the comment that, in the course of working on this, I realised for the first time what an important and all-embracing contribution Dorati has made to our record catalogues over a period of fifty full years!

The discographies are arranged chronologically by composer and are set out in three columns: first column gives place, month and year in which the recording took place; second column gives orchestra and participating soloists; third column contains the catalogue issue numbers (first issues, subsequent editions in the most important territories in the formats of 78, 45, LP and CD). I am always glad to hear from record collectors who can supply further catalogue numbers or any other information relating to recordings. Selected unpublished tapes, mainly from radio transmissions, are included in the hope that they might still be located and found worthy of publication.

I aim to avoid abbreviations whenever possible, but it is necessary in the case of certain orchestras, whose names recur with great frequency. For this volume they are:-

BPO	Berlin Philharmonic
CO	Cleveland Orchestra
LPO	London Philharmonic
LSO	London Symphony
NYPSO	New York Philharmonic
RPO	Royal Philharmonic
VPO	Vienna Philharmonic
VSO	Vienna Symphony

John Hunt 1997

Fritz Reiner
1888 -1963

Discography compiled
by John Hunt

ISAAC ALBENIZ (1860-1909)

Fête-Dieu à Séville, arranged by Arbos

Chicago April 1958	CSO	LP: Victor LM 2230/LSC 2230 LP: RCA VICS 1294/GL 42595 LP: Chesky RC 9 CD: RCA/BMG RD 85404

Navarra, arranged by Arbos

Chicago April 1958	CSO	LP: Victor LM 2230/LSC 2230 LP: RCA VICS 1294/GL 42595 LP: Chesky RC 9 CD: RCA/BMG RD 85404

Triana, arranged by Arbos

Chicago April 1958	CSO	LP: RCA LM 2230/LSC 2230 LP: RCA VICS 1294/GL 42595 LP: Chesky RC 9 CD: RCA/BMG RD 85404

JOHANN SEBASTIAN BACH (1685-1750)

Brandenburg Concerto No 1

New York October 1949	Chamber Ensemble	78: Columbia (USA) M 902 LP: Columbia (USA) ML 4281/RL 3104

Brandenburg Concerto No 2

New York December 1949	Chamber Ensemble	78: Columbia (USA) M 902 LP: Columbia (USA) ML 4281/RL 3104

Brandenburg Concerto No 3

New York October 1949	Chamber Ensemble	78: Columbia (USA) M 902 LP: Columbia (USA) ML 4282/RL 3105

Brandenburg Concerto No 4

New York October 1949	Chamber Ensemble	78: Columbia (USA) M 903 LP: Columbia (USA) ML 4282/RL 3105
Chicago November 1956	CSO	Televised performance issued on sound cassette only by Fritz Reiner Society

Brandenburg Concerto No 5

New York November 1949	Chamber Ensemble	78: Columbia (USA) M 903 LP: Columbia (USA) ML 4283/RL 3106

Brandenburg Concerto No 6

New York October 1949	Chamber Ensemble	78: Columbia (USA) M 903 LP: Columbia (USA) ML 4283/RL 3106

Fugue in G minor, arranged by Cailliet

Pittsburgh February 1946	Pittsburgh SO	78: Columbia (USA) M 695 78: Columbia (Switzerland) DZX 42
Chicago November 1957	CSO	Televised performance issued on sound cassette only by Fritz Reiner Society

Piano Concerto in F minor

Chicago	CSO	LP: Victor LM 2287/LSC 2287
February 1958	Tchaikovsky	LP: RCA DPM1-0444
		LM 2287/LSC 2287 not published

Prelude and Fugue in F flat, arranged by Stock

Chicago	CSO	Issued on cassette only by Fritz Reiner
October 1957		Society

Suite No 1

New York	Victor SO	LP: Victor LM 6012
October 1952		LP: HMV ALP 1382
		Excerpts
		LP: Victor LM 1877

Suite No 2

Pittsburgh	Pittsburgh SO	78: Columbia (USA) M 695
February 1946	Caratelli	LP: Columbia (USA) ML 4156
		CD: Dante LYS 126

New York	Victor SO	LP: Victor LM 6012
January 1953	Baker	LP: HMV ALP 1382

Suite No 3

New York	Victor SO	LP: Victor LM 6012
October 1952		LP: HMV ALP 1383
		Excerpts
		45: Victor ERA 215
		45: HMV 7ER 5025
		LP: Victor LM 1877

Suite No 4

New York	Victor SO	LP: Victor LM 6012
October 1952		LP: HMV ALP 1383
		Excerpts
		LP: Victor LM 1877

BELA BARTOK (1881-1945)

Concerto for orchestra

Pittsburgh February 1946	Pittsburgh SO	78: Columbia (USA) M 793 LP: Columbia (USA) ML 4102/P 14143 CD: Dante LYS 093
Chicago October 1955	CSO	LP: Victor LM 1934/LSC 1934 LP: RCA VICS 1110/VICS 2005 CD: RCA/BMG RC 56042/GD 60175/ 09026 615042

Piano Concerto No 1

New York March 1960	NYPSO Serkin	CD: As-Disc AS 526 CD: Arlecchino ARL 198 <u>Also issued on cassette by Fritz Reiner Society</u>

Piano Concerto No 3

Chicago March 1958	CSO Anda	Issued on cassette by Fritz Reiner Society

Divertimento for strings

Chicago February 1957	CSO	Televised performance issued on sound cassette only by Fritz Reiner Society

Hungarian Sketches

Pittsburgh April 1947	Pittsburgh SO	CD: Sony MHK 62343
Chicago December 1958	CSO	LP: Victor LM 2374/LSC 2374/VICS 1160 CD: RCA/BMG GD 60206/09026 615042/ 74321 179072

Miraculous Mandarin, suite

New York December 1946	NBC SO	Issued on cassette by Fritz Reiner Society
New York March 1960	NYPSO	CD: As-Disc AS 526 CD: Arlecchino ARL 198

Music for strings, percussion and celesta

Chicago December 1958	CSO	LP: Victor LM 2374/LSC 2374/VICS 1160 CD: RCA/BMG RC 56042/GD 60175/ 09026 615042

Rumanian Dances, arranged by Weiner

New York January 1952	NBC SO	CD: Music and Arts CD 292

LUDWIG VAN BEETHOVEN (1770-1827)

Symphony No 1

New York 1925-1926	Singer and Reichmann, pianos	Welte piano rolls C 7595-7598 <u>Reiner acted as conductor for this</u> <u>performance by two pianists</u>
Chicago May 1961	CSO	LP: Victor LM 6096/LSC 6096 LP: RCA RB 6500/SB 6500 CD: RCA/BMG GD 60002

Symphony No 2

Pittsburgh March 1945	Pittsburgh SO	78: Columbia (USA) M 597 LP: Columbia (USA) ML 4085/P 14139 CD: Sony MHK 62344 CD: Dante LYS 126

Symphony No 3 "Eroica"

Chicago December 1954	CSO	LP: Victor LM 1899 LP: RCA RB 16001 LP: Melodiya D028559-028560 CD: RCA/BMG 09026 609622

Symphony No 4

Chicago April 1958	CSO	LP: Chicago Symphony Orchestra 88 CD: Chicago Symphony Orchestra CD 88 CD: Arlecchino ARL 44

Symphony No 5

New York 1925-1926	Singer and Reichmann, pianos	Welte piano rolls 7527-7530 <u>Reiner acted as conductor for this</u> <u>performance by two pianists</u>
Chicago May 1959	CSO	LP: Victor LM 2343/LSC 2343 LP: RCA VICS 1161/CCV 5023 CD: RCA/BMG RD 85403

Symphony No 6 "Pastoral"

New York 1925-1926	Singer and Reichmann, pianos	Unpublished Welte piano rolls <u>Reiner acted as conductor for this</u> <u>performance by two pianists</u>
Chicago April 1961	CSO	LP: Victor LM 2614/LSC 2614 LP: RCA RB 6510/SB 6510/VICS 1449 CD: RCA/BMG GD 60002

Symphony No 7

Chicago October 1955	CSO	LP: Victor LM 1991/LSC 1991 LP: RCA SB 2010/VICS 1523 CD: RCA/BMG RC 56376
Chicago 1961	CSO	VHS Video: Teldec 4509 950386 Laserdisc: Teldec 4509 950383 <u>First movement only</u>

Symphony No 8

Chicago February 1958	CSO	Issued on casssette by Fritz Reiner Society

Symphony No 9 "Choral"

Chicago May 1961	CSO CSO Chorus Curtin, Kopleff, McCollum, Gramm	LP: Victor LM 6096/LSC 6096/LSC 3316 LP: RCA RB 6500-6501/SB 6500-6501 CD: RCA/BMG GD 86532/09026 617952

Piano Concerto No 4

Chicago April 1963	CSO Cliburn	LP: Victor LM 2680/LSC 2680 LP: RCA RB 6548/SB 6548 CD: RCA GD 87943

Piano Concerto No 5 "Emperor"

New York April 1952	Victor SO Horowitz	45: Victor WDM 1718 LP: Victor LM 1718 LP: HMV ALP 1280 LP: HMV (France) FALP 240 LP: RCA RB 16114/VH 009/VH 400 CD: RCA/BMG GD 87992
Chicago May 1961	CSO Cliburn	LP: Victor LM 2562/LSC 2562 LP: RCA RB 16262/SB 2133 CD: RCA/BMG GD 87943/09026 619612

Coriolan Overture

Chicago May 1959	CSO	LP: Victor LM 2343/LSC 2343 LP: RCA VICS 1161/CCV 5023 CD: RCA/BMG RD 85403/VD 60534/VD 60652/ 09026 609622

Fidelio Overture

Chicago December 1955	CSO	LP: Victor LM 1991/LSC 1991 LP: RCA SB 2010/VICS 1523 CD: RCA/BMG RD 85403/09026 609622

Fidelio, excerpt (Abscheulicher, wo eilst du hin?)

Detroit January 1938	Detroit SO Rethberg	LP: Ed Smith EJS 255/EJS 425

Ah perfido!, concert aria

1937	Orchestra Rethberg	LP: Operatic Archives OPA 1051-1052

HECTOR BERLIOZ (1803-1869)

Benvenuto Cellini overture

Chicago December 1957	CSO	LP: Chicago Symphony Orchestra 86 CD: Arlecchino ARL 45

Le carnaval romain, overture

New York February 1945	CBS SO	Issued on cassette by Fritz Reiner Society
Chicago December 1957	CSO	LP: Chicago Symphony Orchestra 88 CD: Chicago Symphony Orchestra CD 88 CD: Arlecchino ARL 45

Marche hongroise (La damnation de Faust)

Pittsburgh May 1941	Pittsburgh SO	78: Columbia (USA) M 491/M 585 78: Columbia (Australia) LOX 526

Les nuits d'été

Chicago March 1963	CSO L.Price	LP: Victor LM 2695/LSC 2695 LP: RCA RB 6566/SB 6566 CD: RCA/BMG 09026 612342/ 09026 681532

GEORGES BIZET (1838-1875)

Carmen

New York March- June 1951	Victor SO Shaw Chorale Stevens, Albanese, Peerce, Merrill	45: Victor WDM 1556 LP: Victor LM 6102 LP: HMV ALP 1115-1117 LP: RCA VL 00670 CD: RCA/BMG GD 87981 <u>Excerpts</u> 45: Victor ERB 7011 45: HMV 7ER 5020 LP: Victor LRM 7011 LP: HMV ALP 1416 CD: Metropolitan Opera CD 114 CD: Di Stefano GDS 2203 <u>Ballet music included in this performance contains items from La jolie fille de Perth and L'Arlésienne</u>
New York February 1952	Metropolitan Opera Orchestra & Chorus Stevens, Conner, Tucker, Silveri	Unpublished Met broadcast
New York December 1952	Metropolitan Opera Orchestra & Chorus Stevens, Conner, Tucker, Merrill	Unpublished video recording
New York January 1953	Metropolitan Opera Orchestra & Chorus Barbieri, Güden, Del Monaco, Guarrera	Unpublished Met broadcast

ALEXANDER BORODIN (1833-1887)

Polovtsian March (Prince Igor)

Chicago March 1959	CSO	LP: Victor LM 2423/LSC 2423 LP: RCA VIC 1068/VICS 1652 CD: RCA/BMG RC 56022/09026 619582

JOHANNES BRAHMS (1833-1897)

Symphony No 2

New York March 1960	NYPSO	CD: Arlecchino ARL 131 <u>Also issued on cassette by Fritz Reiner Society</u>

Symphony No 3

Chicago December 1957	CSO	LP: Victor LM 2209/LSC 2209 LP: RCA RB 16080/SB 2007/VICS 1117 CD: RCA/BMG 09026 617932

Symphony No 4

Walthamstow October 1962	RPO	LP: Reader's Digest RD 15-4 LP: RCA AGL1-1961 LP: Quintessence PMC 7182 LP: Chesky CR 6 CD: Chesky CD 6

Piano Concerto No 1

Pittsburgh February 1946	Pittsburgh SO Serkin	78: Columbia (USA) M 652 78: Columbia (Canada) D 178 78: Columbia LX 1162-1167/LX8655-8660 auto LP: Columbia (USA) ML 4100 CD: Dante LYS 127
Chicago April 1954	CSO Rubinstein	45: Victor ERD 1831 LP: Victor LM 1831 LP: HMV ALP 1297 LP: RCA GL 12044 /ARL1-2044/RL 12044 CD: RCA/BMG RD 85668/09026 612632

Piano Concerto No 2

Chicago February 1958	CSO Gilels	LP: Victor LM 2219/LSC 2219/CCV 5042 LP: RCA RB 16142/SB 2032/VICS 1026 LP: Melodiya D015333-015334/ S0517-0518 CD: RCA/BMG RD 85406/VD 60536/VD 60654
Chicago May 1961	CSO Cliburn	LP: Victor LM 2581/LSC 2581 LP: RCA RB 6554/SB 6554 CD: RCA/BMG GD 87942

English Columbia catalogues list a version of the concerto on LX 1276-1281/ LX 8713-8718 with Serkin and Pittsburgh SO/Reiner, but this in fact the American Columbia performance conducted by Ormandy

Violin Concerto

Chicago February 1955	CSO Heifetz	LP: Victor LM 1903/LSC 1903 LP: HMV ALP 1334 LP: RCA RB 16117 CD: RCA/BMG GD 85402/90926 614952/ 09026 617782/09026 617422

Double Concerto

Philadelphia June 1951	Philadelphia Orchestra Milstein, Piatigorsky	45: Victor WDM 1609 LP: Victor LM 1191 LP: HMV (France) FALP 171 CD: RCA/BMG 09026 614852 Orchestra named on this recording as Robin Hood Dell Orchestra

Academic Festival Orchestra

New York November 1937	Curtis SO	LP: Desmar IPA 5001-5002 CD: VAI Audio VAIA 1020

Tragic Overture

Chicago December 1957	CSO	LP: Victor LM 2209/LSC 2209 LP: RCA RB 16080/SB 2059 CD: RCA/BMG RD 85406

Alto Rhapsody

New York October 1950	Victor SO Shaw Chorale Anderson	45: Victor WDM 1532 LP: Victor LM 1146 LP: HMV ALP 1138

Haydn Variations

Chicago December 1953	CSO	Televised performance issued on sound cassette only by Fritz Reiner Society

Hungarian Dances: No 1 in G minor, No 5 in G minor, No 6 in D, No 7 in A, No 12 in D minor, No 13 in D, No 19 in B minor and No 21 in E minor

Pittsburgh February 1946	Pittsburgh SO	78: Columbia (USA) X 309 LP: Columbia (USA) ML 4116 CD: Arlecchino ARL 131/Dante LYS 127
Vienna June 1960	VPO	LP: Decca LXT 5609/SXL 2249/VIV 18 LP: RCA CM 9267/CS 6198 CD: Decca 417 6962/448 5682

AARON COPLAND (1900-1990)

Clarinet Concerto

New York June 1951	NBC SO Goodman	CD: As-Disc AS 628 CD: Legend LGD 122

The Tender Land, suite

Chicago April 1958	CSO	CD: Chicago Symphony Orchestra CD 90

CLAUDE DEBUSSY (1862-1918)

La mer

Chicago February 1960	CSO	LP: Victor LM 2462/LSC 2462 LP: RCA RB 16257/SB 2128 CD: RCA/BMG RD 87018/GD 60875/ 09026 680792

Ibéria (Images)

Pittsburgh November 1941	Pittsburgh SO	78: Columbia (USA) M 491 78: Columbia (Australia) LOX 524-526 LP: Columbia (USA) ML 4021 CD: Dante LYS 83
Chicago March 1957	CSO	LP: Victor LM 2222/LSC 2222 LP: RCA SB 2044/VICS 1025/VICS 1199 CD: RCA/BMG RD 85720/GD 60179

Danse, arranged by Ravel

Pittsburgh April 1947	Pittsburgh SO	78: Columbia (USA) X 296

Nuages et fêtes (Nocturnes)

New York November 1938	NYPSO	78: World's Greatest Music SR 19 CD: Pearl GEMMCDS 9922 CD: Dante LYS 83
Chicago March 1957	CSO	Televised performance issued on sound cassette only by Fritz Reiner Society

Petite suite, arranged by Büsser

New York January 1952 (19 January)	NBC SO	CD: Music and Arts CD 292
New York January 1952 (21 January)	NBC SO	45: Victor WDM 1724 LP: Victor LM 1724

Prélude à l'après-midi d'un faune

New York November 1938	NYPSO	78: World's Greatest Music SR 19 CD: Dante LYS 83

LEO DELIBES (1836-1891)

Lakmé, excerpt (Sous le dôme épais)

Detroit April 1941	Detroit SO Jepson	LP: Ed Smith EJS 445 <u>Second singer in this duet unidentified</u>

FREDERICK DELIUS (1862-1934)

Irmelin Prelude

Chicago February 1954	CSO	Televised performance issued on sound cassette only by Fritz Reiner Society

GARDENIA DENSMORE

Spring Fancy

Detroit January 1938	Detroit SO Rethberg	LP: Ed Smith EJS 425

GAETONO DONIZETTI (1797-1848)

L'elisir d'amore, excerpt (Una furtiva lagrima)

Date not confirmed	Orchestra Crooks	LP: Ed Smith EJS 488 <u>As this is a compilation LP with various conductors, it is not fully certain that Reiner is the conductor</u>

ANTONIN DVORAK (1841-1904)

Symphony No 9 "From the New World"

New York 1925-1926	Singer and Robinson, pianos	Welte piano rolls 7864/7867/7871/7875 <u>Reiner acted as conductor for this performance by two pianists</u>
Chicago November 1957	CSO	LP: Victor LM 2214/LSC 2214 LP: RCA SB 2031 CD: RCA/BMG RC 56062/09026 625872

Slavonic Dances: No 1 in C, No 3 in A flat, No 8 in G minor, No 9 in B major and No 10 in E minor

Vienna June 1960	VPO	LP: Decca LXT 5609/SXL 2249/VIV 18 LP: RCA CM 9267/CS 6198 CD: Decca 417 6962/448 5682

Carnival Overture

Chicago January 1956	CSO	LP: Victor LM 1999 LP: RCA VICS 1424/VICS 1531 CD: RCA/BMG RC 56062/VD 60537/ VD 60655/09026 625872

MANUEL DE FALLA (1876-1946)

El amor brujo

Pittsburgh February 1946	Pittsburgh SO Brice	78: Columbia (USA) M 633 LP: Columbia (USA) ML 2006 CD: Dante LYS 148
Chicago March 1963	CSO L.Price	LP: Victor LM 2695/LSC 2695 LP: RCA RB 6566/SB 6566 CD: RCA/BMG RD 85404/09026 625862

El sombrero de 3 picos, 3 Dances

Chicago April 1958	CSO	LP: Victor LM 2230/LSC 2230 LP: RCA VICS 1294/GL 42595 LP: Chesky RC 9 CD: RCA/BMG RD 85404

La vida breve, Interlude and Dance

Chicago April 1958	CSO	LP: Victor LM 2230/LSC 2230 LP: RCA VICS 1294/GL 42595 LP: Chesky RC 9 CD: RCA/BMG RD 85404

CESAR FRANCK (1822-1890)

Symphony in D minor

New York 1925-1926	Singer and Reiner, pianos	Welte piano rolls 7708-7711

GEORGE GERSHWIN (1898-1937)

Symphonic Portrait of Porgy and Bess, arranged by Bennett

Pittsburgh March 1945	Pittsburgh SO	78: Columbia (USA) M 572 LP: Columbia (USA) ML 2019

MIKHAIL GLINKA (1804-1857)

Kamarinskaya

Pittsburgh February 1946	Pittsburgh SO	78: Columbia (USA) 12715D CD: Sony awaiting publication

Ruslan and Ludmila, Overture

Chicago March 1959	CSO	LP: Victor LM 2423/LSC 2423 LP: RCA RB 6543/SB 6543/VIC 1068 CD: RCA/BMG RC 56052/GD 60176/ 09026 619582/74321 212902

CHRISTOPH WILLIBALD GLUCK (1714-1787)

Orfeo ed Euridice, Minuet and Dance of the Blessed Spirits

New York June 1953	Victor SO	45: Victor ERA 215 45: HMV 7ER 5025 LP: Victor LM 2141

Orfeo ed Euridice, excerpt (Che farò senza Euridice?)

New York March 1951	Victor SO Stevens	45: Victor ERA 138/WDM 9010 LP: Victor LM 9010

Orfeo ed Euridice, excerpt (Che puro ciel!)

New York March 1951	Victor SO Stevens	45: Victor WDM 9010 LP: Victor LM 9010

CHARLES GOUNOD (1818-1893)

Faust, excerpt (Avant de quitter ces lieux)

Detroit December 1938	Detroit SO Bonelli	LP: Ed Smith EJS 445

ENRIQUE GRANADOS (1867-1916)

Goyescas, Intermezzo

Chicago April 1958	CSO	LP: Victor LM 2230/LSC 2230 LP: Chesky RC 9 CD: RCA/BMG RD 85404

FRANZ JOSEF HAYDN (1732-1809)

Symphony No 88

Chicago February 1960	CSO	LP: Victor LM 6087/LSC 6087 LP: RCA VICS 1366 CD: RCA/BMG 09026 607292

Symphony No 94 "Surprise"

New York 1925-1926	Singer and Reichmann, pianos	Welte piano rolls 7545-7548 <u>Reiner acted as conductor for this performance by two pianists</u>

Symphony No 95

New York September 1963	His SO	LP: Victor LM 2742/LSC 2742 LP: RCA RB 6548/SB 6548/VICS 2007 CD: RCA/BMG 09026 607292 <u>Reiner's final recording sessions</u>

Symphony No 101 "Clock"

New York September 1963	His SO	LP: Victor LM 2742/LSC 2742/VICS 2007 LP: RCA RB 6548/SB 6548/GL 42292 CD: RCA/BMG 09026 607292 <u>Reiner's final recording sessions; GL 42292 (an Italian issue) incorrectly names orchestra as Royal Philharmonic</u>

Symphony No 104 "London"

Chicago November 1957	CSO	LP: Chicago Symphony Orchestra 88 CD: Chicago Symphony Orchestra CD 88 CD: Arlecchino ARL 44

PAUL HINDEMITH (1895-1963)

Cello Concerto

Chicago	CSO	LP: Chicago Symphony Orchestra 88
December 1957	Starker	CD: Chicago Symphony Orchestra CD 88

JOSEF HOFMANN (1876-1957)

Chromaticon for piano and orchestra

New York	Curtis SO	LP: Desmar IPA 5001-5002
November 1937	Hofmann	CD: VAI Audio VAIA 1020

ARTHUR HONEGGER (1892-1955)

Concertino for piano and orchestra

New York	Columbia SO	LP: Columbia (USA) ML 2156
July 1949	Levant	

ALAN HOVHANESS (Born 1911)

Symphony No 2 "Mysterious Mountain"

Chicago	CSO	LP: Victor LM 2251/LSC 2251
April 1958		LP: RCA VICS 1295
		CD: RCA/BMG RC 55733/09026 619572

ENGELBERT HUMPERDINCK (1854-1921)

Dream Pantomime (Hänsel und Gretel)

New York	Victor SO	45: Victor 49-3442
October 1950		CD: RCA/BMG 09026 617922

DMITRY KABALEVSKY (1904-1987)

Colas Breugnon, overture

Pittsburgh March 1945	Pittsburgh SO	78: Columbia (USA) M 585 78: Columbia LX 1002/LX 8563 CD: Sony MHK 62343
Chicago March 1959	CSO	LP: Victor LM 2423/LSC 2423 LP: RCA VIC 1068 CD: RCA/BMG RC 56022/09026 619582

ZOLTAN KODALY (1882-1967)

Dances from Galanta

Pittsburgh March 1945	Pittsburgh SO	CD: Sony MHK 62343
Chicago February 1954	CSO	CD: Chicago Symphony Orchestra CD 90

Peacock Variations

New York March 1960	NYPSO	CD: As-Disc AS 526 CD: Arlecchino ARL 198 Also issued on cassette by Fritz Reiner Society

ROLF LIEBERMANN (Born 1910)

Concerto for jazzband and orchestra

Chicago December 1954	CSO	45: Victor ERB 56 LP: Victor LM 1888

FRANZ LISZT (1811-1886)

Mephisto Waltz

Chicago December 1955	CSO	45: Victor SEP 13 LP: Victor LM 1999 LP: RCA SB 2059/VIC 1205/VICS 1205 CD: RCA/BMG 09026 612462

Totentanz for piano and orchestra

New York March 1951	Victor SO	45: Victor WDM 1615 LP: Victor LM 1615 LP: HMV (France) FALP 172
Chicago February 1959	CSO	LP: Victor LM 2127/LSC 2127 LP: RCA VIC 1205/VICS 1205 CD: RCA/BMG 09026 612502

GUSTAV MAHLER (1860-1911)

Symphony No 4

Chicago December 1958	CSO Della Casa	LP: Victor LM 2364/LSC 2364 LP: RCA RB 16205/SB 2081 CD: RCA/BMG RD 85248/74321 212862

Das Lied von der Erde

Chicago November 1959	CSO Forrester, Lewis	LP: Victor LM 6087/LSC 6087 CD: RCA/BMG RC 52482/GD 60178

Lieder eines fahrenden Gesellen

Pittsburgh February 1946	Pittsburgh SO Brice	78: Columbia (USA) X 267 LP: Columbia (USA) ML 4108 CD: Dante LYS 148

FELIX MENDELSSOHN-BARTHOLDY (1809-1947)

Symphony No 4 "Italian"

Chicago February 1954	CSO	Televised performance issued on sound cassette only by Fritz Reiner Society

Hebrides Overture

Chicago January 1956	CSO	LP: Victor LM 2071 LP: RCA SB 2059/VICS 1531 CD: RCA/BMG 09026 617932

A Midsummer Night's Dream: Overture, Scherzo, Intermezzo, Nocturne and Wedding March

Philadelphia June 1951	Philadelphia Orchestra	45: Victor WDM 1724/WEPR 38 LP: Victor LM 41/LM 1724 <u>WEPR 38 omits Wedding March; orchestra named on this recording as Robin Hood Dell Orchestra</u>

WOLFGANG AMADEUS MOZART (1756-1791)

Symphony No 31 "Paris"

Chicago April 1961	CSO	CD: Chicago Symphony Orchestra CD 91 <u>Televised performance</u>

Symphony No 35 "Haffner"

Pittsburgh February 1946	Pittsburgh SO	78: Columbia (USA) M 836 LP: Columbia (USA) ML 4156 CD: Sony MHK 62344

Symphony No 36 "Linz"

Chicago April 1954	CSO	LP: Victor LM 6035 LP: HMV ALP 1403

Symphony No 39

Chicago April 1954	CSO	LP: Victor LM 6035 LP: HMV ALP 1403 CD: RCA/BMG 09026 625582

Symphony No 40

New York 1925-1926	Singer and Reichmann, pianos	Unpublished Welte piano rolls <u>Reiner acted as conductor for this</u> <u>performance by two pianists</u>
Pittsburgh April 1947	Pittsburgh SO	78: Columbia (USA) M 727 LP: Columbia (USA) ML 2008 CD: Sony MHK 62344
Chicago April 1954	CSO	LP: Victor LM 6035 LP: HMV ALP 1330 CD: RCA/BMG 09026 625582

Symphony No 41 "Jupiter"

New York 1925-1926	Reiner and Singer, pianos	Unpublished Welte piano rolls
Chicago April 1954	CSO	LP: Victor LM 6035 LP: HMV ALP 1330 LP: RCA VICS 1366 CD: RCA/BMG RC 56376

Piano Concerto No 25

Chicago February 1958	CSO Tchaikovsky	LP: Victor LM 2287/LSC 2287 LP: RCA VIC 1167/VICS 1167

Bassoon Concerto

Chicago November 1956	CSO Sharrow	Televised performance issued on sound cassette only by Fritz Reiner Society

Divertimento No 11 K251

New York September 1954	NBC SO	LP: Victor LM 1952

Divertimento No 17 K334

Chicago April 1955	CSO	LP: Victor LM 1966

Serenade No 9 "Posthorn"

Chicago November 1956	CSO	Televised performance issued on sound cassette only by Fritz Reiner Society

Serenade No 13 "Eine kleine Nachtmusik"

Chicago December 1954	CSO	LP: Victor LM 1966 CD: RCA/BMG 09026 625582

Ein musikalischer Spass

New York September 1954	NBC SO	LP: Victor LM 1952

Don Giovanni

New York January 1951	Metropolitan Opera Orchestra & Chorus Resnik, Welitsch, Connor, Conley, Silveri, Alvary, Moscona	CD: Arlecchino ARLA 75-76 Excerpts LP: MRF Records MRF 1 LP: Melodram MEL 096 CD: Melodram MEL 27042
New York December 1952	Metropolitan Opera Zadel, Rigal, Munsel, Peerce, Siepi, Kunz, Alvary, Ernster	Unpublished Met broadcast

Don Giovanni, overture

Chicago March 1959	CSO	LP: Victor LM 2287/LSC 2287 LP: RCA VIC 1167/VICS 1167 CD: RCA/BMG RC 56521/VD 60484/VD 60610/ VD 60640/VD 60670

Don Giovanni, excerpt (Mi tradì)

San Francisco October 1938	San Francisco SO Rethberg	LP: Ed Smith UORC 105

Don Giovanni, excerpt (Or sai chi l'onore)

New York February 1950	Metropolitan Opera Orchestra Welitsch, De Paolis	78: Columbia (USA) X 340 78: Columbia LB 124 78: Columbia (Germany) LW 61 45: Philips ABE 10074 LP: Columbia (USA) ML 2118/3216 0077 LP: CBS 61088 CD: Polyhymnia 21212 CD: Myto MCD 954135

Don Giovanni, excerpt (Non mi dir)

New York	Metropolitan	78: Columbia (USA) X 340
February 1950	Opera Orchestra	78: Columbia LB 121
	Welitsch	78: Columbia (Germany) LW 57
		45: Philips ABE 10074
		LP: Columbia (USA) ML 2118/3216 0077
		LP: Philips SBR 6255
		LP: CBS 61088
		CD: Myto MCD 954135

Le nozze di Figaro

New York	Metropolitan Opera	LP: Robin Hood RHR 514
March 1952	Orchestra & Chorus	CD: As-Disc AS 1108-1109
	De los Angeles,	CD: Legend LGD 117-118
	Conner, Miller,	CD: Arlecchino ARLA 68-70
	Siepi, Valdengo	

Le nozze di Figaro, overture

Chicago	CSO	Issued on cassette only by Fritz Reiner
March 1963		Society

Le nozze di Figaro, excerpt (Non so più)

New York	Victor SO	45: Victor WDM 9010
March 1951	Stevens	LP: Victor LM 9010

Le nozze di Figaro, excerpt (Voi che sapete)

New York	Victor SO	45: Victor WDM 9010
March 1951	Stevens	LP: Victor LM 9010
		CD: Metropolitan Opera MET 114

MODEST MUSSORGSKY (1839-1881)

Night on Bare Mountain, arranged by Rimsky-Korsakov

Pittsburgh March 1945	Pittsburgh SO	78: Columbia (USA) 12407D
Chicago March 1959	Chicago SO	LP: Victor LM 2423/LSC 2423 LP: RCA VIC 1068 CD: RCA/BMG RC 56022/09026 619582

Pictures from an exhibition, arranged by Ravel

Chicago December 1959	CSO	LP: Victor LM 2201/LSC 2201 LP: RCA RB 16072/SB 2001 CD: RCA/BMG RD 85407/09026 614012/ 09026 619582

Boris Godunov, excerpts (Monologue, Hallucination and Farewell)

New York July 1944	NYPSO Kipnis	LP: Discocorp RR 210 CD: As-Disc AS 628 CD: Legend LGD 122 CD: Music and Arts CD 867

SERGEI PROKOFIEV (1891-1953)

Symphony No 5

Chicago April 1958	CSO	CD: Chicago Symphony Orchestra CD 90 <u>Also issued on cassette by Fritz Reiner</u> <u>Society</u>

Alexander Nevsky

Chicago March 1959	CSO CSO Chorus Elias	LP: Victor LM 2395/LSC 2395 LP: RCA RB 6530/SB 6530/VICS 1652/ GL 11966 CD: RCA/BMG RC 56052/GD 60176

Lieutenant Kije, suite

Chicago March 1957	CSO	LP: Victor LM 2150/LSC 2150 LP: RCA VIC 1290/VICS 1290 LP: Chesky RC 10 CD: RCA/BMG RC 56052/GD 60176/ 09026 619572

Peter and the Wolf

New York June 1949	NBC SO Melchior	Victor unpublished <u>May have circulated on Legato cassette</u> <u>ALD 1818</u>

SERGEI RACHMANINOV (1873-1943)

Piano Concerto No 1

Chicago March 1957	CSO Janis	LP: Victor LM 2127/LSC 2127 LP: RCA VIC 1101

Piano Concerto No 2

Chicago
January 1956
	CSO
	Rubinstein
		LP: Victor LM 6039/LM 2068/LSC 2068
		LP: HMV ALP 1413
		LP: RCA RB 16088/SB 2043/SB 2139/
		    VCS 7070/DPS 2014/AGL1-5212/
		    CRL7-0725
		CD: RCA/BMG RD 84934

Chicago March- April 1962	CSO Cliburn	LP: Victor LM 2601/LSC 2601 LP: RCA RB 6502/SB 6502 CD: RCA/BMG RD 85912/09026 619612/ 07863 559122

Piano Concerto No 3

New York June 1951	Victor SO Horowitz	45: Victor WDM 1575 LP: Victor LM 1178 LP: HMV ALP 1017 LP: HMV (France) FALP 180 LP: Electrola WALP 1017 LP: RCA VH 004/VH 400 CD: RCA/BMG GD 87754

Rhapsody on a theme of Paganini

Philadelphia June 1951	Philadelphia Orchestra Kapell	45: Victor WDM 1576 LP: Victor LM 126/LM 9026 <u>Excerpt</u> 78: Victor 10-4210 78: HMV DA 2057 45: Victor 49-4210

Chicago
January 1956
	CSO
	Rubinstein
		LP: Victor LM 2087/LM 2430/LM 6039/
		    LSC 2087/LSC 2430/LSC 3338/
		    LSC 6039
		LP: HMV ALP 1414
		LP: RCA RB 16141/RB 16276/SB 2144/
		    AGL1-5205/ARL1-4409/CRL7-0725
		CD: RCA/BMG RD 84934

Isle of the Dead

Chicago April 1957	CSO	LP: Victor LM 2183/LSC 2183 LP: RCA SB 2042/VIC 1205/VICS 1205 LP: Chesky RC 11 CD: RCA/BMG 09026 612502

MAURICE RAVEL (1875-1937)

Alborada del gracioso

Chicago April 1957	CSO	LP: Victor LM 2222/LSC 2222 LP: RCA SB 2044/VICS 1025/VICS 1199 CD: RCA/BMG RC 55720/GD 60179

Daphnis et Chloé, 2nd suite

New York September 1945	NBC SO	Issued on cassette by Fritz Reiner Society

Pavane pour une infante défunte

Chicago
March 1957
	CSO	LP: Victor LM 2183/LM 2222/LSC 2183/
		    LSC 2222
		LP: RCA SB 2042/VICS 1199
		LP: Chesky RC 11
		CD: RCA/BMG RC 55720/GD 60179/
		    09026 612502

Rapsodie espagnole

Chicago November 1956	CSO	LP: Victor LM 2183/LSC 2183 LP: RCA SB 2042 LP: Chesky RC 11 CD: RCA/BMG RC 55720/GD 60179/ 09026 612502

Le tombeau de Couperin

New York January 1952 (19 January)	NBC SO	CD: Music and Arts CD 292
New York January 1952 (21 January)	NBC SO	45: Victor WDM 1724 LP: Victor LM 1724

La valse

Pittsburgh April 1947	Pittsburgh SO	78: Columbia (USA) X 296 LP: Columbia (USA) ML 4021
Chicago March 1960	CSO	CD: Chicago Symphony Orchestra CD 90 Also issued on cassette by Fritz Reiner Society

Valses nobles et sentimentales

Chicago April 1957	CSO	LP: Victor LM 2222/LSC 2222 LP: RCA SB 2044/VICS 1025/VICS 1199 CD: RCA/BMG RC 55720/GD 60179

OTTORINO RESPIGHI (1879-1936)

Fontane di Roma

Chicago
October 1959
	CSO	LP: Victor LM 2436/LSC 2436
		LP: RCA RB 16231/SB 2103/VICS 1565/
		    GL 42169
		LP: Chesky RC 5
		CD: RCA/BMG RD 85407/09026 614012/
		    09026 680792

Pini di Roma

Chicago
October 1959
	CSO	LP: Victor LM 2436/LSC 2436
		LP: RCA RB 16231/SB 2103/VICS 1565/
		    GL 42169
		LP: Chesky RC 5
		CD: RCA/BMG RD 85407/09026 614012/
		    09026 680792

NIKOLAI RIMSKY-KORSAKOV (1844-1908)

Scheherazade

Chicago February 1960	CSO	LP: Victor LM 2446/LSC 2446 LP: Chesky RC 4 LP: RCA VICS 1480 CD: RCA/BMG RD 87018/GD 60875 09026 681682

RICHARD RODGERS (1902-1979)

Carousel Waltz, arranged by Walker

Pittsburgh February 1946	Pittsburgh SO	78: Columbia (USA) 12322D

GIOACHINO ROSSINI (1792-1868)

Il barbiere di Siviglia, overture

Chicago   CSO   LP: Victor LM 2318/LSC 2318/CCV 5020
November 1959   LP: RCA RB 16192/SB 2075/VICS 1079
                                  CD: RCA/BMG GD 60387

Il signor Bruschino, overture

Pittsburgh   Pittsburgh SO   78: Columbia (USA) M 836
February 1946

Chicago   CSO   LP: Victor LM 2318/LSC 2318/CCV 5020
November 1959   LP: RCA RB 16192/SB 2075/VICS 1079
                                  CD: RCA/BMG GD 60387

La cenerentola, overture

Chicago   CSO   LP: Victor LM 2318/LSC 2318/CCV 5020
November 1959   LP: RCA RB 16192/SB 2075/VICS 1079
                                  CD: RCA/BMG GD 60387

La gazza ladra, overture

Chicago   CSO   LP: Victor LM 2318/LSC 2318/CCV 5020
November 1959   LP: RCA RB 16192/SB 2075/VICS 1079
                                  CD: RCA/BMG 60387

Guilleaume Tell, overture

Chicago	CSO	LP: Victor LM 2318/LSC 2318/CCV 5020
November 1959		LP: RCA RB 16192/SB 2075/VICS 1079
		CD: RCA/BMG GD 60387

La scala di seta, overture

Chicago	CSO	LP: Victor LM 2318/LSC 2318/CCV 5020
November 1958		LP: RCA RB 16192/SB 2075/VICS 1079
		CD: RCA/BMG GD 60387

L'italiana in Algeri overture may also have been recorded at these Chicago Rossini sessions, but was not published

ANTON RUBINSTEIN (1829-1894)

Piano Concerto No 4

New York	Curtis SO	LP: Desmar IPA 5001-5002
November 1937	Hofmann	CD: VAI Audio VAIA 1020

CAMILLE SAINT-SAENS (1835-1921)

Cello Concerto

New York	Victor SO	45: Victor WDM 1538
December 1950	Piatigorsky	LP: Victor LM 1187

ERIK SATIE (1866-1925)

Gymnopédies Nos 1 and 3, arranged by Debussy

Chicago	CSO	CD: Chicago Symphony Orchestra CD 90
March 1960		Also issued on cassette by Fritz Reiner Society

DOMENICO SCARLATTI (1685-1757)

Le donne di buon umore, suite arranged by Tommasini

Chicago March 1954	CSO	Televised performance issued on sound cassette only by Fritz Reiner Society

FRANZ SCHUBERT (1797-1828)

Symphony No 5

Chicago April 1960	CSO	LP: Victor LM 2516/LSC 2516 LP: RCA RB 16263/SB 2134 CD: RCA/BMG 09026 617932

Symphony No 8 "Unfinished"

New York 1925-1926	Singer and Reichmann, pianists	Welte piano rolls 7549-7550 <u>Reiner acted as conductor for this performance by two pianists</u>
Chicago March 1960	CSO	LP: Victor LM 2516/LSC 2516 LP: RCA RB 16263/SB 2134 CD: RCA/BMG RD 85403

ROBERT SCHUMANN (1810-1856)

Symphony No 2

Chicago October 1957	CSO	LP: Chicago Symphony Orchestra 86 CD: Arlecchino ARL 199

Piano Concerto

Chicago February 1959	CSO Janis	LP: RCA ARP1-4668
Chicago April 1960	CSO Cliburn	LP: Victor LM 2455/LSC 2455 LP: RCA RAI 3002/SRA 6001 CD: RCA/BMG GD 60420/09026 626912

ARNOLD SCHOENBERG (1874-1951)

Verklärte Nacht

Chicago November 1957	CSO	LP: Chicago Symphony Orchestra 86 CD: Arlecchino ARL 199

DIMITRI SHOSTAKOVITCH (1906-1975)

Symphony No 6

New York August 1943	NYPSO	CD: As-Disc AS 628 CD: Legend LGD 122
Pittsburgh March 1945	Pittsburgh SO	78: Columbia (USA) M 585 78: Columbia LX 998-1002/LX 8563-8567 auto LP: Columbia ML 4249 CD: Dante LYS 093 CD: Sony MHK 62343

BEDRICH SMETANA (1824-1884)

The Bartered Bride, overture

Chicago December 1955	CSO	LP: Victor LM 1999/LSC 1999 LP: RCA VICS 1424/VICS 1531 CD: RCA/BMG RC 56062/09026 625872

JOHN STAFFORD SMITH (1750-1836)

The Star-spangled Banner

Chicago November 1957	CSO	LP: Victor AHF 1003 **Published for American Heritage Foundation**

JOHANN STRAUSS (1825-1899)

An der schönen blauen Donau, waltz

Chicago April 1960	CSO	LP: Victor LM 2500/LSC 2500 LP: RCA RB 16035/VICS 1742 CD: RCA/BMG RD 85405/GD 60177/ GD 60844/09026 681602

Die Fledermaus, excerpts

New York September 1950	Victor SO Shaw Chorale Munsel, Resnik, Stevens, Peerce, Melton, Merrill <u>Sung in English</u>	78: Victor DM 1457 45: Victor WDM 1457 LP: Victor LM 1114 LP: RCA RB 16109

Kaiserwalzer

Chicago April 1960	CSO	LP: Victor LM 2500/LSC 2500 LP: RCA RB 16035/VICS 1742 CD: RCA/BMG RD 85405/GD 60177/ GD 60844/09026 681602

Künstlerleben, waltz

Chicago April 1960	CSO	LP: Victor LM 2500/LSC 2500 CD: RCA/BMG RD 85405/GD 60177/GD 60844

Morgenblätter, waltz

Chicago April 1960	CSO	LP: Victor LM 2500/LSC 2500 LP: RCA RB 16035 CD: RCA/BMG RD 85405/GD 60177/ GD 60844/09026 681602

Rosen aus dem Süden, waltz

Pittsburgh February 1946	Pittsburgh SO	78: Columbia (USA) 12941D LP: Columbia (USA) ML 4116 CD: Dante LYS 044-045
Chicago April 1960	CSO	LP: Columbia LM 2500/LSC 2500 LP: RCA VICS 1127 CD: RCA/BMG RD 85405/GD 60177/ GD 60844/09026 681602

Schatzwalzer

Pittsburgh November 1941	Pittsburgh SO	78: Columbia (USA) 11800D 78: Columbia (Australia) LOX 555 78: Columbia (Argentina) 266070 78: Columbia (Brazil) 30-5014 LP: Columbia (USA) ML 4116 CD: Dante LYS 44-45
Chicago April 1960	CSO	LP: Victor LM 2500/LSC 2500 LP: RCA VICS 1127 CD: RCA/BMG RD 85405/GD 60177/ GD 60844/09026 681602

Unter Donner und Blitz, polka

Chicago April 1960	CSO	LP: Victor LM 2500/LSC 2500 LP: RCA VICS 1127/VICS 1742 CD: RCA/BMG RD 85405/GD 60177/ GD 60844/09026 681602

Wiener Blut, waltz

Pittsburgh January 1941	Pittsburgh SO	78: Columbia (USA) 11579D LP: Columbia (USA) ML 4116 CD: Dante LYS 044-045
Chicago April 1960	CSO	LP: Victor LM 2500/LSC 2500 LP: RCA VICS 1127/VICS 1742 CD: RCA/BMG RD 85405/GD 60177/ GD 60844/09026 681602

JOSEF STRAUSS (1827-1870)

Dorfschwalben aus Oesterreich, waltz

Chicago April 1957	CSO	LP: Victor LM 2112/LSC 2112 LP: RCA RB 16035 CD: RCA/BMG RD 85405/GD 60177/ 　　 GD 60844/09026 681602

Mein Lebenslauf ist Lieb' und Lust, waltz

Chicago April 1960	CSO	LP: Victor LM 2500/LSC 2500 CD: RCA/BMG RD 85405/GD 60177/GD 60844

RICHARD STRAUSS (1860-1949)

Allerseelen

Detroit February 1938	Detroit SO Pauly	LP: Ed Smith EJS 425

Also sprach Zarathustra

Chicago March 1954	CSO	45: Victor ERA 1806 LP: Victor LM 1806/LSC 1806 LP: HMV ALP 1214 LP: RCA VIC 1265/VICS 1265/CCV 5040 CD: RCA/BMG RC 55721/09026 609302/ 　　 09026 614942
Chicago April- May 1962	CSO	LP: Victor LM 1609/LSC 2609 LP: RCA RB 6518/SB 6518 LP: Mobile Fidelity MFSL 1-322 CD: RCA/BMG GD 86722

Der Bürger als Edelmann, suite

Pittsburgh February 1946	Pittsburgh SO	78: Columbia (USA) M 693 LP: Columbia (USA) ML 2062 CD: Dante LYS 148 <u>Excerpts</u> LP: Columbia (USA) ML 4800

Der Bürger als Edelmann, excerpts from the suite

Chicago April 1956	CSO	LP: Victor LM 6047/LM 2222/LSC 6047/ LSC 2222 LP: RCA VICS 1199/VICS 1295 CD: RCA/BMG RC 55721/09026 609302

Burleske for piano and orchestra

Chicago March 1957	CSO Janis	LP: Victor LM 2127/LSC 2127 LP: RCA VIC 1101 CD: RCA/BMG RD 85734/09026 617962/ 74321 212862

Don Juan

Pittsburgh January 1941	Pittsburgh SO	78: Columbia (USA) X 190 78: Columbia (India) LX 25008-25009 LP: Columbia (USA) ML 2079/ML 4800 CD: Dante LYS 044-045
Chicago December 1954	CSO	45: Victor ERB 56 LP: Victor LM 1888/LSC 1888 LP: RCA VICS 1392 CD: RCA/BMG RC 55721/GD 60206
Chicago February 1960	CSO	LP: Victor LM 2462/LSC 2462 LP: RCA RB 16257/SB 2128/VIC 1265/ VICS 1265 CD: RCA/BMG 15408/09026 681702

Don Quixote

Pittsburgh November 1941	Pittsburgh SO Piatigorsky	78: Columbia (USA) M 506 LP: Columbia (USA) RL 3027 CD: Dante LYS 044-045 CD: Sony awaiting publication <u>Excerpt</u> CD: Sony Masterworks Heritage Sampler SSK 6368
Chicago March 1958	CSO Starker	Issued on cassette by Fritz Reiner Society
Chicago April 1959	CSO Janigro	LP: Victor LD 2384/LDS 2384 LP: RCA RB 16227/SB 2099/VICS 1561 LP: Melodiya D026127-026128 CD: RCA/BMG RD 85734/09026 617962 09026 681702

Elektra

New York February 1952	Metropolitan Opera Orchestra & Chorus Varnay, Wegner, Höngen, Svanholm, Schöffler	LP: Private edition SJS 704-705 LP: Metropolitan Opera MET 9 CD: Arlecchino ARL 20-22

Elektra, excerpts: Weh, ganz allein!; Was willst du, fremder Mensch?; Elektra! Schwester!

Chicago April 1956	CSO Chicago Opera Borkh, Yeend, Schöffler	LP: Victor LM 6047/LSC 6047 LP: RCA VICS 2009 CD: RCA/BMG RC 56032/GD 60874

Ein Heldenleben

Pittsburgh November 1947	Pittsburgh SO	78: Columbia (USA) M 748 LP: Columbia (USA) ML 4138/P 14148
Chicago March 1954	CSO	45: Victor ERD 1807 LP: Victor LM 1807/LSC 1807 LP: HMV ALP 1209 LP: RCA VIC 1042 CD: RCA/BMG RCD 15408/09026 614942 <u>Reiner's first recording with CSO</u>

Morgen

Detroit February 1938	Detroit SO Pauly	LP: Ed Smith EJS 425

Der Rosenkavalier

New York November 1949	Metropolitan Opera Orchestra & Chorus Steber, Berger, Stevens, Di Stefano, List, Thompson	Unpublished video recording <u>Opening of Met 1949-1950 season</u>
New York December 1949	Metropolitan Opera Orchestra & Chorus Steber, Berger, Stevens, Di Stefano, List, Thompson	CD: Arlecchino ARL 37-39
New York February 1951	Metropolitan Opera Orchestra & Chorus Steber, Berger, Novotna, Baum, Krenn, Thompson	Unpublished Met broadcast
New York February 1953	Metropolitan Opera Orchestra & Chorus Varnay, Conner, Stevens, Hayward, Koreh, Brownlee	LP: Melodram MEL 441 <u>Excerpts</u> CD: Gala GL 100.512

Der Rosenkavalier, excerpt (Mir ist die Ehre widerfahren)

New York April 1951	Victor SO Berger, Stevens	45: Victor WDM 9010 LP: Victor LM 9010/LM 6171 CD: Metropolitan Opera MET 114

Der Rosenkavalier, excerpt (Ist ein Traum, kann nicht wirklich sein)

New York April 1951	Victor SO Berger, Stevens	45: Victor WDM 9010/ERA 138 LP: Victor LM 9010/LM 1847 LP: RCA RL 85177 LP: Melodiya D21371-21372 CD: Metropolitan Opera MET 114 CD: RCA/BMG 09026 615802

Der Rosenkavalier, waltzes arranged by Reiner

Chicago April 1957	CSO	LP: Victor LM 2112/LSC 2112 LP: RCA RB 16035/VICS 1561 LP: Melodiya D21371-21372 CD: RCA/BMG RC 55721/09026 609302/ 09026 681602

Metropolitan OPERA HOUSE
GRAND OPERA SEASON 1949-1950
EDWARD JOHNSON General Manager

MONDAY EVENING, NOVEMBER 21, 1949, AT 8 O'CLOCK
OPENING PERFORMANCE

DER ROSENKAVALIER
(THE ROSE CAVALIER)
Opera in three acts
By Hugo von Hofmannsthal

MUSIC by RICHARD STRAUSS

Princess von Werdenberg	Eleanor Steber
Baron Ochs von Lerchenau	Emanuel List
Octavian	Risë Stevens
Von Faninal	Hugh Thompson
Sophie, his daughter	Erna Berger (debut)
Marianne	Thelma Votipka
Valzacchi, an intriguer	Peter Klein (debut)
Annina, his consort	Martha Lipton
Commissary of Police	Lorenzo Alvary
Major-domo of the Princess	Emery Darcy
Major-domo of von Faninal	Paul Franke
Notary	Gerhard Pechner
Innkeeper	Leslie Chabay
A singer	Giuseppe Di Stefano
Three orphans	Paula Lenchner / Maxine Stellman / Thelma Altman
A milliner	Lois Hunt (debut)
A hairdresser	Matthew Vittucci
Leopold, a flunky	Ludwig Burgstaller
Animal vendor	Leslie Chabay
A negro boy	Peggy Smithers

Conductor	Fritz Reiner
Stage director	Herbert Graf
Chorus master	Kurt Adler

POSITIVELY NO ENCORES ALLOWED
THE MANAGEMENT REQUESTS THE AUDIENCE TO REFRAIN
FROM APPLAUSE AS LONG AS THE MUSIC CONTINUES
Correct librettos for sale in the lobby
KNABE PIANO USED EXCLUSIVELY

Salome

New York March 1949	Metropolitan Opera Orchestra Welitsch, Thorborg, Jagel, Janssen	LP: Ed Smith EJS 158 LP: MRF Records MRF 1 LP: BJR Records BJR 156 LP: Melodram MEL 039 CD: Melodram MEL 27042 <u>Parts of Closing scene may be</u> <u>taken by EJS from March 1949</u> <u>studio performance (see below)</u>
New York January 1952	Metropolitan Opera Orchestra Welitsch, Höngen, Svanholm, Hotter	LP: Discocorp SID 724/IGI 293 LP: Metropolitan Opera MET 9 CD: Myto MCD 952125 Excerpts LP: Melodram MEL 096 CD: Melodram MEL 26511/CDI 204 004

Salome, excerpt (Du wolltest mich nicht deinen Mund küssen lassen)

New York March 1949	Metropolitan Opera Orchestra Welitsch	78: Columbia (USA) X 316 78: Columbia LX 1241-1242 45: Philips ABE 10025 LP: Columbia (USA) ML 2048/ML 4795/ VC 806/3216 0077 LP: Columbia 33C 1011 LP: Columbia (Germany) 33WC 1011 LP: CBS 61088 CD: Myto MCD 954135
Chicago December 1955	CSO Borkh	LP: Victor LM 6047/LSC 6047 LP: RCA VICS 1392 CD: RCA/BMG RC 56032/GD 60874

Salome, excerpt (Dance of the 7 veils)

Chicago March 1954	CSO	45: Victor ERD 1806 LP: Victor LM 1806 LP: HMV ALP 1214 CD: RCA/BMG RC 56032/GD 60874 Excerpt LP: Victor SRL 12

Sinfonia domestica

Chicago November 1956	CSO	LP: Victor LM 2103/LSC 2103 LP: RCA VIC 1104/VICS 1104 CD: RCA/BMG GD 60388

Till Eulenspiegels lustige Streiche

New York September 1950	Victor SO	45: Victor WDM 1580 LP: Victor LM 1180 LP: HMV (France) FALP 177
New York January 1952	NBC SO	CD: Music and Arts CD 292
Vienna September 1956	VPO	45: Victor ERA 2077 LP: Victor LM 2077/LSC 2077 LP: RCA SB 2036/VIC 1004 LP: Decca ECS 674 LP: London STS 15582 CD: Decca 448 5682
Chicago February 1957	CSO	Televised performance issued on sound cassette only by Fritz Reiner Society

Tod und Verklärung

New York September 1950	Victor SO	45: Victor WDM 1579 LP: Victor LM 1180 LP: HMV (France) FALP 177 CD: RCA/BMG GD 60388
Vienna September 1956	VPO	LP: Victor LM 2077/LSC 2077 LP: RCA SB 2036/VIC 1004 LP: Decca ECS 674 LP: London STS 15582

IGOR STRAVINSKY (1882-1971)

Le baiser de la fée

Chicago April 1958	CSO	LP: Victor LM 2251/LSC 2251 LP: RCA VICS 1295 CD: RCA/BMG RD 85733/09026 619572/ 74321 212982

Le chant du rossignol

Chicago November 1956	CSO	LP: Victor LM 2150/LSC 2150 LP: RCA VIC 1290/VICS 1290 LP: Chesky RC 10 CD: RCA/BMG RC 55733

The Rake's Progress

New York February 1953	Metropolitan Opera Orchestra & Chorus Güden, Thebom, Lipton, Conley, Harrell, Scott	CD: Datum 90003 US premiere performance

PIOTR TCHAIKOVSKY (1840-1893)

Symphony No 4

Chicago November 1957	CSO	Issued on cassette by Fritz Reiner Society

Symphony No 5

New York 1925-1926	Bacon and Robinson, pianos	Unpublished Welte piano rolls Reiner acted as conductor for this performance by two pianists

Waltz (Symphony No 5)

New York September 1950	Victor SO	45: Victor WDM 1539 45: HMV 7ER 5022 LP: Victor LM 103

Symphony No 6 "Pathétique"

New York 1925-1926	Bacon and Robinson, pianos	Welte piano rolls 7563-7567 <u>Reiner acted as conductor for this</u> <u>performance by two pianists</u>
Chicago April 1957	CSO	LP: Victor LM 2216/LSC 2216 LP: RCA VIC 1163/VICS 1163 CD: RCA/BMG RC 56022/09026 612462

Piano Concerto No 1

Chicago October 1955	CSO Gilels	45: Victor ERC 1969 LP: Victor LM 1969 LP: HMV ALP 1402 LP: RCA RB 16115/VICS 1039

Violin Concerto

Chicago
April 1957
	CSO
	Heifetz
		LP: Victor LM 2129/LSC 2129
		LP: RCA RB 16038/SB 2002/DPS 2002
		CD: RCA/BMG RC 51011/GD 85933/
		    09026 614952/09026 617432/
		    09026 617782

Violin Concerto, abridged version of first movement

New York September 1946	NYPSO Heifetz	VHS Video: RCA/BMG 60883-G VHS Video: Teldec 4509 950386 Laserdisc: Teldec 4509 950383 <u>From the film Carnegie Hall</u>

Casse noisette, selection from the ballet

Chicago March 1959	CSO	LP: Victor LM 2328/LSC 2328/INTS 1022 LP: RCA RB 16236/SB 2107/VICS 1460 CD: RCA/BMG RC 55642 Excerpts CD: RCA/BMG 09026 618672/09026 626642

Casse noisette, waltz

New York September 1950	Victor SO	45: Victor WDM 1539/ERA 83 45: HMV 7ER 5022 LP: Victor LM 103

1812 Overture

Chicago January 1956	CSO	45: Victor ERA 291 LP: Victor LM 1999/LM 2241/LSC 2241 LP: RCA SB 2059/VICS 1531 CD: RCA/BMG RD 85642/09026 612462

Evgeny Onegin, waltz

New York September 1950	Victor SO	45: Victor WDM 1539 LP: Victor LM 103

Francesca da Rimini

Chicago November 1953	CSO	Issued on cassette by Fritz Reiner Society

Marche militaire (Suite No 1)

Pittsburgh March 1945	Pittsburgh SO	CD: Sony Masterworks Heritage Sampler SSK 6368
Chicago March 1959	CSO	LP: Victor LM 2423/LSC 2423 LP: RCA VIC 1068 CD: RCA/BMG RC 56022/09026 619582

Marche slave

Chicago March 1959	CSO	LP: Victor LM 2423/LSC 2423 LP: RCA VIC 1068/VICS 1676 CD: RCA/BMG RC 56422/09026 619582

Sleeping Beauty, waltz

New York September 1950	Victor SO	45: Victor WDM 1539 45: HMV 7ER 5022 LP: Victor LM 103

Swan Lake, waltz

New York September 1950	Victor SO	45: Victor WDM 1539 45: HMV 7ER 5022 LP: Victor LM 103

RALPH VAUGHAN WILLIAMS (1872-1958)

Fantasia on a theme by Thomas Tallis

Chicago November 1957	CSO	LP: Chicago Symphony Orchestra 86

GIUSEPPE VERDI (1813-1901)

Falstaff

New York February 1949	Metropolitan Opera Orchestra & Chorus Albanese, Resnik, Elmo, Di Stefano, Valdengo, Warren	LP: Ed Smith EJS 250

Requiem

Chicago April 1958	CSO CSO Chorus Rysanek, Resnik, Lloyd, Tozzi	LP: Melodram MEL 238 Orchestra and chorus incorrectly described as Chicago Lyric Opera
Vienna May-June 1960	VPO Wiener Singverein L.Price, Elias, Bjoerling, Tozzi	LP: Victor LD 6091/LDS 6091 LP: RCA RE 25026-25027/SER 4526-4527 LP: Decca GOM 617-618/GOS 617-618/DJB 2003 LP: London OSA 1294 CD: Decca 421 6082 Excerpts LP: Decca GRV 4/GRV 10 CD: Decca 440 4022

RICHARD WAGNER (1813-1883)

Der fliegende Holländer

New York December 1950	Metropolitan Opera Orchestra & Chorus Varnay, Glaz, Svanholm, Hayward, Hotter, Nilssen	LP: Ed Smith UORC 149 LP: Raritas OPR 5

Der fliegende Holländer, excerpt (Die Frist ist um)

London June 1937 (7 and 11 June)	LPO Janssen	LP: Ed Smith EJS 514-515 LP: Rococo 1008 LP: Discocorp RR 469 LP: Historical Recording Enterprises HRE 234 CD: Arlecchino ARL 35-36 CD: Legato SRO 808

Der fliegende Holländer, excerpt (Weit komm' ich her)

London June 1937 (7 and 11 June)	LPO Janssen, Weber	LP: Ed Smith EJS 514-515 LP: Rococo 1008 LP: Discocorp RR 469 LP: Historical Recording Enterprises HRE 234 CD: Arlecchino ARL 35-36 CD: Legato SRO 808

Der fliegende Holländer, excerpt (Summ und brumm)

London June 1937 (7 and 11 June)	LPO Covent Garden Chorus Flagstad, Jarred	LP: Ed Smith EJS 514-515/EJS 123 LP: Rococo 1008 LP: Discocorp RR 469 LP: Historical Recording Enterprises HRE 234 CD: Arlecchino ARL 35-36 CD: Legato SRO 808

Der fliegende Holländer, excerpt (Traft ihr das Schiff)

London	LPO	LP: Ed Smith EJS 514-515/EJS 183
June 1937	Covent Garden	LP: Rococo 1008
(7 and 11	Chorus	LP: Harvest H 1005
June)	Flagstad	LP: Discocorp RR 469
		LP: Legendary Recordings LR 120
		LP: Historical Recording Enterprises HRE 234
		LP: Orpheum 8404
		CD: Legendary Recordings LRCD 1015
		CD: Memoir CDMOIR 403
		CD: Arlecchino ARL 35-36
		CD: Legato SRO 808

Der fliegende Holländer, excerpt (Mein Kind, du siehst mich auf der Schwelle!)

London	LPO	LP: Ed Smith EJS 514-515/EJS 123
June 1937	Janssen, Weber	LP: Rococo 1008
(7 and 11		LP: Discocorp RR 469
June)		LP: Historical Recording Enterprises HRE 234
		CD: Arlecchino ARL 35-36
		CD: Legato SRO 808

Der fliegende Holländer, excerpt (Wie aus der Ferne)

London	LPO	LP: Ed Smith EJS 514-515/EJS 123
June 1937	Flagstad,	LP: Rococo 1008
(7 and 11	Janssen	LP: Discocorp RR 469
June)		LP: Historical Recording Enterprises HRE 234
		CD: Arlecchino ARL 35-36
		CD: Legato SRO 808

Der fliegende Holländer, excerpt (Steuermann, lass die Wacht!)

London	LPO	LP: Ed Smith EJS 514-515
June 1937	Covent Garden	LP: Rococo 1008
(7 and 11	Chorus	LP: Discocorp RR 469
June)		LP: Historical Recording Enterprises HRE 234
		CD: Arlecchino ARL 35-36
		CD: Legato SRO 808

Der fliegende Holländer, excerpt (Was muss ich hören?...to end of opera)

London	LPO	LP: Ed Smith EJS 514-515
June 1937	Flagstad, Jarred,	LP: Rococo 1008
(7 and 11	Lorenz, Janssen,	LP: Discocorp RR 469
June)	Weber	LP: Historical Recording Enterprises HRE 234
		CD: Memoir CDMOIR 403
		CD: Arlecchino ARL 35-36
		CD: Legato SRO 808

All issues from 7 and 11 June 1937 performances are taken from unpublished HMV technical test pressings in the matrix series 2EA 5600-5618

Der fliegende Holländer, unspecified extracts

London	LPO	Unpublished HMV technical
June 1937	Covent Garden	test pressings
(16 June)	Chorus	
	Flagstad, Jarred,	
	Ralf, Janssen,	
	Vogel	

Götterdämmerung, excerpts (Zu neuen Taten; Waltraute scene)

New York	NYPSO	LP: Ed Smith ANNA 1008/EJS 166-167
July 1937	Easton, Meisle,	LP: International Record Collectors Club IRCC 7022
	Althouse	ANNA 1008 incorrectly dated London 1936

Götterdämmerung, Siegfried's Rhine Journey

New York	NYPSO	LP: Ed Smith ANNA 1008/EJS 166-167
July 1937		ANNA 1008 incorrectly dated London 1936
Chicago	CSO	LP: Victor LM 2441/LSC 2441/VICS 1165
April 1959		CD: RCA/BMG RD 84738/09026 617922

Götterdämmerung, Siegfried's Funeral March

Chicago	CSO	LP: Victor LM 2441/LSC 2441/VICS 1165
April 1959		CD: RCA/BMG RD 84738/09026 617922

Lohengrin, Prelude

Philadelphia February 1932	Philadelphia Orchestra	Issued on cassette by Fritz Reiner Society <u>Recording incomplete; Bell Telephone</u> <u>Laboratories experimental recording</u>
Pittsburgh November 1941	Pittsburgh SO	78: Columbia (USA) M 549/11772D 78: Columbia (Canada) 15637 LP: Columbia (USA) ML 4054 CD: Dante LYS 044-045

Lohengrin, Act 3 Prelude

Pittsburgh January 1941	Pittsburgh SO	78: Columbia (USA) M 549/11644D LP: Columbia (USA) ML 4054 CD: Dante LYS 044-045
New York October 1950	Victor SO	45: Victor ERA 185 CD: RCA/BMG 09026 617922

Die Meistersinger von Nürnberg

New York March 1952	Metropolitan Opera Orchestra & Chorus Wegner, Glaz, Hopf, Holm, Schöffler, Janssen, Pechner	CD: Arlecchino ARL 40-43
New York January 1953	Metropolitan Opera Orchestra & Chorus De los Angeles, Glaz, Hopf, Holm, Greindl, Kunz, Pechner	Unpublished Met broadcast
Vienna November 1955	VPO Vienna Opera Chorus Seefried, Anday, Beirer, Dickie, Schöffler, Frick, Kunz	CD: Melodram CDM 47083

Die Meistersinger von Nürnberg, Overture

New York November 1938	NYPSO	78: World's Greatest Music SR 12 CD: Dante LYS 83
Pittsburgh January 1941	Pittsburgh SO	78: Columbia (USA) M 549/11580D LP: Columbia (USA) ML 4054
Chicago April 1959	CSO	LP: Victor LM 2441/LSC 2441/VICS 1165 CD: RCA/BMG RD 84738/09026 617922

Die Meistersinger von Nürnberg, suite (Act 3 Prelude, Dance of the Apprentices and Entry of the Masters)

Pittsburgh November 1941	Pittsburgh SO	78: Columbia (USA) X 218/J 79 CD: Dante LYS 044-045
Chicago April 1959	CSO	LP: Victor LM 2441/LSC 2441/VICS 1165 CD: RCA/BMG RD 84738/09026 617922

Die Meistersinger von Nürnberg, fragments from Nightwatchman's Call and Act 3 Prelude

Philadelphia November 1931	Philadelphia Orchestra	Issued on cassette by Fritz Reiner Society <u>Bell Telephone Laboratories experimental recording</u>

Parsifal, Prelude

New York November 1938	NYPSO	78: World's Greatest Music SR 12-13/ S 106-107 CD: Pearl GEMMCDS 9922 CD: Dante LYS 83

Parsifal, Good Friday Music

Chicago March 1958	CSO	LP: Chicago Symphony Orchestra 88 CD: Chicago Symphony Orchestra CD 88 CD: Arlecchino ARL 45

Parsifal, fragments from Act 1 Transformation, Klingsor's Castle and Good Friday Music

Philadelphia November 1931	Philadelphia Orchestra	Issued on cassette by Fritz Reiner Society <u>Bell Telephone Laboratories experimental recording</u>

Parsifal, excerpt (Vom Bade kehrt der König heim....So ward es dir verhiessen)

London April 1937	LPO Covent Garden Chorus Ralf, Janssen, Weber	LP: Ed Smith UORC 130 <u>Section from Mein Sohn Amfortas.. Durch Mitleid wissend der reine Tor also on Discocorp IGI 379, where it was incorrectly described as a Bayreuth performance conducted by Karl Muck</u>

Parsifal, excerpt (Ich sah sie welken....to end of opera)

London May 1937	LPO Covent Garden Chorus Ralf, Janssen, Weber	LP: Ed Smith UORC 130 <u>Section from Ja! Wehe!...leuchtet euch der Gral also on Discocorp IGI 379, where it was incorrectly described as a Bayreuth performance conducted by Furtwängler</u>

Rienzi, Overture

Chicago March 1958	CSO	LP: Chicago Symphony Orchestra 86 CD: Arlecchino ARL 45

Siegfried, Forest murmurs

Pittsburgh January 1941	Pittsburgh SO	78: Columbia (USA) M 549 78: Columbia (Australia) LOX 542 LP: Columbia (USA) ML 4054 CD: Dante LYS 044-045

Tannhäuser, Venusberg Music

Pittsburgh January 1941	Pittsburgh SO	78: Columbia (USA) X 193 78: Columbia (Canada) J 54 CD: Dante LYS 044-045

Tannhäuser, Entry of the Guests

New York October 1950	Victor SO	45: Victor ERA 185 CD: RCA/BMG 09026 617922

Tristan und Isolde

London June 1936	LPO Covent Garden Chorus Flagstad, Kalter, Melchior, Janssen, List	LP: Ed Smith EJS 465 LP: Discocorp RR 471 LP: Discoreale DR 10027-10030 CD: VAI Audio VAIA 1004 CD: Radio Years RY 39-41 Act 1 complete & last two thirds of Act 3 CD: EMI CHS 764 0372 Prelude CD: EMI CDM 565 9182/CMS 565 9152 EMI CHS 764 0372 incorrectly stated that entire performance was conducted by Beecham; Radio Years incorrectly states that the performance took place in New York
New York December 1950	Metropolitan Opera Orchestra & Chorus Traubel, Thebom, Vinay, Schöffler, Nilssen	Unpublished Met broadcast

Tristan und Isolde, Act 2

Los Angeles November 1937	San Francisco SO Flagstad, Meisle, Melchior, Hehn, List	CD: Legato LCD 145

Tristan und Isolde, Prelude and Liebestod

Chicago March 1958	CSO	LP: Chicago Symphony Orchestra 88 CD: Chicago Symphony Orchestra CD 88 CD: Arlecchino ARL 45

Tristan und Isolde, fragments from Tristan's Vision and Death

Philadelphia November 1931	Philadelphia Orchestra	Issued on cassette by Fritz Reiner Society Bell Telephone Laboratories experimental recording

Die Walküre, Act 2

San Francisco November 1936	San Francisco SO Flagstad, Lehmann, Meisle, Melchior, Schorr, List	LP: Ed Smith EJS 234 LP: Discocorp RR 426 LP: Edizione lirica EL 004 CD: Legato LCD 133 CD: Minerva MN 34/Grammofono AB 78555 LP editions have closing passage obliterated by radio announcer: this has been edited out by Legato and replaced by Wotan's final words from another Schorr recording

Die Walküre, Ride of the Valkyries

Pittsburgh March 1940	Pittsburgh SO	78: Columbia (USA) M 549 LP: Columbia (USA) ML 4054 CD: Dante LYS 044-045 This is the only published item from Reiner's first Pittsburgh recording sessions: it is understood that other unspecified Wagner pieces were attempted but not published

CARL MARIA VON WEBER (1786-1826)

Abu Hassan, overture

Chicago November 1956	CSO	Televised performance issued on sound cassette only by Fritz Reiner Society

Aufforderung zum Tanz, arranged by Berlioz

Chicago April 1957	CSO	LP: Victor LM 2112/LSC 2112 LP: RCA RB 16035 LP: Melodiya D026593-026594 CD: RCA/BMG RC 56125/09026 612502/ 09026 681602

JAROMIR WEINBERGER (1896-1967)

Polka and Fugue (Schwanda the Bagpiper)

Chicago January 1956	CSO	LP: Victor LM 1999/LSC 1999 LP: RCA VICS 1424 CD: RCA/BMG RC 56062/09026 625872

LEO WEINER (1885-1960)

Divertimento No 1

Pittsburgh   Pittsburgh SO   CD: Sony MHK 62343
March 1945

FOR THE 13TH CONSECUTIVE YEAR
THE TEXAS COMPANY
PRESENTS
THE METROPOLITAN OPERA BROADCASTS

Enjoy the world's great operas, broadcast in their entirety every Saturday afternoon, direct from the stage of the Metropolitan Opera House in New York City.

NEXT SATURDAY, DECEMBER 6TH, MOZART'S
DON GIOVANNI
with Hilde Zadek, Patrice Munsel, Jan Peerce, Cesare Siepi and Delia Rigal
(cast subject to change)
CONDUCTOR: FRITZ REINER

MILTON CROSS — one of America's favorite music personalities, adds life and color to the operas on the air through his informative commentaries.

THE OPERA QUIZ — provides a chance for the radio audience to match its musical wits against the experts during intermission time. You are welcome to address questions with which you would like to challenge the experts to: The Opera Quiz, The Texas Company, 135 East 42nd Street, New York 17, N. Y.

OPERA NEWS ON THE AIR — conducted by Boris Goldovsky, brings you interesting interviews with famous guest stars and musicologists.

Over a coast-to-coast network in U. S. and the Dominion of Canada. WJZ in New York City.

THE TEXAS COMPANY

Antal Dorati
1906 -1988

Discography compiled by Richard Chlupaty and John Hunt

ISAAC ALBENIZ (1860-1909)

Iberia, suite arranged by Arbos

Minneapolis
April 1957
	Minneapolis SO	LP: Mercury MG 50146/SR 90007/
		   MMA 11081/AMS 16002/SRI 75101
		LP: Wing MGW 14063/MGW 14085/
		   SRW 18063/SRW 18085
		LP: Mercury (France) 839.816
		<u>Excerpts</u>
		45: Mercury XEP 9052

PETER VAN ANROOY (1879-1954)

Piet Hein Rhapsody

Den Haag 1953	Residentie Orchestra	LP: Philips S06036R

ANTON ARENSKY (1861-1906)

Variations on a theme of Tchaikovsky

Vienna June 1958	Philharmonia Hungarica	LP: Mercury MG 50200/MG 50346/SR 90200/ SR 90346/MMA 11091/AMS 16040 <u>Also issued on Philips/Fontana LP</u>

GEORGES AURIC (1899-1983)

Overture

London August 1965	LSO	LP: Mercury MG 50435/SR 90435 LP: Philips AL 3637/SAL 3637/412 0281 CD: Mercury 434 3352

BELA BARTOK (1881-1945)

Concerto for orchestra

Minneapolis December 1953	Minneapolis SO	LP: Mercury MG 50035/MRL 2521/MMA 11082 LP: Concert Hall CM 2300
Wembley July 1962	LSO	LP: Mercury MG 50378/SR 90378/SRI 75105 LP: Fontana (Holland) ZKY 894 020 CD: Mercury 432 0172
Budapest Date not confirmed	Hungarian State SO	LP: Hungaroton LPX 11437/SLPX 11437 CD: Hungaroton HCD 11437
Amsterdam June 1983	Concertgebouw Orchestra	LP: Philips 411 1321 CD: Philips 411 1322

Music for strings, percussion and celesta

Vienna June 1958	Philharmonia Hungarica	LP: Philips 6500 931/6527 139 CD: Philips 426 6612
London June 1960	LSO	LP: Mercury MG 50515/SR 90515 CD: Mercury 434 3572
London June 1960	LSO	Unpublished radio broadcast
Detroit November 1983	Detroit SO	LP: Decca 411 8941 CD: Decca 411 8942

Violin Concerto No 1

London February 1965	New Philharmonia Menuhin	LP: EMI ASD 2323/1C 063 00333/SXLP 30533 LP: Angel 36438 CD: EMI CMS 763 9842/CDM 763 9852

Violin Concerto No 2

Dallas January 1946	Dallas SO Menuhin	78: Victor M 1120 78: HMV DB 6361-6365/DB 9291-9295 auto CD: RCA/BMG 09026 613952
New York February 1957	Minneapolis SO Menuhin	LP: Mercury MG 50140/SR 90003/SRI 75002 LP: Wing MGW 14104/SRW 18104 CD: Mercury 434 3502
London February 1965	New Philharmonia Menuhin	LP: ALP 2281/ASD 2281/SXLP 30533/ 1C 063 00303 LP: Angel 36360 CD: EMI CDM 763 9852

Viola Concerto

London September 1966	New Philharmonia Menuhin	LP: EMI ASD 2323/1C 063 00333 LP: Angel 36438 CD: EMI CMS 763 9842/CDM 763 9852

Dance Suite

Vienna June 1958	Philharmonia Hungarica	LP: Mercury MG 50183/MG 50533/SR 90183/ SR 90533/MMA 11121/AMS 16068 LP: Philips 6500 931 CD: Mercury 432 0172

Divertimento for strings

Minneapolis 1950	Minneapolis SO	45: Victor WDM 1596 LP: Victor LM 1185
Vienna June 1958	Philharmonia Hungarica	LP: Mercury MG 50132/SR 90132/ MMA 11077/AMS 16027 LP: Philips CFL 1022/698 004CL
Watford July 1964	BBC SO	LP: Mercury MG 50416/SR 90416/SRI 75118 LP: Philips AL 3569/SAL 3569/6527 139 CD: Mercury 434 3622
Budapest Date not confirmed	Hungarian State SO	LP: Hungaroton LPX 11437/SLPX 11437 CD: Hungaroton HCD 11437

Hungarian Sketches

Minneapolis November 1956	Minneapolis SO	LP: Mercury MG 50132/SR 90132/MRL 2565/ MMA 11082/AMS 16025 CD: Mercury 432 0052 <u>Excerpts</u> LP: Philips 6599 013

Mikrokosmos, Bourrée and From the diary of a fly, arranged by Serly

Vienna June 1958	Philharmonia Hungarica	LP: Mercury MG 50183/MG 50338/SR 90183/ SR 90338/MMA 11121/AMS 16068 LP: Philips 6500 931 CD: Mercury 432 0172

2 Pictures

Detroit 1978	Detroit SO	LP: Decca SXL 6897
Amsterdam June 1983	Concertgebouw Orchestra	LP: Philips 411 1321 CD: Philips 411 1322

2 Portraits

Vienna June 1958	Philharmonia Hungarica	LP: Mercury MG 50183/SR 90183/ MMA 11121/AMS 16068 LP: Philips 6500 931 CD: Mercury 432 0172

2 Rumanian Dances

Vienna June 1958	Philharmonia Hungarica	LP: Mercury MG 50179/SR 90179/MRL 2595/ MMA 11077/AMS 16027

Rumanian Folk dances

Minneapolis
November
1956
	Minneapolis SO	LP: Mercury MG 50132/SR 90132/MRL 2562/
		    MRL 2565/MMA 11077/AMS 16027/
		    SRI 75105
		CD: Mercury 432 0052

Suite No 1

Detroit 1978	Detroit SO	LP: Decca SXL 6897

Suite No 2

Minneapolis November 1955	Minneapolis SO	LP: Mercury MG 50098/SR 90098/SR 90533/ MRL 2502/MMA 11068 CD: Mercury 434 3502

Bluebeard's Castle

London July 1962	LSO Szönyi, Székély	LP: Mercury MG 50311/SR 90311/ MMA 11190/AMS 16140 LP: Philips 6500 931/6768 600 CD: Mercury 434 3252
Stockholm February 1982	Stockholm PO	CD: Bis BISCD 421-424 <u>Short orchestral rehearsal extract only</u>

The Miraculous Mandarin, ballet

London June 1963	BBC SO	Unpublished radio broadcast
Watford July 1964	BBC SO BBC Chorus	LP: Mercury MG 50416/SR 90416 LP: Philips AL 3569/SAL 3569/ 6500 931/6768 600 CD: Mercury 434 3622 <u>Excerpts</u> LP: Mercury MG 50531/SR 90531/SRI 75030 LP: Philips 6582 011
Detroit November 1983	Detroit SO	LP: Decca 411 9841 CD: Decca 411 9842/448 2762

The Miraculous Mandarin, suite from the ballet

Chicago January 1954	Chicago SO	LP: Mercury MG 50038/MG 50151/ MRL 2541/MMA 11068
Stockholm February 1970	Stockholm PO	CD: Bis BISCD 421-424

ANTAL DORATI Conducting the MINNEAPOLIS SYMPHONY ORCHESTRA

Berlioz
Roman Carnival Overture

Debussy
Three Nocturnes
Nuages
Fêtes
Sirènes

Mercury RECORDS

Ravel
Pavane pour une Infante Défunte
Alborada del Gracioso

The Wooden Prince, ballet

Watford June 1964	LSO	LP: Mercury MG 50426/SR 90246 LP: Philips AL 3670/SAL 3670/ 6500 931/6768 600 CD: Mercury 434 3572

Sonata for 2 pianos and percussion

Wembley June 1960	LSO members Frid, Ponse	LP: Mercury MG 50515/SR 90515 CD: Mercury 434 3622

3 Village scenes

Budapest Date not confirmed	Chamber ensemble Gyor Choir Farago, Adam	LP: Hungaroton LPX 11510/SLPX 11510 CD: Hungaroton HCD 31047

Hungarian Folksongs, selection

Budapest Date not confirmed	Budapest SO Liszt Academy Choir	LP: Hungaroton LPX 11510/SLPX 11510

Székély Songs for unaccompanied chorus

Budapest Date not confirmed	Liszt Academy Choir	CD: Hungaroton HCD 31047

LUDWIG VAN BEETHOVEN (1770-1827)

Symphony No 1

West Ham May 1975	RPO	LP: Mercury SRI 75121 LP: DG 2721 199/2535 334 LP: Metronom (Germany) 140.164

Symphony No 2

West Ham May 1975	RPO	LP: Mercury SRI 75122 LP: DG 2721 199/2535 334 LP: Metronom (Germany) 140.187

Symphony No 3 "Eroica"

Minneapolis February 1957	Minneapolis SO	LP: Mercury MG 50141/SR 90011/SRI 75067 LP: Wing MGW 14047/SRW 18047/WL 1046 LP: Philips GL 5805/642 236L/839 534Y
West Ham May 1975	RPO	LP: Mercury SRI 75123 LP: DG 2721 199/2535 335 LP: Metronom (Germany) 140.163

Symphony No 4

Minneapolis November 1955	Minneapolis SO	LP: Mercury MG 50100/MMA 11016 LP: Wing MGW 14042/SRW 18042/WL 1033
West Ham May 1975	RPO	LP: Mercury SRI 75124 LP: DG 2721 199/2535 218 LP: Metronom (Germany) 140.187

86 Dorati

Symphony No 5

Minneapolis February 1955	Minneapolis SO	LP: Mercury MG 50017/MRL 2539 LP: Wing MGW 14016/SRW 18016/WL 1011
Watford July 1962	LSO	LP: Mercury MG 50317/SR 90317 LP: Philips 839 530
West Ham May 1975	RPO	LP: Mercury SRI 75125 LP: DG 2721 199/2535 216/2870 482 LP: Metronom (Germany) 140.141

Symphony No 6 "Pastoral"

Vienna 1958	VSO	LP: Philips SCFL 104/698 018L/875 007CY
Watford July 1962	LSO	LP: Mercury MG 50415/SR 90415 LP: Philips 6531 009
West Ham May 1975	RPO	LP: Mercury SRI 75119 LP: DG 2721 199/2535 219 LP: Metronom (Germany) 140.142

Symphony No 7

Watford July 1963	LSO	LP: Mercury MG 50523/SR 90523
West Ham May 1975	RPO	LP: Mercury SRI 75120 LP: DG 2721 199/2535 336 LP: Metronom (Germany) 140.186

Symphony No 8

Minneapolis November 1955	Minneapolis	LP: Mercury MG 50100/MMA 11016 LP: Wing MGW 14042/SRW 18042/WL 1033
West Ham May 1975	RPO	LP: Mercury SRI2-77013 LP: DG 2721 199/2726 073 LP: Metronom (Germany) 140.164

Symphony No 9 "Choral"

Walthamstow July 1975	RPO Brighton Festival Chorus Farley, Hodgson, Burrows, Bailey	LP: Mercury SRI2-77013 LP: DG 2721 199/2726 073 LP: Metronom (Germany) 140.143

Symphony No 9 "Choral", extract from final movement

Stockholm December 1967- September 1976	Stockholm PO S.Björling	CD: Bis BISCD 421-424 Composite extract taken from two separate performances in the years shown

Piano Concerto No 3

London December 1967	LPO Rubinstein	CD: Hunt CD 567/CDHP 567

Piano Concerto No 4

Watford July 1963	LSO Bachauer	LP: Mercury MG 50381/SR 90381 LP: Philips 6547 005 LP: Fontana (Holland) ZKY 894 087 CD: Mercury 432 0182
London December 1967	LPO Rubinstein	CD: Hunt CD 567/CDHP 567 Also unpublished video recording

Piano Concerto No 5 "Emperor"

London December 1967	LPO Rubinstein	CD: Hunt CD 567/CDHP 567

Violin Concerto

Watford June 1961	LSO Szigeti	LP: Mercury MG 50358/SR 90358 LP: Fontana (Holland) ZKY 894 021 Issued on CD in Japan by Seven Seas

Missa Solemnis

London August 1966	BBC SO BBC Chorus Harper, Höffgen, Young, Wiemann	Unpublished radio broadcast
Berlin July 1988	European SO Maryland University Choir Kieberg, Lang, Cochran, Krutikov	CD: Bis BISCD 406-407 <u>Includes rehearsal extract</u>

Coriolan, overture

Minneapolis February 1953	Minneapolis SO	LP: Mercury MG 50017/MRL 2539 LP: Wing MGW 14016/MGW 14032/SRW 18016/ SRW 18032/WL 1011/WL 1019
West Ham May 1975	RPO	Mercury/DG unpublished

Egmont, overture

Minneapolis February 1953	Minneapolis SO	LP: Mercury MG 50017/MRL 2539 LP: Wing MGW 14016/MGW 14037/SRW 18016/ SRW 18037/WL 1011
Watford July 1962	LSO	LP: Mercury MG 50317/SR 90317/ SR2-9134/SRI 75124 LP: Philips 88188DY/839 530
Walthamstow July 1975	RPO	Mercury/DG unpublished

Die Geschöpfe des Prometheus, overture

Wembley June 1960	LSO	LP: Mercury MDG 19/SRD 19/LPS 9000/ LPSC 5000/GL 90/GLS 90/MMA 11143/ AMS 16091/SRI 75122
West Ham May 1975	RPO	Mercury/DG unpublished

Leonore No 3, overture

Minneapolis February 1953	Minneapolis SO	LP: Mercury MG 50017/MRL 2539 LP: Wing MGW 14016/MGW 14037/SRW 18016/ SRW 18037/WL 1011
Wembley June 1960	LSO	LP: Mercury MDG 19/SRD 19/LPS 9000/ LPSC 5000/GL 90/GLS 90/MMA 11143/ AMS 16091/SRI 75121
West Ham May 1975	RPO	Mercury/DG unpublished

Die Weihe des Hauses, overture

Watford July 1962	LSO	LP: Mercury MG 50317/SR 90317/SRI 75125 LP: Philips 839 530

Wellington's Victory

Wembley June 1960	LSO Deems Taylor	LP: Mercury MG 50054/SR 90054/MGD 19/ SRD 19/LPS 9000/LPSC 5000/GL 90/ GLS 90/MMA 11143/AMS 16091/ SRI 75142 LP: Philips AL 3461/SAL 3461/5130 514 LP: Fontana (Holland) ZKY 894.028 CD: Mercury 416 4482/434 3602

London Philharmonic Orchestra

Principal Conductor and Artistic Adviser BERNARD HAITINK · Leader RODNEY FRIEND · President SIR ADRIAN BOULT

Antal Dorati CONDUCTOR

Artur Rubinstein SOLOIST

BEETHOVEN · *Piano Concerto No. 3 in C minor*
Piano Concerto No. 4 in G
Piano Concerto No. 5 in E flat
(Emperor)

Tonight's concert is being broadcast in its entirety by the BBC (Radio 3), and in addition, the performance of the Piano Concerto No 4 is being recorded by BBC TV for future transmission.

Royal Festival Hall GENERAL MANAGER JOHN DENISON CBE

Thursday 7 December 1967 at 8 pm

Programme 2/-

This concert is presented by the London Philharmonic Orchestra Limited in association with the London Orchestral Concert Board representing the Arts Council of Great Britain and the Greater London Council

ALBAN BERG (1885-1935)

3 pieces for orchestra

Watford	LSO	LP: Mercury MG 50316/SR 90316
July 1962		LP: Philips AL 3539/SAL 3539/838 409AY
		CD: Mercury 432 0062

Lulu, symphonic suite

Watford	LSO	LP: Mercury MG 50278/SR 90278/SRI 75066/
June 1961	Pilarczyk	MMA 11167/AMS 16117
		CD: Mercury 432 0062

Wozzeck, fragments

Watford	LSO	LP: Mercury MG 50278/SR 50278/SRI 75066/
June 1961	Pilarczyk	MMA 11167/AMS 16117
		CD: Mercury 434 3252

HECTOR BERLIOZ (1803-1869)

Symphonie fantastique

Minneapolis December 1953	Minneapolis SO	LP: Mercury MG 50034/MRL 2532 LP: Wing MGW 14005/SRW 18005/WL 1004 LP: Pickwick S-4040

Benvenuto Cellini

London 1964	BBC SO BBC Chorus Veasey, Cameron, Garrard Sung in English	CD: Music and Arts CD 618

Le carnaval romain, overture

Minneapolis February 1952	Minneapolis SO	45: Mercury EP 15051 LP: Mercury MG 50005/MRL 2516 LP: Wing MGW 14009/SRW 18009/WL 1045

La damnation de Faust, suite: Ballet des sylphes, Menuet des follets and Marche hongroise

Amsterdam September 1959	Concertgebouw Orchestra	LP: Philips 835 062AY/6530 020 Marche hongroise only 45: Philips 313 123SF/SBF 275 LP: Philips 6882 100
Amsterdam January 1982	Concertgebouw Orchestra	LP: Philips 6514 219/6769 089

Roméo et Juliette, excerpts from the Dramatic symphony: Romeo alone, Capulet's ball, Love scene and Queen Mab scherzo

Walthamstow October 1962	RPO	LP: Reader's Digest RD3-15/RDS3-15/ RDM 1027/RDS 9633

Roméo et Juliette, Love scene

Amsterdam September 1959	Concertgebouw Orchestra	LP: Philips 835 062AY/6530 020/6585 026

FRANZ BERWALD (1796-1868)

Symphony No 2 "Sinfonia capricieuse"

Stockholm October 1967	Stockholm PO	LP: RCA VIC 1319/VICS 1319 LP: EMI (Sweden) SP 141/RIKSLP 13 CD: Swedish Society SCD 1046

WILLIAM BILLINGS (1746-1800)

Be glad then America, anthem

Washington 1973-1974	National SO	LP: London OS 26442 <u>Not issued in Europe</u>

GEORGES BIZET (1839-1875)

L'Arlésienne, suites 1 and 2

Paris June 1960	Lamoureux Orchestra	LP: Philips CFL 1061/SCFL 117/698 030CL CD: Philips 442 2722

Carmen, suites 1 and 2

Paris May 1959	Lamoureux Orchestra	LP: Philips CFL 1061/SCFL 117/698 030CL CD: Philips 442 2722

Jeux d'enfants, suite

London September 1937	LPO	78: HMV C 2940-2941 78: Electrola EH 1091-1092 78: Victor M 510 CD: Dutton CDAX 8005

ERNEST BLOCH (1880-1959)

Sinfonia breve

Minneapolis April 1960	Minneapolis SO	LP: Mercury MG 50288/SR 90288/SRI 75116/ 　　MMA 11177/AMS 16127 LP: Composers' Recordings CRIS 248 CD: Mercury 434 3292

KARL BLOMDAHL (1916-1968)

Symphony No 2

Stockholm January 1971	Stockholm PO	LP: EMI 4E 061 35142 <u>Orchestra described on label as</u> <u>Swedish RO</u>

Forma territonans

Stockholm October 1967	Stockholm PO	LP: RCA VIC 1319/VICS 1319 LP: Caprice CAP 1016 CD: Caprice CAP 21365

Sysyphos, ballet suite

Stockholm October 1967	Stockholm PO	LP: RCA VIC 1319/VICS 1319 LP: Caprice CAP 1016 CD: Caprice CAP 21365

LUIGI BOCCHERINI (1743-1805)

Scuola di ballo, ballet arranged by Françaix

London July 1939	LPO	78: Columbia DX 944-945

ALEXANDER BORODIN (1833-1887)

Symphony No 2

Minneapolis February 1952	Minneapolis SO	LP: Mercury MG 50004/MRL 2550/ MGW 14010/SRW 18010 LP: Philips SFL 14026/850 454

Prince Igor, overture

Walthamstow
June 1959
	LSO	LP: Mercury MG 50265/MG 50324/MG 50346/
		       SR 90265/SR 90324/SR 90346/
		       MMA 11154/AMS 16102/SRI 75016
		LP: Philips 6582 012
		CD: Mercury 434 3732

Prince Igor, Polovtsian dances

Walthamstow
July 1956
	LSO
	LSO Chorus
		45: Mercury XEP 9046/SEX 15003
		LP: Mercury MG 50122/MG 50265/MG 50327/
		       SR 90122/SR 90265/SR 90327/MRL 2537/
		       SR2-9130/MMA 11058/AMS 18070
		LP: Wing MGW 14070/SRW 18070
		LP: Philips SFL 14024/6582 012
		LP: Metronom (Germany) 140.170
		CD: Mercury 434 3082

In the Steppes of Central Asia

Walthamstow June 1959	LSO	Mercury unpublished

JOHANNES BRAHMS (1833-1897)

Symphony No 1

Watford June 1959	LSO	LP: Mercury MG 50268/SR 90268/ MMA 11135/AMS 16082 LP: Philips SFL 14080/700 136WGY CD: Mercury 434 3802

Symphony No 2

Minneapolis December 1957	Minneapolis SO	LP: Mercury MG 50171/SR 90171/MMA 11049 LP: Wing MGW 14052/SRW 18052/WL 1047 LP: Philips SFL 14011/700 424WGY LP: Pickwick S-4046 CD: Mercury 434 3802

Symphony No 3

Minneapolis April 1955	Minneapolis SO	LP: Mercury MG 50072/MMA 11138 LP: Wing MGW 14032/SRW 18032/WL 1019
Watford July 1963	LSO	LP: Mercury MG 50502/SR 90502 CD: Mercury 434 3802

Symphony No 4

Watford July 1963	LSO	LP: Mercury MG 50503/SR 90503 CD: Mercury 434 3802

Piano Concerto No 2

Walthamstow May 1967	RPO Bachauer	LP: Reader's Digest RD4 603-04 CD: Chesky CD 36

Violin Concerto

Den Haag June 1949	Residentie Orchestra Neveu	CD: Music and Arts CD 837
Watford July 1962	LSO Szeryng	LP: Mercury MG 50308/SR 90308/ MMA 11184/AMS 16134 LP: Philips AL 3538/SAL 3538/SFM 23021 LP: Contour CC 7523 LP: Metronom (Germany) 140.129 CD: Mercury 434 3182 <u>Excerpt</u> CD: Mercury 442 5412

Haydn Variations

Watford July 1957	LSO	LP: Mercury MG 50154/SR 90154 LP: Philips GL 5824/SGL 5824 CD: Mercury 434 3262

Academic Festival Overture

Minneapolis November 1955	Minneapolis SO	LP: Mercury MG 50072/MG 50336/MG 50503/ SR 90336/SR 90503/MMA 11138 LP: Philips GL 5824/SGL 5824

Tragic Overture

Minneapolis November 1955	Minneapolis SO	LP: Mercury MG 50072/MG 50336/SR 90336/ MMA 11138/SR2-9134 LP: Philips GL 5824/SGL 5824

Song of Destiny

London 1966	BBC SO BBC Chorus	Unpublished radio broadcast
Stockholm May 1988	Stockholm PO Stockholm Philharmonic Chorus	CD: Bis unpublished

Hungarian Dance No 1 in G minor

Watford	LSO	45: Mercury XEP 9028/SEX 15004
July 1957		LP: Mercury MG 50154/MG 50336/SR 90154/
		SR 90336/MMA 11051/AMS 16006/SRI 75024
		LP: Philips GL 5824/SGL 5824/
		6527 032/6582 017
		CD: Mercury 434 3262

Hungarian Dance No 2 in D minor

Watford	LSO	45: Mercury XEP 9028/SEX 15004
July 1957		LP: Mercury MG 50154/MG 50336/SR 90154/
		SR 90336/MMA 11051/AMS 16006/SRI 75024
		LP: Philips GL 5824/SGL 5824/
		6527 032/6582 017
		CD: Mercury 434 3262

Hungarian Dance No 3 in F

Watford	LSO	LP: Mercury MG 50437/SR 90437/SRI 75024
July-		LP: Philips 6582 017
August 1965		CD: Mercury 434 3262

Hungarian Dance No 4 in F sharp minor

Watford	LSO	LP: Mercury MG 50437/SR 90437/SRI 75024
July-		LP: Philips 6582 017
August 1965		CD: Mercury 434 3262

Hungarian Dance No 5 in G minor

Watford	LSO	45: Mercury XEP 9028/SEX 15004
July 1957		LP: Mercury MG 50154/MG 50336/SR 90154/
		SR 90336/MMA 11051/AMS 16006/SRI 75024
		LP: Philips GL 5824/SGL 5824/
		6527 032/6582 017
		CD: Mercury 434 3262

Dorati

Hungarian Dance No 6 in D

Watford   LSO
July 1957

LP: Mercury MG 50154/MG 50336/SR 90154/
        SR 90336/MMA 11051/AMS 16006/SRI 75024
LP: Philips GL 5824/SGL 5824/
        6527 032/6582 017
CD: Mercury 434 3262

Hungarian Dance No 7 in A

Watford   LSO
July 1957

45: Mercury XEP 9028/SEX 15004
LP: Mercury MG 50154/MG 50336/SR 90154/
        SR 90336/MMA 11051/AMS 16006/SRI 75024
LP: Philips GL 5824/SGL 5824/
        6527 032/6582 017
CD: Mercury 434 3262

Hungarian Dance No 10 in F

Watford   LSO
July–
August 1965

LP: Mercury MG 50437/SR 90437/SRI 75024
LP: Philips 6582 017
CD: Mercury 434 3262

Hungarian Dance No 11 in D minor

Watford   LSO
July 1957

45: Mercury XEP 9028/SEX 15004
LP: Mercury MG 50154/MG 50336/SR 90154/
        SR 90336/MMA 11051/AMS 16006/SRI 75024
LP: Philips GL 5824/SGL 5824/
        6527 032/6582 017
CD: Mercury 434 3262

Hungarian Dance No 12 in D minor

Watford   LSO
July–
August 1965

LP: Mercury MG 50437/SR 90437/SRI 75024
LP: Philips 6582 017
CD: Mercury 434 3262

Hungarian Dance No 15 in B flat

Watford   LSO
July–
August 1965

LP: Mercury MG 50437/SR 90437/SRI 75024
LP: Philips 6582 017
CD: Mercury 434 3262

Hungarian Dance No 17 in F sharp minor

Watford	LSO	LP: Mercury MG 50437/SR 90437/SRI 75024
July-		LP: Philips 6582 017
August 1965		CD: Mercury 434 3262

Hungarian Dance No 18 in D

Watford	LP: Mercury MG 50437/SR 90437/SRI 75024
July-	LP: Philips 6582 017
August 1965	CD: Mercury 434 3262

Hungarian Dance No 19 in B minor

Watford	LSO	LP: Mercury MG 50437/SR 90437/SRI 75024
July-		LP: Philips 6582 017
August 1965		CD: Mercury 434 3262

Hungarian Dance No 20 in E minor

Watford	LSO	LP: Mercury MG 50437/SR 90437/SRI 75024
July-		LP: Philips 6582 017
August 1965		CD: Mercury 434 3262

Hungarian Dance No 21 in E minor

Watford	LSO	45: Mercury XEP 9028/SEX 15004
July 1957		LP: Mercury MG 50154/MG 50336/SR 90154/ SR 90336/MMA 11051/AMS 16006/SRI 75024
		LP: Philips GL 5824/SGL 5824/ 6527 032/6582 017
		CD: Mercury 434 3262

BENJAMIN BRITTEN (1913-1976)

Variations and Fugue on a theme of Purcell

Minneapolis November 1954	Minneapolis SO Deems Taylor	LP: Mercury MG 50047/MG 50055/ MRL 2533/MMA 11023 LP: Wing MGW 14033/SRW 18033/WL 1036 LP: Philips SFL 14010 MG 50047 is version without narrative
London March 1965	RPO Connery	LP: Decca LK 4801/PFS 4104/SPA 520/VIV 40 LP: London 55005/21007 CD: Pickwick IMPX 9009 CD: Decca 444 1042/450 0242

Our Hunting Fathers

Boston April 1965	BBC SO Harper	Unpublished radio broadcast

Spring Symphony

London February 1981	BBC SO BBC Singers Armstrong, Walker, Rolfe-Johnson	Unpublished radio broadcast

MAX BRUCH (1838-1920)

Concerto for 2 pianos and orchestra

London November 1973	LSO Berkovsky, Twining	LP: EMI 1C 063 02493 LP: Angel 36997

Kol Nidrei

Watford July 1962	LSO Starker	LP: Mercury MG 50303/SR 90303/ MMA 1183/AMS 16133/SRI 75045 LP: Philips SFM 23020 LP: Fontana (Holland) ZKY 894 024 LP: Metronom (Germany) 140.169 LP: Contour CC 7585 CD: Mercury 420 8732/432 0012

NICOLO CASTIGLIONE (Born 1932)

Apreludes

London October 1965	BBC SO	Unpublished radio broadcast

EMMANUEL CHABRIER (1841-1894)

Cotillon, ballet music arranged by Rieti

London July 1938	LPO	78: Columbia DX 877-878 78: Columbia (France) LFX 701-702 78: Columbia (USA) X 113 78: Columbia (Argentina) DOX 585-586

FREDERIC CHOPIN (1810-1849)

Piano Concerto No 1

Watford July 1963	LSO Bachauer	LP: Mercury MG 50368/SR 90368 CD: Mercury 434 3742

Piano Concerto No 2

Watford June 1964	LSO Bachauer	LP: Mercury MG 50432/SR 90432 CD: Mercury 434 3742
Amsterdam June- July 1983	Concertgebouw Orchestra Schiff	LP: Philips 411 9421 CD: Philips 411 9422

FRANCESCO CILEA (1866-1950)

L'Arlesiana, excerpt (E la solita storia)

New York September 1947	Victor SO Tagliavini	78: Victor MO 1191/VO 13 78: HMV DB 6869 LP: Victor LM 1202/LM 20062

AARON COPLAND (1900-1990)

Symphony No 3

Minneapolis February 1953	Minneapolis SO	LP: Mercury MG 50018/MG 50421/ SR 90421/MMA 11050 Recorded under auspices of Koussevitzky Music Foundation

Dance Symphony

Detroit May 1981	Detroit SO	LP: Decca SXDL 7547 CD: Decca 414 2732/430 7052/448 2612

Appalachian Spring, ballet

Watford June 1961	LSO	LP: Mercury MG 50246/SR 90246/ MMA 11172/AMS 16122 CD: Mercury 434 3012 Excerpt CD: Mercury 442 5412
Detroit November 1984	Detroit SO	LP: Decca 414 4571 CD: Decca 414 4572/430 7052

Billy the Kid, ballet

Watford June 1961	LSO	LP: Mercury MG 50246/SR 90246/ MMA 11172/AMS 16122 CD: Mercury 434 3012

Billy the Kid, waltz

Dallas February 1947	Dallas SO	78: Victor M 1214 45: Victor WDM 1214

Danzon cubano

Minneapolis December 1957	Minneapolis SO	45: Mercury XEP 9004 LP: Mercury MG 50172/SR 90172/ MMA 11005/AMS 16021 CD: Mercury 434 3012

Fanfare for the Common Man

Detroit May 1981	Detroit SO	LP: Decca SXDL 7547 CD: Decca 414 2732/430 7052

Rodeo, 4 dance episodes

Dallas February 1947	Dallas SO	78: Victor M 1214 45: Victor WDM 1214 LP: Victor LM 32
Minneapolis December 1957	Minneapolis SO	LP: Mercury MG 50172/SR 90172/ MMA 11005/AMS 16021 CD: Mercury 434 3292 Excerpts 45: Mercury XEP 9004 LP: Mercury MG 50494/SR 90494
Detroit May 1981	Detroit SO	LP: Decca SXDL 7547/416 5511 CD: Decca 414 2732/430 7052/448 2612

El salon Mexico

Minneapolis December 1957	Minneapolis SO	LP: Mercury MG 50172/SR 90172/ MMA 11005/AMS 16021 Excerpt LP: Mercury MB 1001
Detroit May 1981	Detroit SO	LP: Decca SXDL 7547 CD: Decca 414 2732/430 7052/448 2612

LUIGI DALLAPICCOLA (1904-1975)

Il prigionero

Washington April 1974	National SO University of Maryland Choir Barrera, Mazzieri, Emile	LP: Decca HEAD 10

Requiescant

London February 1966	BBC SO	Unpublished radio broadcast

ALEXANDER DARGOMIZHKY (1813-1869)

Russalka, ballet music

London September 1937	LPO	78: Columbia DX 804 78: Columbia (Germany) DWX 1603 78: Columbia (USA) 69126D

CLAUDE DEBUSSY (1862-1918)

Images (Ibéria)

Washington April 1974	National SO	LP: Decca SXL 6742 LP: London 6968

3 Nocturnes

Minneapolis February 1952	Minneapolis SO Cecilian Singers	LP: Mercury MG 50005/MG 50025/MRL 2516 LP: Wing MGW 14029/SRW 18029
Washington April 1974	National SO Oratorio Society Choir	LP: Decca SXL 6742 LP: London CS 6968

LEO DELIBES (1836-1891)

Coppélia, ballet

Minneapolis
December 1957
	Minneapolis SO	LP: Mercury OL2-105/SR2-9005/
		    MG 50185-50186/SR 90185-90186/
		    MMA 11000-11001/AMS 16018-16019/
		    SRI2-77004
		LP: Wing SRW2-19050
		LP: Philips GL 5780-5781/SGL 5780-5781/
		    SFL 14100-14101/6780 253
		CD: Mercury 434 3132
		<u>Excerpts</u>
		45: Mercury XEP 9018/XEP 9026
		LP: Mercury MG 50328/MG 50494/
		    SR 90328/SR 90494
		LP: Wing MGW 14087/SRW 18087
		LP: Philips 839 536

ERNO DOHNANYI (1877-1960)

Wedding Waltz (The Veil of Pierette)

Vienna June 1958	Philharmonia Hungarica	45: Mercury XEP 9076/SEX 15020 LP: Mercury MG 50190/SR 90190/ MMA 11116/AMS 16063 LP: Wing WL 1208 CD: Mercury 434 3382

GAETONO DONIZETTI (1797-1848)

L'elisir d'amore, excerpt (Una furtiva lagrima)

New York September 1947	Victor SO Tagliavini	78: Victor MO 1191/VO 13 78: HMV DB 6856 LP: Victor LM 1202 LP: EMI EX 769 7411 CD: EMI CHS 769 7412

ANTAL DORATI (1906-1988)

Symphony No 1

Minneapolis April 1960	Minneapolis SO	LP: Mercury MG 50248/MG 50499/ SR 90248/SR 90499
London April 1966	BBC SO	Unpublished radio broadcast
Stockholm January 1972	Stockholm PO	CD: Bis BISCD 408

Symphony No 2 "Querela pacis"

Stockholm May 1988	Stockholm PO	CD: Bis BISCD 408

Piano Concerto

Washington October 1975	National SO Alpenheim	LP: Turnabout

Madrigal Suite for choir and small orchestra

London April 1966	BBC SO BBC Chorus	Unpublished radio broadcast

Die Stimmen, for bass and orchestra

Stockholm October 1978	Stockholm PO Lagger	LP: Bachtele Verlag SBV 003

<u>Other compositions by Dorati not involving a conductor were recorded and published on the Mercury and Philips labels</u>

ANTONIN DVORAK (1841-1904)

Symphony No 7

Watford July 1963	LSO	LP: Mercury MG 50516/SR 90516 CD: Mercury 434 3122

Symphony No 8

Watford June 1959	LSO	LP: Mercury MG 50236/SR 90236/ MMA 11128/AMS 16075 LP: Wing MGW 14080/SRW 18080 LP: Concert Hall CMS 2445/SMS 2445 CD: Mercury 434 3122

Symphony No 9 "From the New World"

Den Haag 1953	Residentie Orchestra	LP: Philips ABL 3021/A00154L LP: Epic LC 3001
Amsterdam September 1959	Concertgebouw Orchestra	LP: Philips ABL 3309/SABL 161/GL 5848/ SGL 5848/SFL 14030/6701 006/6582 014 LP: Fontana ZKY 894.007/839 502 CD: Philips 442 4012
London December 1966	New Philharmonia	LP: Decca LK 4880/PFS 4128/JB 37 LP: London 21025/15567 LP: Contour CC 7579 CD: Decca 448 9472
London February 1976	RPO	LP: Turnabout TV 34702

Violin Concerto

Minneapolis March 1951	Minneapolis SO Milstein	78: Victor M 1537 45: Victor WDM 1537 LP: Victor LM 1147 LP: HMV (France) FALP 158/FALP 241

Cello Concerto

Watford July 1962	LSO Starker	LP: Mercury MG 50303/SR 90303/ MMA 11183/AMS 16133/SRI 75045 LP: Philips SFM 23020 LP: Fontana (Holland) ZKY 894.024 LP: Contour CC 7585 CD: Mercury 420 8732/432 0012

American Suite

London October 1983	RPO	LP: Decca 411 7351 LP: London 71024 CD: Decca 430 7022

Carnival Overture

Watford
June 1959
	LSO	LP: Mercury MG 50236/MG 50323/MG 50516/
		      SR 90236/SR 90323/SR 90516/
		      MMA 11128/AMS 16075
		LP: Wing MGW 14080/SRW 18080
		LP: Concert Hall CM 2445/SMS 2445

Czech Suite

Detroit June 1980	Detroit SO	LP: Decca SXDL 7522 LP: London 71024 CD: Decca 414 3702/436 4762/ 443 0152/448 2452

In Nature's Realm, overture

Amsterdam October 1986	Concertgebouw Orchestra	LP: Philips 420 6071 CD: Philips 420 6072

Nocturne for strings

Detroit June 1980	Detroit SO	LP: Decca SXDL 7522 LP: London 71024 CD: Decca 414 3702/436 4762

Polka in B flat

Detroit June 1980	Detroit SO	LP: Decca SXDL 7522 LP: London 71024 CD: Decca 414 3702/436 4762

Polonaise in E flat

Detroit June 1980	Detroit SO	LP: Decca SXDL 7522 LP: London 71024 CD: Decca 414 3702/436 4762

Prague Waltzes

Detroit June 1980	Detroit SO	LP: Decca SXDL 7522 LP: London 71024 CD: Decca 448 2452/436 4762/443 0152

Requiem

Edinburgh September 1970	Stockholm PO and Chorus Soloists	Unpublished radio broadcast

Slavonic Dance No 1 in C

Minneapolis
April 1958
	Minneapolis SO	45: Mercury XEP 9030
		LP: Mercury MG50193-50194/SR90193-90194/
		    MG 50335/SR 90335/MMA 11029-11030/
		    AMS 16046-16047/SR2-9007/SRI2-77001
		LP: Wing MGW 14082/SRW 18082
		LP: Philips GL 5832/SGL 5832/6527 032

Bamberg 1975	Bamberg SO	LP: Turnabout TV 34582 LP: Turnabout (France) FSM 73001
London September- October 1983	RPO	LP: Decca 411 7351/417 2671 CD: Decca 411 7352/417 7492/430 7352/ 436 4762

Slavonic Dance No 2 in E minor

Minneapolis
April 1958
	Minneapolis SO	45: Mercury XEP 9039/EP 40041
		LP: Mercury MG50193-50194/SR90193-90194/
		    MG 50335/SR 90335/MMA 11029-11030/
		    AMS 16046-16047/SR2-9007/SRI2-77001
		LP: Wing MGW 14082/SRW 18082
		LP: Philips GL 5832/SGL 5832

Bamberg 1975	Bamberg SO	LP: Turnabout TV 34582 LP: Turnabout (France) FSM 73001
London September- October 1983	RPO	LP: Decca 411 7351 CD: Decca 411 7352/417 7492/430 7352/ 436 4762

Slavonic Dance No 3 in A flat

Minneapolis
April 1958
	Minneapolis SO	45: Mercury XEP 9030
		LP: Mercury MG50193-50194/SR90193-90194/
		    MG 50335/SR 90335/MMA 11029-11030/
		    AMS 16046-16047/SR2-9007/SRI2-77001
		LP: Wing MGW 14082/SRW 18082
		LP: Philips GL 5832/SGL 5832/6527 032

Bamberg 1975	Bamberg SO	LP: Turnabout TV 34582 LP: Turnabout (France) FSM 73001
London September- October 1983	RPO	LP: Decca 411 7351/417 2671 CD: Decca 411 7352/417 7492/430 7352/ 436 4762

Slavonic Dance No 4 in F

Minneapolis
April 1958
	Minneapolis SO	45: Mercury XEP 9063/SEX 15014
		LP: Mercury MG50193-50194/SR90193-90194/
		    MG 50335/SR 90335/MMA 11029-11030/
		    AMS 16046-16047/SR2-9007/SRI2-77001
		LP: Wing MGW 14082/SRW 18082
		LP: Philips GL 5832/SGL 5832/6527 032

Bamberg 1975	Bamberg SO	LP: Turnabout TV 34582 LP: Turnabout (France) FSM 73001
London September- October 1983	RPO	LP: Decca 411 7351 CD: Decca 411 7352/417 7492/430 7352

Slavonic Dance No 5 in A

Minneapolis
April 1958
	Minneapolis SO	45: Mercury XEP 9039/EP 40041
		LP: Mercury MG50193-50194/SR90193-90194/
		    MG 50335/SR 90335/MMA 11029-11030/
		    AMS 16046-16047/SR2-9007/SRI2-77001
		LP: Wing MGW 14082/SRW 18082
		LP: Philips GL 5832/SGL 5832/6527 032

Bamberg 1975	Bamberg SO	LP: Turnabout TV 34582 LP: Turnabout (France) FSM 73001
London September- October 1983	RPO	LP: Decca 411 7351 CD: Decca 411 7352/417 7492/430 7352

Slavonic Dance No 6 in D

Minneapolis
April 1958
	Minneapolis SO	LP: Mercury MG50193-50194/SR90193-90194/
		    MG 50335/SR 90335/MMA 11029-11030/
		    AMS 16046-16047/SR2-9007/SRI2-77001
		LP: Wing MGW 14082/SRW 18082
		LP: Philips GL 5832/SGL 5832/6527 032

Bamberg 1975	Bamberg SO	LP: Turnabout TV 34582 LP: Turnabout (France) FSM 73001
London September- October 1983	RPO	LP: Decca 411 7351 CD: Decca 411 7352/417 7492/430 7352

Slavonic Dance No 7 in C minor

Minneapolis
April 1958
	Minneapolis SO	45: Mercury XEP 9030
		LP: Mercury MG50193-50194/SR90193-90194/
		    MG 50335/SR 90335/MMA 11029-11030/
		    AMS 16046-16047/SR2-9007/SRI2-77001
		LP: Wing MGW 14082/SRW 18082
		LP: Philips GL 5832/SGL 5832/6527 032

Bamberg 1972	Bamberg SO	LP: Turnabout TV 34582 LP: Turnabout (France) FSM 73001
London September- October 1983	RPO	LP: Decca 411 7351 CD: Decca 411 7352/417 7492/430 7352/

Slavonic Dance No 8 in G minor

Minneapolis
April 1958
	Minneapolis SO	45: Mercury XEP 9030
		LP: Mercury MG50193-50194/SR90193-90194/
		    MG 50335/SR 90335/MMA 11029-11030/
		    AMS 16046-16047/SR2-9007/SRI2-77001
		LP: Wing MGW 14082/SRW 18082
		LP: Philips GL 5832/SGL 5832/6527 032

Bamberg 1972	Bamberg SO	LP: Turnabout TV 34582 LP: Turnabout (France) FSM 73001
London September- October 1983	RPO	LP: Decca 411 7351/417 2671 CD: Decca 411 7352/417 7492/430 7352/ 436 4762

Slavonic Dance No 9 in B

Minneapolis
April 1958
	Minneapolis SO	LP: Mercury MG50193-50194/SR90193-90194/
		    MG 50335/SR 90335/MMA 11029-11030/
		    AMS 16046-16047/SR2-9007/SRI2-77001
		LP: Wing MGW 14082/SRW 18082
		LP: Philips GL 5832/SGL 5832

Bamberg 1975	Bamberg SO	LP: Turnabout TV 34582 LP: Turnabout (France) FSM 73001
London September- October 1983	RPO	LP: Decca 411 7351 CD: Decca 411 7352/417 7492/ 430 7352/448 9912

Slavonic Dance No 10 in E minor

Minneapolis
April 1958
	Minneapolis SO	45: Mercury XEP 9039/EP 40041
		LP: Mercury MG50193-50194/SR90193-90194/
		    MG 50335/SR 90335/MMA 11029-11030/
		    AMS 16046-16047/SR2-9007/SRI2-77001
		LP: Wing MGW 14082/SRW 18082
		LP: Philips GL 5832/SGL 5832

Bamberg 1975	Bamberg SO	LP: Turnabout TV 34582 LP: Turnabout (France) FSM 73001
London September- October 1983	RPO	LP: Decca 411 7351/417 2671 CD: Decca 411 7352/417 7492/430 7352/ 436 4762/448 9912

Slavonic Dance No 11 in F

Minneapolis
April 1958
	Minneapolis SO	LP: Mercury MG50193-50194/SR90193-90194/
		    MG 50335/SR 90335/MMA 11029-11030/
		    AMS 16046-16047/SR2-9007/SRI2-77001
		LP: Wing MGW 14082/SRW 18082
		LP: Philips GL 5832/SGL 5832

Bamberg 1975	Bamberg SO	LP: Turnabout TV 34582 LP: Turnabout (France) FSM 73001
London September- October 1983	RPO	LP: Decca 411 7351 CD: Decca 411 7352/417 7492/ 430 7352/448 9912

Slavonic Dance No 12 in D flat

Minneapolis
April 1958
	Minneapolis SO	LP: Mercury MG50193-50194/SR90193-90194/
		    MG 50335/SR 90335/MMA 11029-11030/
		    AMS 16046-16047/SR2-9007/SRI2-77001
		LP: Wing MGW 14082/SRW 18082
		LP: Philips GL 5832/SGL 5832

Bamberg 1975	Bamberg SO	LP: Turnabout TV 34582 LP: Turnabout (France) FSM 73001
London September- October 1983	RPO	LP: Decca 411 7351 CD: Decca 411 7352/417 7492/ 430 7352/448 9912

Slavonic Dance No 13 in B flat

Minneapolis
April 1958
	Minneapolis SO	45: Mercury XEP 9039/EP 40041
		LP: Mercury MG50193-50194/SR90193-90194/
		    MG 50335/SR 90335/MMA 11029-11030/
		    AMS 16046-16047/SR2-9007/SRI2-77001
		LP: Wing MGW 14082/SRW 18082
		LP: Philips GL 5832/SGL 5832

Bamberg 1975	Bamberg SO	LP: Turnabout TV 34582 LP: Turnabout (France) FSM 73001
London September- October 1983	RPO	LP: Decca 411 7351 CD: Decca 411 7352/417 7492/ 430 7352/448 9912

Slavonic Dance No 14 in B flat

Minneapolis
April 1958
	Minneapolis SO	LP: Mercury MG50193-50194/SR90193-90194/
		      MG 50335/SR 90335/MMA 11029-11030/
		      AMS 16046-16047/SR2-9007/SRI2-77001
		LP: Wing MGW 14082/SRW 18082
		LP: Philips GL 5832/SGL 5832

Bamberg 1975	Bamberg SO	LP: Turnabout TV 34582 LP: Turnabout (France) FSM 73001
London September- October 1983	RPO	LP: Decca 411 7351 CD: Decca 411 7352/417 7492/ 430 7352/448 9912

Slavonic Dance No 15 in C

Minneapolis
April 1958
	Minneapolis SO	45: Mercury XEP 9063/SEX 15014
		LP: Mercury MG50193-50194/SR90193-90194/
		      MG 50335/SR 90335/MMA 11029-11030/
		      AMS 16046-16047/SR2-9007/SRI2-77001
		LP: Wing MGW 14082/SRW 18082
		LP: Philips GL 5832/SGL 5832

Bamberg 1975	Bamberg SO	LP: Turnabout TV 34582 LP: Turnabout (France) FSM 73001
London September- October 1983	RPO	LP: Decca 411 7351 CD: Decca 411 7352/417 7492/ 430 7352/448 9912

Slavonic Dance No 16 in A flat

Minneapolis
April 1958
	Minneapolis SO	LP: Mercury MG50193-50194/SR90193-90194/
		      MG 50335/SR 90335/MMA 11029-11030/
		      AMS 16046-16047/SR2-9007/SRI2-77001
		LP: Wing MGW 14082/SRW 18082
		LP: Philips GL 5832/SGL 5832

Bamberg 1975	Bamberg SO	LP: Turnabout TV 34582 LP: Turnabout (France) FSM 73001
London September- October 1983	RPO	LP: Decca 411 7351 CD: Decca 411 7352/417 7492/ 430 7352/448 9912

Slavonic Rhapsody No 1 in D

Amsterdam September 1956	Concertgebouw Orchestra	LP: Philips L09003-09004L/6701 008

Slavonic Rhapsody No 2 in G minor

Amsterdam October 1957	Concertgebouw Orchestra	LP: Philips L09003-09004L/6701 008

Slavonic Rhapsody No 3 in A flat minor

Den Haag 1953	Residentie Orchestra	LP: Philips NBR 6010
Detroit April 1978	Detroit SO	LP: Decca SXL 6896 LP: London 71195 CD: Decca 425 0872

EDWARD ELGAR (1857-1934)

Pomp and Circumstance March No 1

Amsterdam September 1959	Concertgebouw Orchestra	45: Philips ABE 10245/313 123SF/SBF 275 LP: Philips 6780 753 LP: Reader's Digest RDS 6997/2588

GEORGE ENESCU (1881-1955)

Rumanian Rhapsody No 1

Watford June 1960	LSO	LP: Mercury MG 50235/SR 90235/SRI 75018/ MMA 11153/AMS 16101 LP: Philips 6747 394 CD: Mercury 432 0152
Detroit April 1978	Detroit SO	LP: Decca SXL 6896 LP: London 71195 CD: Decca 425 0872

Rumanian Rhapsody No 2

Watford June 1960	LSO	LP: Mercury MG 50235/SR 90235/SRI 75018/ MMA 11153/AMS 16101 CD: Mercury 434 3262

FREDERIC D'ERLANGER (1868-1943)

Les cent baisers, ballet

London September 1937	LPO	78: HMV C 3098-3099 78: Victor M 511 <u>Excerpts</u> 78: Victor 12-376

ESPEJO

Tzigane for violin and orchestra

Los Angeles 1940s	Hollywood Bowl SO Elman	CD: Eklipse EKR 1404

MANUEL DE FALLA (1876-1946)

El amor brujo

New York June 1944	Ballet Theatre Orchestra L'Argentinita	78: Decca (USA) DA 390 <u>Dorati's first recording with an American orchestra</u>

La vida breve, Interlude and Dance No 1

Minneapolis
April 1957
	Minneapolis SO	45: Mercury XEP 9052
		LP: Mercury MG 50146/SR 90007/MMA 11081/
		    AMS 16002/SRI 75101
		LP: Mercury (France) 839.816
		LP: Wing MGW 14063/MGW 14085/
		    SRW 18063/SRW 18085
		CD: Mercury 432 8292
		<u>Dance only</u>
		LP: Mercury SR2-9130

Harpsichord Concerto

Watford July 1964	BBC SO Puyana	Mercury unpublished

7 canciones populares espanolas

London 1960	LSO Berganza	Unpublished radio broadcast

PAUL FETLER (Born 1920)

Contrasts for orchestra

Minneapolis April 1960	Minneapolis SO	LP: Mercury MG 50282/SR 90282/ MMA 11151/AMS 16099 CD: Mercury 434 3292

CAROLUS FODOR (1786-1846)

Symphony No 4

Den Haag Date not confirmed	Residentie Orchestra	LP: Residentie Orchestra 6812 901-6812 906 CD: Olympia OCD 501

JEAN FRANCAIX (Born 1912)

Concertino for piano and orchestra

Watford August 1965	LSO C.Françaix	LP: Mercury MG 50435/SR 90435 LP: Philips AL 3637/SAL 3637/412 0281 CD: Mercury 434 3352

CESAR FRANCK (1822-1890)

Symphony in D minor

London February 1976	RPO	LP: Turnabout TV 34663

Variations symphoniques pour piano et orchestre

London February 1976	RPO Alpenheim	LP: Turnabout TV 34663

ROBERTO GERHARD (1896-1970)

Symphony No 1

London March 1964	BBC SO	LP: HMV ALP 2063/ASD 613 LP: Angel 60071 LP: Argo ZRG 752

Concerto for orchestra

Boston April 1965	BBC SO	Unpublished radio broadcast

Dances from Don Quixote

London March 1964	BBC SO	LP: HMV ALP 2063/ASD 613 LP: Angel 60071 LP: Argo ZRG 752

The Plague

London April 1969	BBC SO BBC Singers Murray	Unpublished radio broadcast
Washington April 1974	National SO and Chorus McCowen	LP: Decca HEAD 6
London February 1981	BBC SO BBC Singers Rippon	Unpublished radio broadcast

GEORGE GERSHWIN (1898-1937)

An American in Paris

Minneapolis December 1957	Minneapolis SO	LP: Mercury MG 50290/MG 50431/SR 90290/ SR 90431/MMA 11004/MMA 11185/ AMS 16135 LP: Wing WL 1206 LP: Philips GL 5820/SGL 5820/ 6513 003/6582 019 CD: Mercury 434 3292/434 3652

Porgy and Bess, symphonic suite arranged by Bennett

Minneapolis December 1952	Minneapolis SO	LP: Mercury MG 50016/MG 50394/SR 90016/ SR 90394/MRL 2506/MMA 11004/ MMA 11185/AMS 16135 LP: Wing WL 1206 LP: Philips GL 5820/SGL 5820
Detroit October 1982	Detroit SO	LP: Decca 410 1101 CD: Decca 410 1102/430 7122

ALBERTO GINASTERA (Born 1916)

Variaciones concertantes

Minneapolis November 1954	Minneapolis SO	LP: Mercury MG 50047/SR 90047/MRL 2533

ALEXANDER GLAZUNOV (1865-1936)

The Seasons, ballet

Dallas 1949	Dallas SO	78: Victor M 1072

MORTON GOULD (Born 1913)

Spirituals

Minneapolis February 1953	Minneapolis SO	45: Mercury EP 15028 LP: Mercury MG 50016/SR 90016/MRL 2506 LP: Wing MGW 14034/SRW 18034

EDVARD GRIEG (1843-1907)

Peer Gynt, suite no 1

Vienna 1958	VSO	45: Philips CFE 15037/494 016EE LP: Epic LC 3606 LP: Philips SCFL 102/EFR 2009/SFL 14043 <u>Excerpts</u> 45: Philips EFF 545

Peer Gynt, suite no 2

Vienna 1958	VSO	LP: Philips EFR 2009/SFL 14043 LP: Epic LC 3606 <u>Excerpts</u> 45: Philips EFF 545 LP: Philips SCFL 102

Piano Concerto

New York August 1949	Victor SO Rubinstein	78: Victor M 1343 45: Victor WDM 1343/ERB 16 LP: Victor LM 1018 LP: HMV ALP 1065

FERDE GROFE (1892-1972)

Grand Canyon, suite

Detroit October 1982	Detroit SO	LP: Decca 410 1101 CD: Decca 410 1102/430 7122

Mississippi suite

Detroit October 1982	Detroit SO	LP: Decca 410 1101 CD: Decca 410 1102

GEORGE FRIDERIC HANDEL (1685-1759)

Messiah

Washington 1982	Smithsonian Orchestra University of Maryland and Cathedral Choirs Mathis, Bowman, Ahnsjö, Krause	LP: Intersound DMM 232 CD: Intersound CDD 232

Music for the Royal Fireworks, arranged by Harty

Watford July 1957	LSO	LP: Mercury MG 50158/SR 90158/MMA 11017/ AMS 16031/SRI 75005

Water Music, suite arranged by Harty

Watford July 1957	LSO	LP: Mercury MG 50158/SR 90158/MMA 11017/ AMS 16031/SRI 75005

DORÁTI

BUDAPEST CHORUS

**CHILDREN'S CHORUS
OF THE HUNGARIAN RADIO AND TELEVISION**

HUNGARIAN STATE ORCHESTRA

JÓZSEF SIMÁNDY
/TENOR/

KODÁLY

**OP. 13
PSALMUS
HUNGARICUS**

LPX 11392

STEREO — MONO

**PEACOCK
VARIATIONS**

FRANZ JOSEF HAYDN (1732-1809)

Symphony "A" in B flat

Marl June 1970- June 1972	Philharmonia Hungarica	LP: Decca HDNK 47-48 LP: London STS 15316-15317 CD: Decca 425 9352/448 5312

Symphony "B" in B flat

Marl June 1970- June 1972	Philharmonia Hungarica	LP: Decca HDNK 47-48 LP: London STS 15316-15317 CD: Decca 425 9352/448 5312

Symphony No 1

Marl June 1970- June 1972	Philharmonia Hungarica	LP: Decca HDNA 1-6 LP: London STS 15310-15315 CD: Decca 430 1002/425 9002/448 5312

Symphony No 2

Marl June 1970- June 1972	Philharmonia Hungarica	LP: Decca HDNA 1-6 LP London STS 15310-15315 CD: Decca 430 1002/425 9002/448 5312

Symphony No 3

Marl June 1970- June 1972	Philharmonia Hungarica	LP: Decca HDNA 1-6 LP: London STS 15310-15315 CD: Decca 430 1002/425 9002/448 5312

Symphony No 4

Marl June 1970- June 1972	Philharmonia Hungarica	LP: Decca HDNA 1-6 LP: London STS 15310-15315 CD: Decca 430 1002/425 9002/448 5312

Haydn symphonies/continued

Symphony No 5

| Marl June 1970– June 1972 | Philharmonia Hungarica | LP: Decca HDNA 1-6
LP: London STS 15310-15315
CD: Decca 430 1002/425 9002/448 5312 |

Symphony No 6 "Le matin"

| Marl June 1970– June 1972 | Philharmonia Hungarica | LP: Decca HDNA 1-6
LP: London STS 15310-15315
CD: Decca 430 1002/421 6272/425 9002 448 5312 |

Symphony No 7 "Le midi"

| Marl June 1970– June 1972 | Philharmonia Hungarica | LP: Decca HDNA 1-6
LP: London STS 15310-15315
CD: Decca 430 1002/421 6272/425 9002 448 5312 |

Symphony No 8 "Le soir"

| Marl June 1970– June 1972 | Philharmonia Hungarica | LP: Decca HDNA 1-6
LP: London STS 15310-15315
CD: Decca 430 1002/421 6272/425 9002 448 5312 |

Symphony No 9

| Marl June 1970– June 1972 | Philharmonia Hungarica | LP: Decca HDNA 1-6
LP: London STS 15310-15315
CD: Decca 430 1002/425 9002/448 5312 |

Symphony No 10

| Marl June 1970– June 1972 | Philharmonia Hungarica | LP: Decca HDNA 1-6
LP: London STS 15310-15315
CD: Decca 430 1002/425 9002/448 5312 |

Symphony No 11

| Marl June 1970– June 1972 | Philharmonia Hungarica | LP: Decca HDNA 1-6
LP: London STS 15310-15315
CD: Decca 430 1002/425 9002/448 5312 |

Haydn symphonies/continued

Symphony No 12

Marl June 1970- June 1972	Philharmonia Hungarica	LP: Decca HDNA 1-6 LP: London STS 15310-15315 CD: Decca 430 1002/425 9002/448 5312

Symphony No 13

Marl June 1970- June 1972	Philharmonia Hungarica	LP: Decca HDNA 1-6 LP: London STS 15310-15315 CD: Decca 430 1002/425 9002/448 5312

Symphony No 14

Marl June 1970- June 1972	Philharmonia Hungarica	LP: Decca HDNA 1-6 LP: London STS 15310-15315 CD: Decca 430 1002/425 9002/448 5312

Symphony No 15

Marl June 1970- June 1972	Philharmonia Hungarica	LP: Decca HDNA 1-6 LP: London STS 15310-15315 CD: Decca 430 1002/425 9002/448 5312

Symphony No 16

Marl June 1970- June 1972	Philharmonia Hungarica	LP: Decca HDNA 1-6 LP: London STS 15310-15315 CD: Decca 430 1002/425 9002/448 5312

Symphony No 17

Marl June 1970- June 1972	Philharmonia Hungarica	LP: Decca HDNA 1-6 LP: London STS 15310-15315 CD: Decca 430 1002/425 9052/448 5312

Symphony No 18

Marl June 1970- June 1972	Philharmonia Hungarica	LP: Decca HDNA 1-6 LP: London STS 15310-15315 CD: Decca 430 1002/425 9052/448 5312

Haydn symphonies/continued

Symphony No 19

| Marl
June 1970-
June 1972 | Philharmonia
Hungarica | LP: Decca HDNA 1-6
LP: London STS 15310-15315
CD: Decca 430 1002/425 9052/448 5312 |

Symphony No 20

| Marl
June 1970-
June 1972 | Philharmonia
Hungarica | LP: Decca HDNB 7-12/SDD 468
LP: London STS 15257-15262
CD: Decca 430 1002/425 9052/448 5312 |

Symphony No 21

| Marl
June 1970-
June 1972 | Philharmonia
Hungarica | LP: Decca HDNB 7-12/SDD 468
LP: London STS 15257-15262
CD: Decca 430 1002/425 9002/448 5312 |

Symphony No 22

| Marl
June 1970-
June 1972 | Philharmonia
Hungarica | LP: Decca HDNB 7-12/SDD 468
LP: London STS 15257-15262
CD: Decca 430 1002/425 9052/448 5312 |

Symphony No 22 "Philosopher", second version

| Marl
June 1970-
June 1972 | Philharmonia
Hungarica | LP: Decca HDNK 47-48
LP: London STS 15316-15317
CD: Decca 448 5312/448 5312 |

Symphony No 23

| Marl
June 1970-
June 1972 | Philharmonia
Hungarica | LP: Decca HDNB 7-12
LP: London STS 15257-15262
CD: Decca 430 1002/425 9052/448 5312 |

Symphony No 24

| Marl
June 1970-
June 1972 | Philharmonia
Hungarica | LP: Decca HDNB 7-12
LP: London STS 15257-15262
CD: Decca 430 1002/425 9052/448 5312 |

Haydn symphonies/continued

Symphony No 25

Marl June 1970- June 1972	Philharmonia Hungarica	LP: Decca HDNB 7-12/SDD 457 LP: London STS 15257-15262 CD: Decca 430 1002/425 9052/448 5312

Symphony No 26 "Lamentatione"

Marl June 1970- June 1972	Philharmonia Hungarica	LP: Decca HDNB 7-12/SDD 457 LP: London STS 15257-15262 CD: Decca 430 1002/425 9052/448 5312

Symphony No 27

Marl June 1970- June 1972	Philharmonia Hungarica	LP: Decca HDNB 7-12/SDD 457 LP: London STS 15257-15262 CD: Decca 430 1002/425 9052/448 5312

Symphony No 28

Marl June 1970- June 1972	Philharmonia Hungarica	LP: Decca HDNB 7-12/SDD 457 LP: London STS 15257-15262 CD: Decca 430 1002/425 9052/448 5312

Symphony No 29

Marl June 1970- June 1972	Philharmonia Hungarica	LP: Decca HDNB 7-12/SDD 458 LP: London STS 15257-15262 CD: Decca 430 1002/425 9052/448 5312

Symphony No 30 "Allelujah"

Marl June 1970- June 1972	Philharmonia Hungarica	LP: Decca HDNB 7-12/SDD 458 LP: London STS 15257-15262 CD: Decca 430 1002/425 9052/448 5312

Haydn symphonies/continued

Symphony No 31 in D "Horn Signal"

| Marl June 1970- June 1972 | Philharmonia Hungarica | LP: Decca HDNB 7-12/SDD 458 LP: London STS 15257-15262 CD: Decca 430 1002/425 9052/448 5312 |

Symphony No 32

| Marl June 1970- June 1972 | Philharmonia Hungarica | LP: Decca HDNB 7-12 LP: London STS 15257-15262 CD: Decca 430 1002/425 9052/448 5312 |

Symphony No 33

| Marl June 1970- June 1972 | Philharmonia Hungarica | LP: Decca HDNB 7-12 LP: London STS 15257-15262 CD: Decca 430 1002/425 9052/448 5312 |

Symphony No 34

| Marl June 1970- June 1972 | Philharmonia Hungarica | LP: Decca HDNB 7-12 LP: London STS 15257-15262 CD: Decca 430 1002/425 9102/448 5312 |

Symphony No 35

| Marl June 1970- June 1972 | Philharmonia Hungarica | LP: Decca HDNB 7-12 LP: London STS 15257-15262 CD: Decca 430 1002/425 9102/448 5312 |

Symphony No 36

| Marl June 1970- June 1972 | Philharmonia Hungarica | LP: Decca HDNC 13-18 LP: London STS 15249-15254 CD: Decca 430 1002/425 9102/448 5312 |

Symphony No 37

| Marl June 1970- June 1972 | Philharmonia Hungarica | LP: Decca HDNC 13-18 LP: London STS 15249-15254 CD: Decca 430 1002/425 9102/448 5312 |

Haydn symphonies/continued

Symphony No 38

Marl June 1970- June 1972	Philharmonia Hungarica	LP: Decca HDNC 13-18 LP: London STS 15249-15254 CD: Decca 430 1002/425 9102/448 5312

Symphony No 39

Marl June 1970- June 1972	Philharmonia Hungarica	LP: Decca HDNC 13-18 LP: London STS 15249-15254 CD: Decca 430 1002/425 9102/448 5312

Symphony No 40

Marl June 1970- June 1972	Philharmonia Hungarica	LP: Decca HDNC 13-18 LP: London STS 15249-15254 CD: Decca 430 1002/425 9102/448 5312

Symphony No 41

Marl June 1970- June 1972	Philharmonia Hungarica	LP: Decca HDNC 13-18 LP: London STS 15249-15254 CD: Decca 430 1002/425 9102/448 5312

Symphony No 42

Marl June 1970- June 1972	Philharmonia Hungarica	LP: Decca HDNC 13-18/SDD 414 LP: London STS 15249-15254 CD: Decca 430 1002/425 9102/448 5312

Symphony No 43 "Mercury"

Marl June 1970- June 1972	Philharmonia Hungarica	LP: Decca HDNC 13-18/SDD 546 LP: London STS 15249-15254 CD: Decca 430 1002/425 9102/448 5312

Symphony No 44 "Trauer"

Marl June 1970- June 1972	Philharmonia Hungarica	LP: Decca HDNC 13-18/SDD 546 LP: London STS 15249-15254 CD: Decca 430 1002/425 9102/448 5312

Haydn symphonies/continued

Symphony No 45 in "Farewell"

Watford June 1961	LSO	LP: Mercury MG 50280/SR 90280 LP: Philips GL 5819/SGL 5819
Marl June 1970- June 1972	Philharmonia Hungarica	LP: Decca HDNC 13-18/SDD 414 LP: London STS 15249-15254 CD: Decca 430 1002/425 9102/448 5312

Symphony No 46 in B

Marl   Philharmonia   LP: Decca HDNC 13-18
June 1970-   Hungarica   LP: London STS 15249-15254
June 1972   CD: Decca 430 1002/425 9102/448 5312

Symphony No 47 in G

Marl   Philharmonia   LP: Decca HDNC 13-18
June 1970-   Hungarica   LP: London STS 15249-15254
June 1972   CD: Decca 430 1002/425 9102/448 5312

Symphony No 48 "Maria Theresia"

Marl   Philharmonia   LP: Decca HDNC 13-18/SDD 547
June 1970-   Hungarica   LP: London STS 15249-15254
June 1972   CD: Decca 430 1002/425 9152/448 5312

Symphony No 49 "La passione"

Marl   Philharmonia   LP: Decca HDND 19-22/SDD 359/SDD 547
June 1970-   Hungarica   LP: London STS 15127-15130
June 1972   CD: Decca 430 1002/425 9152/448 5312

Symphony No 50 in C

Marl   Philharmonia   LP: Decca HDND 19-22
June 1970-   Hungarica   LP: London STS 15127-15130
June 1972   CD: Decca 430 1002/425 9152/448 5312

Haydn symphonies/continued

Symphony No 51

| Mar1
June 1970-
June 1972 | Philharmonia
Hungarica | LP: Decca HDND 19-22/SDD 359/SDD 415
LP: London STS 15127-15130
CD: Decca 430 1002/425 9152/448 5312 |

Symphony No 52

| Mar1
June 1970-
June 1972 | Philharmonia
Hungarica | LP: Decca HDND 19-22/SDD 415
LP: London STS 15127-15130
CD: Decca 430 1002/425 9152/448 5312 |

Symphony No 53 "L'Imperiale"

| Mar1
June 1970-
June 1972 | Philharmonia
Hungarica | LP: Decca HDND 19-22
LP: London STS 15127-15130
CD: Decca 430 1002/425 9152/448 5312 |

Symphony No 53 "L'Imperiale", first alternative version of final movement

| Mar1
June 1970-
June 1972 | Philharmonia
Hungarica | LP: Decca HDNK 47-48
LP: London STS 15316-15317
CD: Decca 448 5312 |

Symphony No 53 "L'Imperiale", second alternative version of final movement

| Mar1
June 1970-
June 1972 | Philharmonia
Hungarica | LP: Decca HDNK 47-48
LP: London STS 15316-15317
CD: Decca 448 5312 |

Symphony No 53 "L'Imperiale", third alternative version of final movement also known as Overture in D

| Mar1
June 1970-
June 1972 | Philharmonia
Hungarica | LP: Decca HDNK 47-48
LP: London STS 15316-15317
CD: Decca 448 5312 |

Symphony No 54

| Mar1
June 1970-
June 1972 | Philharmonia
Hungarica | LP: Decca HDND 19-22
LP: London STS 15127-15130
CD: Decca 430 1002/425 9152/448 5312 |

Haydn symphonies/continued

Symphony No 55 "Schoolmaster"

Mar1 June 1970- June 1972	Philharmonia Hungarica	LP: Decca HDND 19-22/SDD 415 LP: London STS 15127-15130 CD: Decca 430 1002/425 9152 /448 5312

Symphony No 56

Mar1 June 1970- June 1972	Philharmonia Hungarica	LP: Decca HDND 19-22 LP: London STS 15127-15130 CD: Decca 430 1002/425 9152 /448 5312

Symphony No 57

Mar1 June 1970- June 1972	Philharmonia Hungarica	LP: Decca HDNE 23-26 LP: London STS 15131-15134 CD: Decca 430 1002/425 9152 /448 5312

Symphony No 58

Mar1 June 1970- June 1972	Philharmonia Hungarica	LP: Decca HDNE 23-26 LP: London STS 15131-15134 CD: Decca 430 1002/425 9152 /448 5312

Symphony No 59 "Fire"

Watford August 1965	Bath Festival Orchestra	LP: Mercury MG 50436/SR 90436 LP: Mercury (France) 131.037 LP: Philips 838 431AY Orchestra described for this recording as Festival Chamber Orchestra
Mar1 June 1970- June 1972	Philharmonia Hungarica	LP: Decca HDNE 23-26 LP: London STS 15131-15134 CD: Decca 430 1002/425 9152 /448 5312

Symphony No 60 "Il distratto"

Mar1 June 1970- June 1972	Philharmonia Hungarica	LP: Decca HDNE 23-26/SDD 358 LP: London STS 15131-15134 CD: Decca 430 1002/425 9202 /448 5312

PHILHARMONIA CONCERT SOCIETY LTD
Artistic Director: WALTER LEGGE

PHILHARMONIA ORCHESTRA & CHORUS

DORATI

26 November 1962

ROYAL FESTIVAL HALL

General Manager: T. E. Bean, C.B.E.

PHILHARMONIA CONCERT SOCIETY Ltd

ARTISTIC DIRECTOR:
WALTER LEGGE

PHILHARMONIA ORCHESTRA & CHORUS

CHORUS MASTER: WILHELM PITZ

STRAVINSKY: Suite, The Firebird (1919)

PROKOFIEV: Piano Concerto No 2 in G minor

SHURA CHERKASSKY

WALTON: Belshazzar's Feast

PETER GLOSSOP

ANTAL DORATI

Monday, November 26, 1962, at 8 p.m.

Programme One Shilling and Sixpence

Haydn symphonies/continued

Symphony No 61

Marl	Philharmonia	LP: Decca HDNE 23-26
June 1970-	Hungarica	LP: London STS 15131-15134
June 1972		CD: Decca 430 1002/425 9202/448 5312

Symphony No 62

Marl	Philharmonia	LP: Decca HDNE 23-26
June 1970-	Hungarica	LP: London STS 15131-15134
June 1972		CD: Decca 430 1002/425 9202/448 5312

Symphony No 63 "La roxelane"

Marl	Philharmonia	LP: Decca HDNE 23-26
June 1970-	Hungarica	LP: London STS 15131-15134
June 1972		CD: Decca 430 1002/425 9202/448 5312

Symphony No 63 "La roxelane", earlier version

Marl	Philharmonia	LP: Decca HDNK 47-48
June 1970-	Hungarica	LP: London STS 15316-15317
June 1972		CD: Decca 448 5312

Symphony No 64 "Tempora mutantus"

Marl	Philharmonia	LP: Decca HDNE 23-26
June 1970-	Hungarica	LP: London STS 15131-15134
June 1972		CD: Decca 430 1002/425 9202/448 5312

Symphony No 65

Marl	Philharmonia	LP: Decca HDNF 27-30
June 1970-	Hungarica	LP: London STS 15135-15138
June 1972		CD: Decca 430 1002/425 9202/448 5312

Haydn symphonies/continued

Symphony No 66

Marl June 1970- June 1972	Philharmonia Hungarica	LP: Decca HDNF 27-30 LP: London STS 15135-15138 CD: Decca 430 1002/425 9202/448 5312

Symphony No 67

Marl June 1970- June 1972	Philharmonia Hungarica	LP: Decca HDNF 27-30/SDD 358 LP: London STS 15135-15138 CD: Decca 430 1002/425 9202/448 5312

Symphony No 68

Marl June 1970- June 1972	Philharmonia Hungarica	LP: Decca HDNF 27-30 LP: London STS 15135-15138 CD: Decca 430 1002/425 9202/448 5312

Symphony No 69

Marl June 1970- June 1972	Philharmonia Hungarica	LP: Decca HDNF 27-30 LP: London STS 15135-15138 CD: Decca 430 1002/425 9202/448 5312

Symphony No 70

Marl June 1970- June 1972	Philharmonia Hungarica	LP: Decca HDNF 27-30 LP: London STS 15135-15138 CD: Decca 430 1002/425 9202/448 5312

Symphony No 71

Marl June 1970- June 1972	Philharmonia Hungarica	LP: Decca HDNF 27-30 LP: Decca STS 15135-15138 CD: Decca 430 1002/425 9202/448 5312

Haydn symphonies/continued

Symphony No 72

Marl June 1970- June 1972	Philharmonia Hungarica	LP: Decca HDNF 27-30 LP: London STS 15135-15138 CD: Decca 430 1002/425 9252/448 5312

Symphony No 73 "La chasse"

Marl June 1970- June 1972	Philharmonia Hungarica	LP: Decca HDNG 31-34/SDD 413 LP: London STS 15182-15185 CD: Decca 430 1002/425 9252/448 5312

Symphony No 74

Marl June 1970- June 1972	Philharmonia Hungarica	LP: Decca HDNG 31-34/SDD 413 LP: London STS 15182-15185 CD: Decca 430 1002/425 9252/448 5312

Symphony No 75

Marl June 1970- June 1972	Philharmonia Hungarica	LP: Decca HDNG 31-34 LP: London STS 15182-15185 CD: Decca 430 1002/425 9252/448 5312

Symphony No 76

Marl June 1970- June 1972	Philharmonia Hungarica	LP: Decca HDNG 31-34 LP: London STS 15182-15185 CD: Decca 430 1002/425 9252/448 5312

Symphony No 77

Marl June 1970- June 1972	Philharmonia Hungarica	LP: Decca HDNG 31-34 LP: London STS 15182-15185 CD: Decca 430 1002/425 9252/448 5312

Haydn symphonies/continued

Symphony No 78

| Mar1
June 1970-
June 1972 | Philharmonia
Hungarica | LP: Decca HDNG 31-34
LP: London STS 15182-15185
CD: Decca 430 1002/425 9252/448 5312 |

Symphony No 79

| Mar1
June 1970-
June 1972 | Philharmonia
Hungarica | LP: Decca HDNG 31-34
LP: London STS 15182-15185
CD: Decca 430 1002/425 9252/448 5312 |

Symphony No 80

| Mar1
June 1970-
June 1972 | Philharmonia
Hungarica | LP: Decca HDNG 31-34
LP: London STS 15182-15185
CD: Decca 430 1002/425 9252/448 5312 |

Symphony No 81

| Watford
August
1965 | Bath Festival
Orchestra | LP: Mercury MG 50436/SR 90436
LP: Mercury (France) 131.037
LP: Philips 838 431AY
<u>Orchestra described for this recording</u>
<u>as Festival Chamber Orchestra</u> |

| Mar1
June 1970-
June 1972 | Philharmonia
Hungarica | LP: Decca HDNG 31-34
LP: London STS 15182-15185
CD: Decca 430 1002/425 9252/448 5312 |

Symphony No 82 "L'ours"

| Mar1
June 1970-
June 1972 | Philharmonia
Hungarica | LP: Decca HDNH 35-40/SDD 482
LP: London STS 15229-15234
CD: Decca 430 1002/425 9252/
    448 1942/448 5312 |

Symphony No 83 "La poule"

| Mar1
June 1970-
June 1972 | Philharmonia
Hungarica | LP: Decca HDNH 35-40/SDD 482
LP: London STS 15229-15234
CD: Decca 430 1002/425 9252/
    448 1942/448 5312 |

Haydn symphonies/continued

Symphony No 84

| Marl
June 1970-
June 1972 | Philharmonia
Hungarica | LP: Decca HDNH 35-40/SDD 483
LP: London STS 15229-15234
CD: Decca 430 1002/425 9302/
    448 1942/448 5312 |

Symphony No 85 "La reine"

| Marl
June 1970-
June 1972 | Philharmonia
Hungarica | LP: Decca HDNH 35-40/SDD 483
LP: Decca STS 15229-15234
CD: Decca 430 1002/425 9302/
    448 1942/448 5312 |

Symphony No 86

| Marl
June 1970-
June 1972 | Philharmonia
Hungarica | LP: Decca HDNH 35-40/SDD 484
LP: London STS 15229-15234
CD: Decca 430 1002/425 9302/
    448 1942/448 5312 |

Symphony No 87

| Marl
June 1970-
June 1972 | Philharmonia
Hungarica | LP: Decca HDNH 35-40/SDD 484
LP: London STS 15229-15234
CD: Decca 430 1002/425 9302/
    448 1942/448 5312 |

Symphony No 88

| Marl
June 1970-
June 1972 | Philharmonia
Hungarica | LP: Decca HDNH 35-40/SDD 431
LP: London STS 15229-15234
CD: Decca 430 1002/425 9302/448 5312 |

Symphony No 89

| Marl
June 1970-
June 1972 | Philharmonia
Hungarica | LP: Decca HDNH 35-40/SDD 431
LP: London STS 15229-15234
CD: Decca 430 1002/425 9302/448 5312 |

Haydn symphonies/continued

Symphony No 90

| Marl
June 1970-
June 1972 | Philharmonia
Hungarica | LP: Decca HDNH 35-40/SDD 412
LP: London STS 15229-15234
CD: Decca 430 1002/425 9302/448 5312 |

Symphony No 91

| Marl
June 1970-
June 1972 | Philharmonia
Hungarica | LP: Decca HDNH 35-40
LP: London STS 15229-15234
CD: Decca 430 1002/425 9302/448 5312 |

Symphony No 92 "Oxford"

| Marl
June 1970-
June 1972 | Philharmonia
Hungarica | LP: Decca HDNH 35-40/SDD 412
LP: London STS 15229-15234
CD: Decca 430 1002/425 9302/448 5312 |

Symphony No 93

| Marl
June 1970-
June 1972 | Philharmonia
Hungarica | LP: Decca HDNJ 41-46/SDD 500
LP: London STS 15319-15324
CD: Decca 430 1002/425 9302/
448 5312/452 2562 |

Symphony No 94 "Surprise"

| Vienna
June 1958 | Philharmonia
Hungarica | LP: Mercury MG 50208/SR 90208/
MMA 11139/AMS 16085/SR2-9128
LP: Wing MGW 14077/SRW 18077
LP: Fontana (Holland) ZKY 894089
LP: Metronom (Germany) 140.132 |

| Marl
June 1970-
June 1972 | Philharmonia
Hungarica | LP: Decca HDNJ 41-46/SDD 500/SPA 494
LP: London STS 15319-15324
CD: Decca 430 1002/425 9302/417 7182/
448 5312/452 2562 |

148 Dorati

Haydn symphonies/continued

Symphony No 95

Marl June 1970- June 1972	Philharmonia Hungarica	LP: Decca HDNJ 41-46/SDD 501 LP: London STS 15319-15324 CD: Decca 430 1002/425 9302/ 448 5312/452 2592

Symphony No 96 "Miracle"

Marl June 1970- June 1972	Philharmonia Hungarica	LP: Decca HDNJ 41-46/SDD 501 LP: London STS 15319-15324 CD: Decca 430 1002/425 9352/417 7182/ 448 5312/452 2592

Symphony No 97

Marl June 1970- June 1972	Philharmonia Hungarica	LP: Decca HDNJ 41-46/SDD 502 LP: London STS 15319-15324 CD: Decca 430 1002/425 9352/ 448 5312/452 2562

Symphony No 98

Marl June 1970- June 1972	Philharmonia Hungarica	LP: Decca HDNJ 41-46/SDD 502 LP: London STS 15319-15324 CD: Decca 430 1002/425 9352/ 448 5312/452 2592

Symphony No 99

Marl June 1970- June 1972	Philharmonia Hungarica	LP: Decca HDNJ 41-46/SDD 503 LP: London STS 15319-15324 CD: Decca 430 1002/425 9352/ 448 5312/452 2592

Haydn symphonies/continued

Symphony No 100 "Military"

Watford July 1957	LSO	LP: Mercury MG 50155/MG 50415/SR 90155/ SR 90415/MRL 2592/MMA 11055 LP: Wing MGW 14064/SRW 18064 LP: Philips 6547 009
Marl June 1970- June 1972	Philharmonia Hungarica	LP: Decca HDNJ 41-46/SDD 503 LP: London STS 15319-15324 CD: Decca 430 1002/425 9352/417 7182/ 448 5312/452 2562

Symphony No 101 "Clock"

Watford July 1957	LSO	LP: Mercury MG 50155/MG 50415/SR 90155/ SR 90415/MRL 2592/MMA 11055 LP: Wing MGW 14064/SRW 18064 LP: Philips 6547 009
Marl June 1970- June 1972	Philharmonia Hungarica	LP: Decca HDNJ 41-46/SDD 504/SPA 494 LP: London STS 15319-15324 CD: Decca 430 1002/425 9352/ 448 5312/452 2592

Symphony No 102

Marl June 1970- June 1972	Philharmonia Hungarica	LP: Decca HDNJ 41-46/SDD 504 LP: London STS 15319-15324 CD: Decca 430 1002/425 9352/ 448 5312/452 2592

Symphony No 103 "Drum Roll"

Vienna June 1958	Philharmonia Hungarica	LP: Mercury MG 50208/SR 90208/ MMA 11139/AMS 16085 LP: Wing MGW 14077/SRW 18077 LP: Fontana (Holland) ZKY 894089 LP: Metronom (Germany) 140.132
Marl June 1970- June 1972	Philharmonia Hungarica	LP: Decca HDNJ 41-46/SDD 505 LP: London STS 15319-15324 CD: Decca 430 1002/425 9352/ 448 5312/452 2562

Haydn symphonies/concluded

Symphony No 103 "Drum Roll", alternative version of final movement

Marl June 1970- June 1972	Philharmonia Hungarica	LP: Decca HDNK 47-48 LP: London STS 15316-15317 CD: Decca 448 5312

Symphony No 104 "London"

Marl June 1970- June 1972	Philharmonia Hungarica	LP: Decca HDNJ 41-46/SDD 505 LP: London STS 15319-15324 CD: Decca 430 1002/425 9352/ 448 5312/452 2562

Die Schöpfung

London December 1976	RPO Brighton Festival Chorus Popp, Doese, Hollweg, Luxon Moll	LP: Decca D50 D2 LP: London OSA 12108 CD: Decca 421 6052/443 0272 Excerpt CD: Decca 411 9572

Die Jahreszeiten

London June 1977	RPO Brighton Festival Chorus Cotrubas, Krenn, Sotin	LP: Decca D88 D3 LP: London OSA 13128 CD: Decca 425 7082

Il ritorno di Tobia

London December 1979	RPO Brighton Festival Chorus Hendricks, Zoghby, D.Jones, Langridge, Luxon	LP: Decca D216 D4 LP: London OSA 51445 CD: Decca 440 0382

Sinfonia concertante for wind instruments and orchestra

Marl June 1970- June 1972	Philharmonia Hungarica Ozim, Racz, Engle, Baranyai	LP: Decca HDNH 35-40/SDD 445 LP: London STS 15229-15234 CD: Decca 425 9352/448 5312

Cello Concerto No 1

Bamberg 1975	Bamberg SO Varga	LP: Turnabout TV 34695 LP: Turnabout (France) FSM 43019

Cello Concerto No 2

Bamberg 1975	Bamberg SO Varga	LP: Turnabout TV 34695 LP: Turnabout (France) FSM 43019

Piano Concerto No 2 in D

Bamberg 1975	Bamberg SO Alpenheim	LP: Vox SVBX 5136 LP: Turnabout TV 37090-37092 LP: Turnabout (France) FSM 43031-43033 CD: Vox 11 54992

Piano Concerto No 3 in F

Bamberg 1975	Bamberg SO Alpenheim	LP: Vox SVBX 5136 LP: Turnabout TV 37090-37092 LP: Turnabout (France) FSM 43031-43033 CD: Vox 11 54992

Piano Concerto No 4 in G

Bamberg 1975	Bamberg SO Alpenheim	LP: Vox SBVX 5136 LP: Turnabout TV 37090-37092 LP: Turnabout (France) FSM 43031-43033 CD: Vox 11 54992

152   Dorati

Piano Concerto No 9 in G

Bamberg	Bamberg SO	LP: Vox SVBX 5136
1975	Alpenheim	LP: Turnabout TV 37090-37092
		LP: Turnabout (France) FSM 43031-43033
		CD: Vox 11 54992

Piano Concerto No 11 in D

Bamberg	Bamberg SO	LP: Vox SVBX 5136
1975	Alpenheim	LP: Turnabout TV 37090-37092
		LP: Turnabout (France) FSM 43031-43033
		CD: Vox 11 54992

Divertimento in C for piano, horn and strings

Bamberg	Bamberg SO	LP: Vox SVBX 5136
1975	Alpenheim	LP: Turnabout TV 37090-37092
		LP: Turnabout (France) FSM 43031-43033
		CD: Vox 11 54992

24 Minuets

Marl	Philharmonia	LP: Decca HDNW 90-91
September	Hungarica	CD: Decca 436 2202
1975		

Armida

Epalinges	Lausanne CO	LP: Philips 6769 021
Switzerland	Norman, Burrowes,	CD: Philips 432 4382
September	Ahnsjö, Leggate,	Excerpts
1978	Rolfe-Johnson,	LP: Philips 6527 147/6529 060
	Ramey	CD: Philips 426 6412/434 9872
		CD: BBC Music MM 10

La fedeltà premiata

Epilanges Switzerland June 1975	Lausanne CO Cotrubas, Landy, Valentini-Terrani, Stade, Alva, Titus	LP: Philips 6707 028 CD: Philips 432 4302 Excerpts LP: Philips 6527 218/6527 147 CD: Philips 420 0842/434 9872 CD: BBC Music MM 10

L'incontro improvviso

Epilanges Switzerland June 1979- June 1980	Lausanne CO Zoghby, Marshall, D.Jones, Ahnsjö, Trimarchi, Luxon	LP: Philips 6769 040 CD: Philips 432 4162 Excerpts LP: Philips 6527 218/6527 147 CD: Philips 434 9872 CD: BBC Music MM 10

L'infedeltà delusa

Epilanges Switzerland June 1980	Lausanne CO Mathis, Hendricks, Ahnsjö, Baldin, Devlin	LP: Philips 6769 061 CD: Philips 432 4132 Excerpts LP: Philips 6527 218/6527 147

Il mondo della luna

Epilanges Switzerland September 1977	Lausanne CO Auger, Mathis, Stade, Alva, Rolfe-Johnson, Trimarchi	LP: Philips 6769 003 CD: Philips 432 4202 Excerpts LP: Philips 6527 218/6527 147 CD: Philips 420 0842/434 9872 CD: BBC Music MM 10

L'isola disabitata

Epilanges Switzerland May 1977	Lausanne CO Zoghby, Lerer, Alva, Bruson	LP: Philips 6700 119 CD: Philips 432 4272 Excerpts LP: Philips 6527 218/6527 147 CD: Philips 438 8972 CD: BBC Music MM 10

154 Dorati

Orlando paladino

Epilanges Switzerland June 1976	Lausanne CO Auger, Ameling, Killebrew, Ahnsjö, Shirley, Luxon, Trimarchi	LP: Philips 6703 077 CD: Philips 432 4342 Excerpts LP: Philips 6527 218 CD: Philips 434 9872 CD: BBC Music MM 10

La vera costanza

Epilanges Switzerland May 1976	Lausanne CO Norman, Donath, Ahnsjö, Trimarchi, Ganzarolli	LP: Philips 6707 029 CD: Philips 432 4242 Excerpts LP: Philips 6527 218/6527 147/6527 060 CD: Philips 426 6412/434 9872/454 6932 CD: BBC Music MM 10

AKE HERMANSON (Born 1923)

Symphony No 1

Stockholm September 1973	Stockholm PO	LP: Caprice CAP 1206

PAUL HINDEMITH (1895-1963)

Sinfonia serena

Dallas February 1947	Dallas SO	Unpublished radio broadcast <u>World premiere performance</u>

EMMERICH KALMAN (1882-1953)

Die Csardasfürstin, waltz

Vienna June 1958	Philharmonia Hungarica	45: Mercury XEP 9076/SEX 15020 LP: Mercury MG 50190/MG 50289/MG 50444/ SR 90190/SR 90289/SR 90444/ MMA 11116/AMS 16063 LP: Wing MGW 14087/SRW 18087 CD: Mercury 434 3382 Wing edition incorrectly describes orchestra as Minneapolis SO

CHARLES KOECHLIN (1867-1951)

Les Bandar-Log, symphonic poem

London September- October 1964	BBC SO	LP: HMV ALP 2092/ASD 639 LP: Angel 36295 LP: Argo ZRG 756 CD: EMI CDM 763 9482
London October 1964	BBC SO	Unpublished radio broadcast

ARAM KHACHATURIAN (1903-1978)

Violin Concerto

Watford July 1964	LSO Szeryng	LP: Mercury MG 50393/SR 90393 LP: Philips AL 3503/SAL 3503/838 418AY CD: Mercury 434 3182

Gayaneh, suite

Watford June 1960	LSO	LP: Mercury MG 50209/SR 90209/ MMA 11166/AMS 16116 LP: Wing MGW 14095/SRW 18095/WL 1210 LP: Philips 6527 187 CD: Mercury 434 3232 Excerpts LP: Mercury MG 50293/MG 50516/SR 90293/ SR 90526/SR2-9127 LP: Philips 6882 102 CD: Mercury 442 5412

FINE RECORDING
Conducted By
ANTAL DORATI

WEBER
Overtures: Der Freischütz—Preciosa
        Euryanthe—Oberon
The Concertgebouw Orchestra, Amsterdam
                            GBL 5580

MENDELSSOHN
Calm Sea and Prosperous Voyage
The Hebrides Overture (Fingal's Cave)

SCHUBERT
Overture in the Italian style in C, D.591
The Concertgebouw Orchestra, Amsterdam
                            GBL 5581

TCHAIKOVSKY
Symphony No. 6 in B minor, Op. 74
('Pathétique')
The Vienna Symphony Orchestra
                            CFL 1019

BIZET
Carmen Suites Nos. 1 and 2
L'Arlésienne Suite No. 1
L'Arlésienne Suite No. 2
The Lamoureux Orchestra, Paris
                            CFL 1061

GRIEG
Peer Gynt Suite No. 1, Op. 46

MENDELSSOHN
A Midsummer Night's Dream—
        Overture and Incidental Music
The Vienna Symphony Orchestra
                        SCFL 102 (Stereo)

on  PHILIPS and

PHILIPS RECORDS LTD · STANHOPE HOUSE · STANHOPE PLACE · LONDON W2
Printed by the Shenval Press, London, Hertford and Harlow

ZOLTAN KODALY (1882-1967)

Ballet music

Marl September-December 1973	Philharmonia Hungarica	LP: Decca SXLM 6665-6667/SXL 7614 LP: London 2313/6864

Concerto for orchestra

Marl September-December 1973	Philharmonia Hungarica	LP: Decca SXLM 6665-6667/SXL 6712 LP: London 2313 CD: Decca 443 0062/443 0422

Dances of Galanta

Vienna June 1958	Philharmonia Hungarica	LP: Mercury MG 50179/SR 90179/ MMA 11077/AMS 16027 CD: Mercury 432 0052
Marl September-December 1973	Philharmonia Hungarica	LP: Decca SXLM 6665-6667/SXL 6712/JB 38 LP: London 2313/6864 CD: Decca 425 0342/443 0062/443 0422

Dances of Marosszek

Vienna June 1958	Philharmonia Hungarica	LP: Mercury MG 50179/SR 90179/ MMA 11077/AMS 16027 CD: Mercury 432 0052
Marl September-December 1973	Philharmonia Hungarica	LP: Decca SXLM 6665-6667/SXL 6712/ 414 0761 LP: London 2313/6862 CD: Decca 425 0342/443 0062/443 0422

Hary Janos, suite

Minneapolis 1950	Minneapolis SO	LP: Victor LM 1750
Minneapolis November 1956	Minneapolis SO	LP: Mercury MG 50132/SR 90132/MRL 2565/ MMA 11072/AMS 16025 CD: Mercury 432 0052 Excerpt LP: Mercury MG 50338/MG 50526/ SR 90338/SR 90526 LP: Philips 6882 100
Marl September- December 1973	Philharmonia Hungarica	LP: Decca SXLM 6665-6667/SXL 6712/JB 38 LP: London 2313 CD: Decca 425 0342/443 0062/443 0422
Hilversum May 1974	Netherlands RO	LP: Decca PFS 4355/414 0761 LP: London 21146 CD: Decca 448 9472

Hungarian Rondo

Marl September- December 1973	Philharmonia Hungarica	LP: Decca SXLM 6665-6667/SXL 6714/ 414 0761 LP: London 2313/6864

Hungarian Tunes

Marl September- December 1973	Philharmonia Hungarica	LP: Decca SXLM 6665-6667/SXL 6714 LP: Decca 2313

Jesus and the traders, for unaccompanied chorus

Dallas January 1949	North Texas College Choir	78: Victor M 1331

Minuetto serio

Marl September- December 1973	Philharmonia Hungarica	LP: Decca SXLM 6665-6667/SXL 6713 LP: London 2313

Peacock Variations

Chicago January 1954	Chicago SO	LP: Mercury MG 50038/MMA 11072/MRL 2541
Budapest 1969	Hungarian State Orchestra	LP: Hungaroton SLPX 11392 CD: Hungaroton HCD 11392
Marl September- December 1973	Philharmonia Hungarica	LP: Decca SXLM 6665-6667/SXL 6714/JB 138 LP: London 2313/6864 CD: Decca 425 0342/443 0062/443 0422

Psalmus hungaricus

Dallas January 1949	Dallas SO North Texas College Choir Carelli	78: Victor M 1331
Stockholm December 1967	Stockholm PO and Chorus Simandy	CD: Bis BISCD 421-424
Budapest 1969	Hungarian State Orchestra and Chorus Simandy	LP: Hungaroton SLPX 11392 CD: Hungaroton HCD 11392

Summer evening

Marl September- December 1973	Philharmonia Hungarica	LP: Decca SXLM 6665-6667/SXL 6714 LP: London 2313 CD: Decca 443 0062

Symphony in C

Marl September- December 1973	Philharmonia Hungarica	LP: Decca SXLM 6665-6667/SXL 6713 LP: London 2313 CD: Decca 443 0062

Theatre Overture

Marl September- December 1973	Philharmonia Hungarica	LP: Decca SXLM 6665-6667/SXL 6712 LP: London 2313/6862 CD: Decca 443 0062

JOSEF LANNER (1801-1843)

Die Schönbrunner, waltz

Vienna
June 1958
	Philharmonia
	Hungarica
		LP: Mercury MG 50190/MG 50289/MG 50444/
		    SR 90190/SR 90289/SR 90444/
		    MMA 11116/AMS 16063
		LP: Wing MGW 14087/SRW 18087
		CD: Mercury 434 3382
		<u>Wing edition incorrectly describes
		orchestra as Minneapolis SO</u>

FRANZ LEHAR (1870-1948)

Die lustige Witwe, waltz

Vienna
June 1958
	Philharmonia
	Hungarica
		45: Mercury XEP 9076/SEX 15020
		LP: Mercury MG 50190/MG 50289/MG 50444/
		    SR 90190/SR 90289/SR 90444/
		    MMA 11116/AMS 16063
		LP: Wing MGW 14087/SRW 18087/WL 1208
		CD: Mercury 434 3382
		<u>Wing edition incorrectly describes</u>
		<u>orchestra as Minneapolis SO</u>

FRANZ LISZT (1811-1886)

A Faust Symphony

Amsterdam January 1982	Concertgebouw Orchestra and Chorus Kozma	LP: Philips 6769 089 CD: Philips 442 6422

Piano Concerto No 1

Dallas February 1947	Dallas SO Rubinstein	78: Victor M 1144 78: HMV DB 9487-9488 45: Victor WDM 1144 LP: Victor LM 1018 LP: HMV (France) FALP 162 CD: RCA GD 60046

Christus

Budapest Date not confirmed	Hungarian State Orchestra and Choruses Kincses, Takacs, Nagy, Solyom-Nagy, Polgar	CD: Hungaroton HCD 12831-12833 May also have been issued on Hungaroton LP

Les Préludes

Watford June 1960	LSO	LP: Mercury MG 50214/SR 90214 MMA 11159/AMS 16105 LP: Wing MGW 14084/SRW 18084 LP: Metronom (Germany) 140.170

Hungarian Rhapsody No 1 in F minor

Watford July 1963	LSO	LP: Mercury MG 50371/SR 90371/SRI 75089 LP: Philips GL 5789/SGL 5789/ 6527 202/6570 140 LP: Fontana (Holland) ZKY 894.080 CD: Mercury 432 0152

Hungarian Rhapsody No 2 in D minor

Watford
June 1960
	LSO	LP: Mercury MG 50235/SR 90235/
		  MMA 11153/AMS 16101/SRI 75018
		LP: Philips GL 5789/SGL 5789/ 839 821
		  6527 202/6570 140/6882 100
		CD: Mercury 432 0152

Detroit April 1978	Detroit SO	LP: Decca SXL 6896 LP: London 71195

Hungarian Rhapsody No 3 in D

Watford   LSO
June 1960

LP: Mercury MG 50235/SR 90235/
     MMA 1153/AMS 11601/SRI 75018
LP: Philips 6527 202/6570 140
LP: Victor LSC 2746
CD: Mercury 432 0152

Hungarian Rhapsody No 4 in D minor

Watford   LSO
July 1963

LP: Mercury MG 50371/SR 90371/SRI 75089
LP: Philips GL 5789/SGL 5789/6527 202/
     6570 140/6747 071
LP: Fontana (Holland) ZKY 894080
CD: Mercury 432 0152

Hungarian Rhapsody No 5 in E minor

Watford   LSO
July 1963

LP: Mercury MG 50371/SR 90371/SRI 75089
LP: Philips GL 5789/SGL 5789/
     6527 202/6570 140
LP: Fontana (Holland) ZKY 894080
CD: Mercury 432 0152

Hungarian Rhapsody No 6 in D

Watford   LSO
July 1963

LP: Mercury MG 50371/SR 90371/SRI 75089
LP: Philips GL 5789/SGL 5789/
     6527 202/6570 140
LP: Fontana (Holland) ZKY 894080
CD: Mercury 432 0152

ELIZABETH LUTYENS (1906-1983)

Music for orchestra III

Cheltenham July 1964	BBC SO	Unpublished radio broadcast

GUSTAV MAHLER (1860-1911)

Symphony No 5

Stockholm September 1973	Stockholm PO	LP: Lyssna LY 74-4

Symphony No 6

London September 1979	RPO	Unpublished radio broadcast

Lieder eines fahrenden Gesellen

London September 1979	RPO Luxon	Unpublished radio broadcast

FELIX MENDELSSOHN-BARTHOLDY (1809-1847)

Symphony No 3 "Scotch"

Walthamstow July 1956	LSO	LP: Mercury MG 50123/SR 90123/MMA 11048 LP: Philips SDAL 502 LP: Concert Hall M 2465/SM 2465 CD: Mercury 434 3632

Symphony No 4 "Italian"

Minneapolis April 1952	Minneapolis SO	LP: Mercury MG 50010/MRL 2540 LP: Wing MGW 14006/SRW 18006/WL 1038 LP: Philips SFL 14067/6747 239 LP: Metronom (Germany) 140.137

Violin Concerto

Los Angeles 1940s	Hollywood Bowl SO Elman	CD: Eklipse EKR 1404
Watford July 1964	LSO Szeryng	LP: Mercury MG 50406/SR 90406 LP: Philips AL 3504/SAL 3504/6527 061 CD: Mercury 434 3392

Hebrides, overture

Walthamstow July 1956	LSO	LP: Mercury MG 50123/MG 50323/SR 90123/ SR 90323/MMA 11048 LP: Wing MGW 14056/SRW 18056 LP: Philips SDAL 502 LP: Concert Hall M 2465/SM 2465 CD: Mercury 434 3632
Amsterdam September 1959	Concertgebouw Orchestra	LP: Philips GO5398R/GBL 5581

Meeresstille glückliche Fahrt, overture

Amsterdam September 1959	Concertgebouw Orchestra	LP: Philips GO5398R/GBL 5581

A Midsummer Night's Dream, overture

Vienna 1958	VSO	LP: Philips CFL 1043/SCFL 102/SFL 14043 6747 239 LP: Epic LC 3606

A Midsummer Night's Dream, scherzo

Vienna 1958	VSO	45: Philips 494 015EE LP: Philips CFL 1043/SFL 14043/6747 239 LP: Epic LC 3606

A Midsummer Night's Dream, nocturne

Vienna 1958	VSO	LP: Philips CFL 1043/SCFL 102/SFL 14043 6747 239 LP: Epic LC 3606

A Midsummer Night's Dream, Wedding march

Vienna 1958	VSO	45: Philips 494 015EE LP: Philips CFL 1043/SCFL 102/SFL 14043 6747 239/6747 050 LP: Epic LC 3606

OLIVIER MESSIAEN (1908-1992)

Chronochromie

London September 1964	BBC SO	LP: HMV ALP 2092/ASD 639 LP: Angel 36295 LP: Argo ZRG 756 CD: EMI CDM 763 9482

La transfiguration de Notre Seigneur

Washington April 1972	National SO Westminster Choir Sylvester, Aquino	LP: Decca HEAD 1-2 CD: Decca 425 6162

MENDELSSOHN & MOZART SYMPHONIES

MENDELSSOHN
SYMPHONY No. 4 in A, Op. 90 ("Italian")
MOZART
SYMPHONY No. 40 in G minor, K. 550
MINNEAPOLIS SYMPHONY ORCHESTRA
Conducted by **ANTAL DORATI**

GIACOMO MEYERBEER (1791-1864)

L'Africaine, excerpt (O paradis!)

New York September 1947	Victor SO Tagliavini <u>Sung in Italian</u>	78: Victor MO 1191/VO 13 78: HMV DB 6869 LP: Victor LM 20062

DARIUS MILHAUD (1892-1974)

Le boeuf sur le toit

London August 1965	LSO	LP: Mercury MG 50435/SR 90435 LP: Philips AL 3637/SAL 3637/412 0281 CD: Mercury 434 3352

WOLFGANG AMADEUS MOZART (1756-1791)

Symphony No 31 "Paris"

Minneapolis 1951	Minneapolis SO	45: Victor WDM 1595 LP: Victor LM 1185

Symphony No 36 "Linz"

Walthamstow July 1956	LSO	LP: Mercury MG 50121/SR 90121/ MRL 2562/MMA 11987 LP: Wing MGW 14064/SRW 18064

Symphony No 40

Minneapolis April 1952	Minneapolis SO	LP: Mercury MG 50010/MRL 2540 LP: Wing MGW 14006/SRW 18006/WL 1038 LP: Philips SFL 14067
Watford June 1961	LSO	LP: Mercury MG 50280/SR 90280 LP: Philips GL 5819/SGL 5819/6531 006 LP: Metronom (Germany) 140.135

Eine kleine Nachtmusik

Walthamstow July 1956	LSO	LP: Mercury MG 50121/MG 50412/SR 90121/ SR 90412/MRL 2562/MMA 11087

Allegro in D K121

Watford August 1965	Bath Festival Orchestra	LP: Mercury MG 50438/SR 90438 <u>Orchestra described for this recording</u> <u>as Festival Chamber Orchestra</u>

3 German dances K605

Watford August 1965	Bath Festival Orchestra	LP: Mercury MG 50438/SR 90438 <u>Orchestra described for this recording</u> <u>as Festival Chamber Orchestra</u>

3 Marches K249 and K335

Watford August 1965	Bath Festival Orchestra	LP: Mercury MG 50438/SR 90438 <u>Orchestra described for this recording</u> <u>as Festival Chamber Orchestra</u>

Minuet in C K409

Watford August 1965	Bath Festival Orchestra	LP: Mercury MG 50438/SR 90438 <u>Orchestra described for this recording</u> <u>as Festival Chamber Orchestra</u>

Lucio Silla, overture

Watford August 1965	Bath Festival Orchestra	LP: Mercury MG 50438/SR 90438 <u>Orchestra described for this recording</u> <u>as Festival Chamber Orchestra</u>

Le nozze di Figaro, overture

Walthamstow July 1962	LSO	LP: Mercury SR2-9134

Maurerische Trauermusik

London August 1966	BBC SO	Unpublished radio broadcast

Ave verum corpus

London August 1966	BBC SO BBC Chorus	Unpublished radio broadcast

Kyrie in D minor

London August 1966	BBC SO BBC Chorus	Unpublished radio broadcast

MODEST MUSSORGSKY (1839-1881)

Pictures from an exhibition, arranged by Ravel

Amsterdam February 1952	Concertgebouw Orchestra	LP: Philips ABR 4013/A00607R/GBR 6521 G05309R
Minneapolis April 1959	Minneapolis SO	LP: Mercury MG 50217/MG 50342/SR 90217/ SR 90342/MMA 11100/AMS 16051/ SRI 75025 LP: Philips 6598 402 LP: Fontana (Holland) ZKY 894090 LP: Reader's Digest RDS 6999/RDES 2591 CD: Mercury 434 3462 Excerpt LP: Philips 6882 100

Night on Bare Mountain, arranged by Rimsky-Korsakov

Wembley August 1960	LSO	45: Mercury XEP 9103/SEX 15042 LP: Mercury MG 50214/MG 50342/SR 90214/ SR 90342/MMA 11159/AMS 16105/ SRI 75025 LP: Columbia Record Club (USA) GB 8 LP: Metronom (Germany) 140.170 CD: Mercury 432 0042

Khovantschina, entr'acte and Dance of the Persian Slaves

Minneapolis April 1959	Minneapolis SO	45: Mercury XEP 9071/SEX 15018 LP: Mercury MG 50217/MG 50293/SR 90217/ SR 90293/SR2-9130/MMA 11100/AMS 16051 LP: Fontana (Holland) ZKY 894090

JACQUES OFFENBACH (1819-1880)

Gaité parisienne, arranged by Rosenthal

Minneapolis
April 1957
	Minneapolis SO	LP: Mercury MG 50016/MG 50431/SR 90016/
		    SR 90431/MMA 11038/AMS 16005/
		    SRI 75014
		LP: Philips 6582 019
		CD: Mercury 434 3652
		Excerpts
		LP: Mercury MG 50493/SR 90493
		LP: Philips 6882 104
		Excerpts also issued by Mercury on
		its popular LP label

La belle Hélène, suite arranged by Dorati

Minneapolis April 1950	Minneapolis SO	78: Victor M 1381 45: Victor WDM 1381 LP: Victor LM 22/LM 9033

JULIAN ORBON (Born 1925)

Cantigas del rey

Watford July 1964	BBC SO Harper, Puyana	Mercury unpublished

CARL ORFF (1895-1982)

Carmina burana

London February 1976	RPO Brighton and Southend Choruses Burrowes, Devos, Shirley-Quirk	LP: Decca PFS 4368/JB 78/SPA 555/ 417 7141 LP: London 21153 CD: Decca 417 7142/444 1052/444 1172 Excerpt CD: Belart 450 0152

WAYNE PETERSON (Born 1927)

Free variations for orchestra

Minneapolis April 1959	Minneapolis SO	LP: Mercury MG 50288/SR 90288/ MMA 11177/AMS 16127

ALLAN PETTERSON (1911-1980)

Symphony No 7

Stockholm September 1969	Stockholm PO	LP: Decca SXL 6538 LP: London 6740 LP: Swedish Society SLT 33194 CD: Swedish Society SCD 1002

Symphony No 10

Stockholm Date not confirmed	Stockholm PO	LP: EMI (Sweden) 4E 061 35142

Songs for baritone and orchestra, arranged by Dorati

Stockholm September 1973	Stockholm PO Saeden	LP: Lysnna LY 74-4

176 Dorati

SERGEI PROKOFIEV (1891-1953)

Symphony No 5

Minneapolis November 1959	Minneapolis SO	LP: Mercury MG 50258/MG 50343/SR 90258/ 　　SR 90343/MMA 11126/AMS 16073 LP: Wing MGW 14081/SRW 18081 CD: Mercury 432 7532

Piano Concerto No 3

Dallas January 1949	Dallas SO Kapell	78: Victor M 1326 LP: Victor LM 1058/VIC 1420/GL 85266 CD: RCA/BMG GD 60921

Lieutenant Kijé, suite

Hilversum May 1974	Netherlands RO	LP: Decca PFS 4355 LP: London 21146 CD: Decca 444 1042/448 2732

Love of 3 Oranges, suite

Watford July 1957	LSO	45: Mercury XEP 9042/SEX 15001 LP: Mercury MG 50006/MG 50132/MG 50342/ 　　MG 50531/SR 90006/SR 90132/SR 90342/ 　　SR 90531/MMA 11028/AMS 16009/ 　　SRI 75030 LP: Philips 6582 011 CD: Mercury 432 7532 Excerpts LP: Philips 6882 102 CD: Mercury 442 5412

Peter and the Wolf

London March 1965	RPO Connery	LP: Decca LK 4801/PFS 4104/SPA 520 LP: London 21007 LP: Contour CC 7519 CD: Decca 444 1042/450 0242 CD: Pickwick IMPX 9002

Scythian suite

Watford July 1957	LSO	LP: Mercury MG 50006/MG 50343/MG 50531/ SR 90006/SR 90343/SR 90531/ MMA 11028/AMS 16009/SRI 75030 LP: Philips 6582 011 CD: Mercury 432 7532

SERGEI RACHMANINOV (1873-1943)

Piano Concerto No 2

Minneapolis April 1960	Minneapolis SO Janis	LP: Mercury MG 50260/MG 50448/SR 90260/ SR 90448/MMA 11124/AMS 16071/ SRI 75032 LP: Philips AL 3496/SAL 3496/6780 251 CD: Mercury 432 7592

Piano Concerto No 3

Watford June 1961	LSO Janis	LP: Mercury MG 50260/MG 50283/SR 90260/ SR 90283/MMA 11162/AMS 16109/ SRI 75068 LP: Philips 6582 006/6780 251 CD: Mercury 432 7592

MAURICE RAVEL (1875-1937)

Alborada del gracioso

Minneapolis February 1952	Minneapolis SO	45: Mercury XEP 9012/EP 15000 LP: Mercury MG 50005/MRL 2516/ MGW 14030/SRW 18030

Daphnis et Chloé, ballet

Minneapolis December 1954	Minneapolis SO Macalester Choir	LP: Mercury MG 50040/MG 50048/MMA 11015 <u>Excerpt</u> LP: Mercury OLD 6

Daphnis et Chloé, 2nd suite

Stockholm May 1966	Stockholm PO	CD: Bis BISCD 421-424

Pavane pour une infante défunte

Minneapolis February 1952	Minneapolis SO	45: Mercury XEP 9012/EP 15000 LP: Mercury MG 50005/MRL 2516/ MGW 14029/SRW 18029

Rapsodie espagnole

Detroit April 1978	Detroit SO	LP: Decca SXL 6896 LP: London 71195

OTTORINO RESPIGHI (1879-1936)

Antiche arie e danzo per liuto, suites 1, 2 and 3

Vienna June 1958	Philharmonia Hungarica	LP: Mercury MG 50199/SR 90199/MMA 11078/ AMS 16028/SRI 75009 LP: Philips 6582 010 CD: Mercuru 416 4962/434 3042 <u>Excerpts</u> LP: Mercury SR2-9132 CD: Mercury 442 5412

Feste romane

Minneapolis November 1954	Minneapolis SO	LP: Mercury MG 50046/SR 90046/ MRL 2002/MMA 11095/SRI 75116 LP: Wing MGW 14039/SRW 18039

Fontane di Roma

Minneapolis December 1952	Minneapolis SO	LP: Mercury MG 50011/MRL 2506/MMA 11083 LP: Wing MGW 14035/SRW 18035
Minneapolis April 1960	Minneapolis SO	LP: Mercury MG 50298/SR 90298 LP: Philips 6582 015 CD: Mercury 432 0072

Gli uccelli

Watford July 1957	LSO	LP: Mercury MG 50153/SR 90153/ MMA 11053/AMS 16036/SRI 75023 LP: Philips 6547 043 CD: Mercury 432 0072

Impressioni brasiliane

Watford July 1957	LSO	LP: Mercury MG 50153/SR 90153/MMA 11053/ AMS 16036/SRI 75023 LP: Philips 6547 043 CD: Mercury 432 0072

Pini di Roma

Minneapolis December 1952	Minneapolis SO	LP: Mercury MG 50011/MRL 2506/MMA 11083 LP: Wing MGW 14035/SRW 18035
Minneapolis April 1960	Minneapolis SO	LP: Mercury MG 50298/SR 90298 LP: Philips 6582 015 CD: Mercury 432 0072

Vetrate di chiesa

Minneapolis November 1954	Minneapolis SO	LP: Mercury MG 50046/SR 90046/ MRL 2002/MMA 11095/SRI 75116 LP: Wing MGW 14039/SRW 18039

NIKOLAI RIMSKY-KORSAKOV (1844-1908)

Capriccio espagnol

Walthamstow June 1959	LSO	LP: Mercury MG 50265/SR 90265/ MMA 11154/AMS 16102/SRI 75101 CD: Mercury 434 3082

Le coq d'or, suite

Walthamstow July 1956	LSO	LP: Mercury MG 50122/MG 50344/SR 90122/ SR 90344/MRL 2537/MMA 11058/ AMS 16008/SRI 75016 LP: Wing MGW 14070/SRW 18070 LP: Philips GL 5822/SGL 5822/ SFL 14024/6582 012 CD: Mercury 434 3082 <u>Excerpts</u> LP: Mercury SR2-9130

Russian Easter Festival Overture

Walthamstow June 1959	LSO	LP: Mercury MG 50265/MG 50332/SR 90265/ SR 90332/MMA 11154/AMS 16102 LP: Philips GL 5835/SGL 5835/6567 003 CD: Mercury 434 3082

Scheherazade

London July 1937	LPO	78: HMV C 2968-2972/C 7495-7499 auto 78: Victor M 509 45: Victor WBC 1018 LP: Victor LBC 1018
Minneapolis April 1952	Minneapolis SO	LP: Mercury MG 50009/MRL 2503/MMA 11022 LP: Wing MGW 14008/SRW 18008/WL 1006 Excerpts LP: Mercury MG 50532/SR 90532
Minneapolis December 1958	Minneapolis SO	LP: Mercury MG 50195/MG 50332/SR 90195/ SR 90332/AMS 16057 LP: Philips GL 5835/SGL 5835/6547 028 LP: Fontana (Holland) ZKY 894.027 Excerpt LP: Philips 6882 102

HILDING ROSENBERG (1892-1985)

Voyage to America, Intermezzo and Railway Fugue

Stockholm October 1967	Stockholm PO	LP: RCA VIC 1319/VICS 1319 LP: RIKSLP 13

GIAOCHINO ROSSINI (1792-1868)

Il barbiere di Siviglia, overture

Minneapolis   Minneapolis SO   45: Mercury XEP 9015/EP 40015
March 1957
                                                                        LP: Mercury MG 50139/SR 90139/
                                                                             MMA 11006/AMS 16090/SR2-9130
                                                                       LP: Wing MGW 14055/SRW 18055/WL 1086
                                                                       LP: Readers Digest RDS 9141
                                                                       CD: Mercury 434 3452

La cenerentola, overture

Minneapolis   Minneapolis SO   45: Mercury XEP 9015/EP 40015
March 1957
                                                                        LP: Mercury MG 50139/SR 90139/
                                                                             MMA 11006/AMS 16090
                                                                       LP: Wing MGW 14055/SRW 18055/WL 1086
                                                                       CD: Mercury 434 3452

La gazza ladra, overture

Minneapolis   Minneapolis SO   LP: Mercury MG 50139/SR 90139/
March 1957   MMA 11006/AMS 16090
                                                                       LP: Wing MGW 14055/SRW 18055/WL 1086
                                                                       CD: Mercury 434 3452

L'italiana in Algeri, overture

Minneapolis   Minneapolis SO   45: Mercury XEP 9001
March 1957   LP: Mercury MG 50139/SR 90139/
                                                                       MMA 11006/AMS 16090
                                                                       LP: Wing MGW 14055/SRW 18055/WL 1086
                                                                       CD: Mercury 434 3452

La scala di seta, overture

Minneapolis   Minneapolis SO   45: Mercury XEP 9001
March 1957   LP: Mercury MG 50139/SR 90139/
                                                                       MMA 11006/AMS 16090
                                                                       LP: Wing MGW 14055/SRW 18055/WL 1086
                                                                       CD: Mercury 434 3452

Il signor bruschino, overture

Minneapolis March 1957	Minneapolis SO	LP: Mercury MG 50139/SR 90139/ MMA 11006/AMS 16090 LP: Wing MGW 14055/SRW 18055/WL 1086 CD: Mercury 434 3452

La boutique fantasque, arranged by Respighi

London 1976	RPO	LP: Decca PFS 4407/JB 79 LP: London 21172

Rossiniana, suite arranged by Respighi

London 1976	RPO	LP: Decca PFS 4407/JB 79 LP: London 21172 CD: Decca 444 1062

CAMILLE SAINT-SAENS (1835-1921)

Cello Concerto No 1

Watford June 1964	LSO Starker	LP: Mercury MG 50409/SR 90409 LP: Philips AL 3559/SAL 3559/SFM 23019 839 533 CD: Mercury 432 0102

ERIK SATIE (1866-1925)

Parade, ballet

Watford August 1965	LSO	LP: Mercury MG 50435/SR 90435 LP: Philips AL 3637/SAL 3637/412 0281 CD: Mercury 434 3352

SYMPHONY NO. 3
AARON COPLAND

MMA 11050
(MG 50018)

ANTAL DORATI conducting the MINNEAPOLIS SYMPHONY ORCHESTRA

ARNOLD SCHOENBERG (1874-1951)

5 pieces for orchestra

Watford July 1962	LSO	LP: Mercury MG 50316/SR 90316 LP: Philips AL 3539/SAL 3539/838 409AY CD: Mercury 432 0062

FRANZ SCHUBERT (1797-1828)

Symphony No 8 "Unfinished"

Chicago January 1954	Chicago SO	LP: Mercury MG 50037/MRL 2517 LP: Wing MGW 14018/SRW 18018/WL 1012

Overture in D in the Italian style

Amsterdam September 1959	Concertgebouw Orchestra	LP: Philips GBL 5581/G05398R

GUENTHER SCHULLER (Born 1925)

7 studies on themes of Paul Klee

Minneapolis April 1960	Minneapolis SO	LP: Mercury MG 50282/SR 90282/ MMA 11151/AMS 16099 CD: Mercury 434 3292 <u>Excerpt</u> LP: Mercury MG 50338/SR 90338

ROBERT SCHUMANN (1810-1856)

Symphony No 4

Watford July 1963	LSO	LP: Mercury SR 90511

Piano Concerto

Amsterdam June- July 1983	Concertgebouw Orchestra Schiff	LP: Decca 411 9421 CD: Decca 411 9422

Violin Concerto

Watford July 1964	LSO Szeryng	LP: Mercury MG 50406/SR 90406 LP: Philips AL 3504/SAL 3504/6527 061 CD: Mercury 434 3392

WILLIAM SCHUMAN (1910-1992)

Symphony No 6

Dallas February 1949	Dallas SO	Unpublished radio broadcast <u>World premiere performance</u>

JEAN SIBELIUS (1865-1957)

Symphony No 2

Stockholm October 1967	Stockholm PO	LP: RCA VIC 1318/VICS 1318/CCV 5029 CD: Swedish Society SCD 1046

En Saga

Wembley February 1969	LSO	LP: EMI ASD 2486/1C 063 01987

Luonnatar, for soprano and orchestra

Wembley February 1969	LSO Jones	LP: EMI ASD 2486/1C 063 01987 CD: EMI CDM 565 1822

Night Ride and Sunrise

Wembley February 1969	LSO	LP: EMI ASD 2486/1C 063 01987 CD: EMI CDM 565 1822

The Oceanides

Wembley February 1969	LSO	LP: EMI ASD 2486/1C 063 01987 CD: EMI CDM 565 1822

Valse triste

Wembley June 1960	LSO	LP: Mercury MG 50214/MG 50526/SR 90214/ SR 90526/MMA 11159/AMS 16105 LP: Philips (France) 839 819

NIKOLAOS SKALKOTTAS (1904-1949)

Suite No 2

London January 1966	BBC SO	Unpublished radio broadcast

Other works by Skalkottas were performed in BBC broadcasts with BBC SO

BEDRICH SMETANA (1824-1884)

The Bartered Bride, overture

Minneapolis April 1958	Minneapolis SO	45: Mercury XEP 9035 LP: Mercury MG 50193/SR 90193/MMA 11030/ AMS 16047/SR2-9134/77001

The Bartered Bride, Dance of the Comedians

Minneapolis April 1958	Minneapolis SO	45: Mercury XEP 9063/SEX 15014 LP: Mercury MG 50193/SR 90193/MMA 11030/ AMS 16047/77001

The Bartered Bride, polka

Minneapolis April 1958	Minneapolis SO	45: Mercury XEP 9035 LP: Mercury MG 50193/SR 90193/MMA 11030/ AMS 16047/77001

The Bartered Bride, Furiant

Minneapolis April 1958	Minneapolis SO	45: Mercury XEP 9035 LP: Mercury MG 50193/SR 90193/MMA 11030/ AMS 16047/77001

Ma Vlast

Amsterdam September 1956	Concertgebouw Orchestra	LP: Philips 09003L-09004L Excerpts 45: Philips ABE 10032 LP: Philips 6701 008
Amsterdam October 1986	Concertgebouw Orchestra	LP: Philips 420 6071 CD: Philips 420 6072/442 6412 Excerpt CD: Philips 438 0012

Vltava (Ma Vlast)

Amsterdam February 1952	Concertgebouw Orchestra	LP: Philips NBR 6010/N00620R/A00399L ABL 3195/S06053R LP: Epic LC 3015
Wembley June 1960	LSO	LP: Mercury MG 50214/SR 90214/ MMA 11159/AMS 16105 LP: Philips 6747 126/6747 050 LP: Metronom (Germany) 140.170

JOHN PHILIP SOUSA (1854-1932)

Semper fidelis, march

Amsterdam September 1959	Concertgebouw Orchestra	45: Philips ABE 10245/SABE 2010/ SBF 182/313 122SF

WILHELM STENHAMMAR (1871-1927)

Serenade for orchestra, 3 movements

Stockholm February 1970	Stockholm PO	CD: Bis BISCD 421-424

EDUARD STRAUSS (1835-1916)

Bahn frei!, polka

Minneapolis December 1957	Minneapolis SO	LP: Mercury MG 50178/SR 90178/ MMA 11014/AMS 16024 LP: Philips GL 5816

Doktrinen, waltz

Minneapolis December 1957	Minneapolis SO	45: Mercury XEP 9007 LP: Mercury MG 50178/SR 90178/ MMA 11014/AMS 16024 LP: Philips GL 5816 CD: Mercury 434 3382

JOHANN STRAUSS FATHER (1804-1849)

Lorelei-Rheinklänge

Minneapolis December 1957	Minneapolis SO	LP: Mercury MG 50178/SR 90178/ MMA 11014/AMS 16024 LP: Philips GL 5816

JOHANN STRAUSS (1825-1899)

Aegyptischer Marsch

Minneapolis December 1957	Minneapolis SO	45: Mercury XEP 9007 LP: Mercury MG 50178/SR 90178/ MMA 11014/AMS 16024 LP: Philips GL 5816/6747 176

An der schönen blauen Donau, waltz

London December 1966	LPO	LP: Decca LK 4850/PFS 4117/SPA 155/VIV 2 LP: London 21018

Le beau Danube, suite arranged by Désormière

London July 1936	LPO	78: HMV C 2869-2871/C 7477-7479 auto/ JOX 7000-7002 78: Victor M 414

Champagne polka

Minneapolis
November
1956
	Minneapolis SO	LP: Mercury MG 50131/MG 50289/MG 50293/
		     MG 50444/SR 90008/SR 90289/SR 90293/
		     SR 90444/MMA 11062/AMS 16001
		LP: Philips 6747 176

Eljen a Magyar, polka

Minneapolis December 1957	Minneapolis SO	45: Mercury XEP 9007 LP: Mercury MG 50178/SR 90178/ MMA 11014/AMS 16024 LP: Philips GL 5816/6747 176

Frühlingsstimmen, waltz

New York September 1947	Victor SO Korjus	78: Victor M 1221 78: HMV C 3898 45: Victor WDM 1221

Minneapolis
November
1956
	Minneapolis SO	45: Mercury XEP 9054
		LP: Mercury MG 50131/MG 50289/MG 50293/
		    MG 50444/SR 90008/SR 90289/SR 90293/
		    SR 90444/MMA 11062/AMS 16001
		
		CD: Mercury 434 3382

London December 1966	LPO	LP: Decca LK 4850/PFS 4117/VIV 2 LP: London 21018

G'schichten aus dem Wienerwald, waltz

Minneapolis February 1953	Minneapolis SO	LP: Mercury MG 50019/MMA 11086 LP: Wing MGW 14000/SRW 18000/WL 1000
London December 1966	LPO	LP: Decca LK 4850/PFS 4117/ SPA 155/SPA 205/VIV 2 LP: London 21018

Graduation Ball, ballet arranged by Dorati

Dallas February 1947	Dallas SO	78: Victor M 1180 78: HMV JOX 7006-7009 LP: Victor LM 1061
Minneapolis April 1957	Minneapolis·SO	LP: Mercury MG 50152/SR 90016/MMA 11038/ AMS 16005/SRI 75014 LP: Philips SFL 14119/6747 176 CD: Mercury 434 3652 Excerpts LP: Mercury MG 50494/SR 90494
Vienna December 1976	VPO	LP: Decca SXL 6867 LP: London 70865

194 Dorati

Kaiserwalzer

Minneapolis February 1953	Minneapolis SO	LP: Mercury MG 50019/MMA 11086 LP: Wing MGW 14000/SRW 18000/WL 1000

Künstlerleben, waltz

New York September 1947	Victor SO Korjus	78: Victor M 1221 78: HMV C 3898 78: Electrola EH 1361 78: HMV (Switzerland) FKX 219 45: Victor WDM 1221 45: HMV 7EP 7039 LP: RCA Camden CDS 1095/CAL 427 LP: Melodiya D034445-034446
Minneapolis November 1956	Minneapolis SO	LP: Mercury MG 50131/MG 50289/MG 50293/ MG 50444/SR 90008/SR 90289/SR 90293/ SR 90444/MMA 11062/AMS 16001
London December 1966	LPO	LP: Decca LK 4850/PFS 4117/VIV 2 LP: London 21018

Eine Nacht in Venedig, overture

Minneapolis December 1957	Minneapolis SO	LP: Mercury MG 50178/SR 90178/ MMA 11014/AMS 16024 LP: Philips GL 5816/6747 176

Rosen aus dem Süden, waltz

New York September 1947	Victor SO Korjus	78: Victor M 1221 78: HMV C 3898 78: Electrola EH 1361 78: HMV (Switzerland) FKX 219 45: Victor WDM 1221 45: HMV 7EP 7039 LP: RCA Camden CDS 1095/CAL 427
Minneapolis November 1956	Minneapolis SO	LP: Mercury MG 50131/MG 50289/MG 50293/ MG 50444/MG 50526/SR 90008/SR 90289/ SR 90293/SR 90444/SR 90526/ MMA 11062/AMS 16001 LP: Wing WL 1208 LP: Philips SDAL 502/839 819

Schatzwalzer

New York September 1947	Victor SO Korjus	78: Victor M 1221 45: Victor WDM 1221 LP: RCA Camden CDS 1095/CAL 427 LP: Melodiya D034445-034446

Wein Weib und Gesang, waltz

Minneapolis February 1953	Minneapolis SO	LP: Mercury MG 50019/MMA 11086 LP: Wing MGW 14000/SRW 18000/WL 1000
London December 1966	LPO	LP: Decca LK 4850/PFS 4117/VIV 2 LP: London 21018

Wiener Blut, waltz

New York September 1947	Victor SO Korjus	78: Victor M 1221 45: Victor WDM 1221 LP: RCA Camden CDS 1095/CAL 427
Minneapolis February 1953	Minneapolis SO	LP: Mercury MG 50019/MMA 11086 LP: Wing MGW 14000/SRW 18000/WL 1000

Wiener Bonbons, waltz

Minneapolis
November
1956
	Minneapolis SO	45: Mercury XEP 9054
		LP: Mercury MG 50131/MG 50289/MG 50293/
		    MG 50444/SR 90008/SR 90289/SR 90293/
		    SR 90444/MMA 11062/AMS 16001
		LP: Wing WL 1208
		LP: Philips SDAL 502

ANTAL DORATI conducts the MINNEAPOLIS SYMPHONY ORCHESTRA

RESPIGHI

Vetrate di Chiesa
Feste Romane

A PRODUCT OF THE PYE GROUP OF COMPANIES

JOSEF STRAUSS (1827-1870)

Aquarellen, waltz

Minneapolis December 1957	Minneapolis SO	LP: Mercury MG 50178/SR 90178/ MMA 11014/AMS 16024 LP: Philips GL 5816 CD: Mercury 434 3382

Dorfschwalben aus Oesterreich, waltz

Vienna
June 1958
	Philharmonia
	Hungarica
		LP: Mercury MG 50190/MG 50289/MG 50337/
		    MG 50444/SR 90190/SR 90289/SR 90337/
		    SR 90444/MMA 11116/AMS 16063
		LP: Wing MGW 14087/SRW 18087
		LP: Philips 6736 001
		CD: Mercury 434 3382
		<u>Wing edition incorrectly describes</u>
		<u>orchestra as Minneapolis SO</u>

Sphärenklänge, waltz

Minneapolis December 1957	Minneapolis SO	LP: Mercury MG 50178/SR 90178/ MMA 11014/AMS 16024 LP: Philips GL 5816

RICHARD STRAUSS (1864-1949)

Die ägyptische Helena

Detroit May 1979	Detroit SO Jewell Chorale Jones, Hendricks, Finnilä, Kastu, White	LP: Decca D176 D3 LP: London 13135 CD: Decca 430 3812

Also sprach Zarathustra

Detroit October 1982	Detroit SO	LP: Decca SXDL 7613 LP: London 71113 CD: Decca 410 1462/430 7082

Don Juan

Minneapolis
December
1958
	Minneapolis SO	LP: Mercury MG 50202/MG 50336/SR 90202/
		    SR 90336/MMA 11125/AMS 16072/
		    SRI 75015
		LP: Philips GL 5831/SGL 5831
		LP: Concert Hall CM 2446/SMS 2446
		CD: Mercury 434 3482

Detroit June 1980	Detroit SO	LP: Decca SXDL 7523 LP: London 71025 CD: Decca 400 0852/430 7082

Die Frau ohne Schatten, symphonic fantasy

Detroit November 1983	Detroit SO	LP: Decca 411 8931 CD: Decca 411 8932/444 3442

Ein Heldenleben

Minneapolis December 1952	Minneapolis SO	45: Mercury EP2-501 LP: Mercury MG 50012/MRL 2545/MMA 11069 LP: Wing MGW 14014/SRW 18014 LP: Pickwick S 4041

Macbeth

Detroit October 1982	Detroit SO	LP: Decca SXDL 7613 LP: London 71113 CD: Decca 410 1462/430 7082/444 3442

Der Rosenkavalier, suite arranged by Dorati

Philadelphia July 1950	Philadelphia Orchestra	78: Victor M 1475 45: Victor WDM 1475 LP: Victor LM 48/LM 9033 <u>Orchestra described as Robin Hood</u> <u>Dell Orchestra</u>
Minneapolis December 1955	Minneapolis SO	LP: Mercury MG 50099/SR 90099/MRL 2566/ MMA 11061/AMS 16014/SRI 75015 LP: Wing MGW 14072/SRW 18072 LP: Philips GL 5831/SGL 5831 LP: Concert Hall CM 2309/SMS 2309 CD: Mercury 434 3482
Detroit November 1983	Detroit SO	LP: Decca 411 8931 CD: Decca 411 8932/444 3442

Salome, Dance of the 7 veils

Walthamstow October 1962	RPO	LP: Reader's Digest RDM 1027/RDS3-15 CD: Chesky CD 36

Till Eulenspiegels lustige Streiche

Minneapolis December 1955	Minneapolis SO	45: Mercury XEP 9033 LP: Mercury MG 50099/MG 50334/SR 90099/ SR 90334/MRL 2566/MMA 11061/ AMS 16014/SRI 75015 LP: Wing MGW 14072/MGW 14501/SRW 18072/ SRW 18501 LP: Philips GL 5831/SGL 5831 LP: Concert Hall CM 2309/SMS 2309 CD: Mercury 434 3482 <u>MGW 14501/SRW 18501 has a spoken</u> <u>commentary over-dubbed</u>
Detroit June 1980	Detroit SO	LP: Decca SXDL 7523 LP: London 71025 CD: Decca 400 0852/430 7082

Tod und Verklärung

Minneapolis December 1958	Minneapolis SO	LP: Mercury MG 50202/MG 50334/SR 90202/ SR 90334/MMA 11125/AMS 16072 LP: Philips GL 5831/SGL 5831 LP: Concert Hall CM 2446/SMS 2446 CD: Mercury 434 3482
Detroit June 1980	Detroit SO	LP: Decca SXDL 7523 LP: London 71023 CD: Decca 400 0852/430 7082

IGOR STRAVINSKY (1882-1971)

Apollon musagète

Detroit November 1984	Detroit SO	LP: Decca 414 4571 CD: Decca 414 4572/430 7402

Le baiser de la fée

London July 1939	LPO	78: Columbia DX 949 78: Columbia (USA) 69840D 78: Columbia (Argentina) 266243 78: Columbia (Canada) 15261 78: Columbia (Brazil) 30-5373

Le chant du rossignol

Watford June 1964	LSO	LP: Mercury MG 50387/SR 90387 LP: Philips 6585 003 CD: Mercury 432 0122

4 Etudes for orchestra

Watford July 1964	LSO	LP: Mercury MG 50387/SR 90387 CD: Mercury 434 3312

Fireworks

Watford June 1964	LSO	LP: Mercury MG 50387/SR 90387 CD: Mercury 432 0122

L'oiseau de feu, ballet

Watford   LSO   LP: Mercury MG 50226/SR 90226/MMA 11089/
June 1959   AMS 16038/SRI 75058
                              LP: Philips GL 5827/SGL 5827/6547 003
                              LP: Fontana (Holland) ZKY 894.083
                              LP: Contour 6870 574
                              CD: Mercury 432 0122
                              <u>Excerpts</u>
                              LP: Mercury SR2-9127

London   RPO   LP: Enigma VAR 1022/K 53534
1976   LP: ASV ALH 924
                              LP: Musicmasters (USA) 20051
                              CD: ASV CDQS 6031

Detroit   Detroit SO   LP: Decca 410 1091
October   CD: Decca 410 1092/430 7402/448 2262
1982

L'oiseau de feu, suite (1919 version)

Minneapolis   Minneapolis SO   LP: Mercury MG 50004/MG 50025/MRL 2550
February   LP: Wing MGW 14010/SRW 18010
1952   LP: Philips SFL 14016/850 454

Petrushka (1911 version)

Minneapolis April 1955	Minneapolis SO	LP: Mercury MG 50058/MRL 2523 LP: Wing MGW 14038/SRW 18038/WL 1035 Excerpt LP: Mercury OLD 6

Petrushka (1947 version)

Minneapolis April 1959	Minneapolis SO	LP: Mercury MG 50216/SR 90216/ MMA 11105/AMS 16056 LP: Philips 6582 021/6780 755 CD: Mercury 434 3312 Excerpt LP: Mercury SR2-9127
Detroit June 1980	Detroit SO	LP: Decca SXDL 7521 LP: London 71023 CD: Decca 417 7582/421 0792 This recording includes certain modifications taken from 1911 version

Le sacre du printemps

Minneapolis December 1953	Minneapolis SO	LP: Mercury MG 50030/MRL 2006 LP: Wing MGW 14027/SRW 18027/WL 1034
Minneapolis November 1959	Minneapolis SO	LP: Mercury MG 50253/SR 90253/ MMA 11118/AMS 16065 LP: Philips SFL 14009/6582 021 LP: Fontana (Holland) ZKY 894.023 CD: Mercury 434 3312
Detroit May 1981	Detroit SO	LP: Decca SXDL 7548 LP: London 71048 CD: Decca 400 0842/417 7582/421 0792 448 2262

Scherzo à la russe

Watford June 1964	LSO	LP: Mercury MG 50387/SR 90387 CD: Mercury 432 0122/442 5412

STRAVINSKY

THE FIREBIRD BALLET
(complete)

LONDON SYMPHONY ORCHESTRA

ANTAL DORATI

Scherzo fantastique

Detroit November 1984	Detroit SO	LP: Decca 414 4561 CD: Decca 414 4562

Symphony No 1

Detroit November 1984	Detroit SO	LP: Decca 414 4561 CD: Decca 414 4562

Tango

Watford July 1964	LSO	LP: Mercury MG 50387/SR 90387 CD: Mercury 432 0122

KAROL SZYMANOWSKI (1882-1937)

Symphony No 2

Detroit June 1980	Detroit SO	LP: Decca SXDL 7524 LP: London 71026 CD: Decca 425 6252

Symphony No 3 "Song of the Night"

Detroit June 1980	Detroit SO Jewell Chorale Karczykowski	LP: Decca SXDL 7524 LP: London 71026 CD: Decca 425 6252

PIOTR TCHAIKOVSKY (1840-1893)

Symphony No 1 "Winter Dreams"

Watford July 1965	LSO	LP: Mercury MG 50398-550399/ MG 50468-50473/RR 90398-90399/ SR 90468-90473/OL2-115/SR2-9015/ SR6-9121/SRI3-77009 LP: Philips 6582 016/6599 932

Symphony No 2 "Little Russian"

Watford July 1965	LSO	LP: Mercury MG 50398-50399/ MG 50468-50473/SR 90398-90399/ SR 90468-90473/OL2-115/SR2-9015/ SR6-9121/SRI3-77009 LP: Philips 6599 933

Symphony No 3 "Polish"

Watford July 1965	LSO	LP: Mercury MG 50398-50399/ MG 50468-50473/SR 90398-90399/ SR 90468-90473/OL2-115/SR2-9015/ SRI3-77009/SR6-9121 LP: Philips 6599 934

Symphony No 4

Amsterdam September 1956	Concertgebouw Orchestra	LP: Philips ABL 3195/A 00399L

Wembley
June 1960
	LSO	LP: Mercury MG 50279/MG 50468-50473/
		    SR 90279/SR 90468-90473/SR6-9121/
		    MMA 11168/AMS 16118/SRI 75004
		LP: Philips 6582 022/6599 935
		LP: Metronom (Germany) 140.138
		CD: Mercury 434 3732

Washington May 1973	National SO	LP: Decca SXL 6574 LP: London CS 6793

Symphony No 5

Minneapolis April 1952	Minneapolis SO	LP: Mercury MG 50008 LP: Wing MGW 14013/SRW 18013/WL 1009 LP: Philips 700 164WGY <u>Waltz movement</u> 45: Mercury EP 15001

Watford
June 1961
	LSO	LP: Mercury MG 50255/MG 50468-50473/
		    SR 90255/SR 90468-90473/SR6-9121/
		    MMA 11175/AMS 16125/SRI 75056
		LP: Philips 6582 013
		CD: Mercury 434 3052
		<u>Waltz movement</u>
		LP: Mercury MG 50395/SR 90395
		LP: Wing WL 1209

Symphony No 6 "Pathétique"

Vienna 1958	VSO	LP: Philips CFL 1019/697 010EL/698 001CL

Watford
June 1960
	LSO	LP: Mercury MG 50312/MG 50468-50473/
		    SR 90312/SR 90468-90473/SR6-9121/
		    SRI 75031
		LP: Philips 6582 014/6702 002/420 0381
		LP: Fontana (Holland) ZKY 894.029
		CD: Mercury 434 3532

Sérénade mélancolique for violin and orchestra

Los Angeles 1940s	Hollywood Bowl SO Elman	CD: Eklipse EKR 1404

Violin Concerto

Watford
July 1962
	LSO
	Szeryng
		LP: Mercury MG 50389/MG 50527/
		   SR 90389/SR 90527/OL3-117/SR3-9017/
		   SRI 75032
		LP: Philips AL 3503/SAL 3503/6582 009/
		   6833 120/420 0381

London 1968	LSO Zukerman	LP: CBS 72768/MS 7313

Variations on a Rococo theme

Watford June 1964	LSO Starker	LP: Mercury MG 50409/SR 90409 LP: Philips AL 3559/SAL 3559/ SFM 23019/839 533VGY CD: Mercury 432 0012 Excerpt CD: Mercury 442 5412

Orchestral Suite No 1

Watford August 1966	New Philharmonia	LP: Philips SBAL 22/6768 035/ SAL 3734/6799 002 LP: Mercury OL3-118/SR3-9018/SRI3-77008 CD: Philips 454 2532

Orchestral Suite No 2

Watford August 1966	New Philharmonia	LP: Philips SBAL 22/6768 035/ SAL 3725/6799 002 LP: Mercury OL3-118/SR3-9018/SRI3-77008 CD: Philips 454 2532

Orchestral Suite No 3

Watford
August 1966
	New Philharmonia	LP: Philips SBAL 22/6768 035/
		   SAL 3673/6799 002
		LP: Mercury OL3-118/SR3-9018/SR2-9019/
		   SRI3-77008
		CD: Philips 454 2532

Orchestral Suite No 4 "Mozartiana"

Watford August 1966	New Philharmonia	LP: Philips SBAL 22/6768 035/ SAL 3725/6799 002/6866 027 LP: Mercury OL3-118/SR3-9018/SR2-9019/ SRI3-77008 CD: Philips 454 2532 <u>Schwann catalogues list another Mercury</u> <u>LP set (SR2-9126) containing excerpt from</u> <u>Fourth Suite with Dorati and LSO</u>

The Sleeping Beauty, ballet

Minneapolis April 1955	Minneapolis SO	LP: Mercury OL3-103/OL6-114/ MG 50061-50063/MG 50064-50067/ MRL 2524-2527/MMA 11113-11115/ SR 90350-90355/SR6-9014 LP: Philips GL5706-5708/SFL14016-14018 Excerpts LP: Mercury MG 50118/MG 50493/SR 90493/ SR6-9014/MG 50395/SR 90395/OLD 6/ MMA 11149/SRI 75113 LP: Wing MGW 14012/MGW 14033/SRW 18012/ SRW 18033/WL 1008/WL 1036/WL 1209 LP: Philips SFL 14010
Amsterdam May 1979- January 1981	Concertgebouw Orchestra	LP: Philips 6769 036 CD: Philips 420 7922/446 1662

Swan Lake, ballet

Minneapolis December 1954	Minneapolis SO	LP: Mercury MG 50050-50052/ MG 50068-50070/OL3-102/OL6-114/ SR 90350-90355/SR6-9014/ MRL 2528-2530/MMA 11074-11076 LP: Philips GL 5736-5738/ SFL 14021-14023/6755 011 Excerpts LP: Mercury MG 50395/MG 50493/SR 90395/ SR 90493/MMA 11149 LP: Wing MGW 14025/MGW 14033/SRW 18025/ SRW 18033/WL 1017/WL 1036/WL 1209

Swan Lake, ballet suite

London July-August 1938	LPO	78: Columbia DX 869-872/DX 8132-8135 auto LP: Columbia (USA) RL 3014

The Nutcracker, ballet

Minneapolis   Minneapolis SO   LP: Mercury MG 50031-50032/OL6-114/
December   Minnesota   SR6-9014/SR 90350-90355
1953   University Choir   MRL 2508-2509/MMA 11106-11107
                                      LP: Philips GL 5732-5733/SFL14007-14008
                                      Excerpts
                                      45: Mercury XEP 9010
                                      LP: Mercury MG 50494/SR 90494/MMA 11023
                                      LP: Wing MGW 14011/SRW 18011/WL 1007
                                      LP: Philips 6527 065/6582 018/420 0381
                                      Excerpts also issued by Mercury
                                      on their Popular LP label

Watford   LSO   LP: Mercury MG 50306-50307/OL2-133/
July 1962   LSO Chorus   SR 90306-90307/SR2-9013/
                                          MMA 11193-11194/AMS 16143-16144
                                      LP: Philips 6780 250
                                      CD: Mercury 432 7502
                                      Excerpts
                                      LP: Mercury MG 50395/MG 50528/
                                          SR 90395/SR 90528
                                      LP: Wing WL 1209
                                      LP: Philips 6768 069
                                      CD: Mercury 422 2652/450 1262

Amsterdam   Concertgebouw   LP: Philips 6747 364
June-July   Orchestra   CD: Philips 442 5622
1975   Haarlem Choir   Excerpts
                                      LP: Philips 9500 697/412 9381
                                      CD: Philips 426 1772

Capriccio italien

Minneapolis   Minneapolis SO   LP: Mercury MG 50054/SR 90054/MRL 2514/
December   MMA 11057/AMS 16010/SRI 75001
1955   LP: Philips SDAL 503
                                      CD: Mercury 434 3602
                                      Excerpt
                                      LP: Mercury SR2-9126

Detroit   Detroit SO   LP: Decca SXL 6895/417 2771
April 1978   LP: London CS 7118
                                      CD: Decca 414 4942/417 7422/
                                          443 0032/443 0392

1812 Overture

Minneapolis December 1954	Minneapolis SO Deems Taylor	45: Mercury XEP 9092 LP: Mercury MG 50054/MRL 2514/ MMA 11057/SRI 75142
Minneapolis April 1958	Minneapolis SO Deems Taylor	LP: Mercury MGD 19/SRD 19/SR 90054/ AMS 16010/SRI 75001/GL 90/GLS 90/ LP: Philips AL 3461/SAL 3461/SDAL 502 LP: Fontana (Holland) ZKY 894.028 CD: Mercury 416 4482/434 3602
Detroit April 1978	Detroit SO	LP: Decca SXL 6895/417 2771 LP: London CS 7118 CD: Decca 414 4942/417 7082/417 7422 443 0032/443 0392

Evgeny Onegin, waltz

Minneapolis December 1958	Minneapolis SO	LP: Mercury MG 50201/MG 50293/MG 50395/ SR 90201/SR 90293/SR 90395/ MMA 11112/AMS 16059 LP: Wing MGW 14076/SRW 18076/WL 1209 LP: Philips SDAL 503 CD: Mercury 434 3052

Evgeny Onegin, polonaise

Minneapolis December 1958	Minneapolis SO	LP: Mercury MG 50201/MG 50293/MG 50395/ SR 90201/SR 90293/SR 90395/ MMA 11112/AMS 16059 LP: Wing MGW 14076/SRW 18076 CD: Mercury 434 3052

Fatum, symphonic poem

Washington April 1974	National SO	LP: Decca SXL 6694 LP: London CS 6891 CD: Decca 417 7422/443 0032/443 0392

Francesca da Rimini

Minneapolis December 1958	Minneapolis SO	LP: Mercury MG 50201/SR 90201/ MMA 11112/AMS 16059 LP: Wing MGW 14076/SRW 18076 CD: Mercury 434 3732
Washington May 1973	National SO	LP: Decca SXL 6627 LP: London CS 6841 CD: Decca 443 0032/443 0392

Hamlet, fantasy overture

Washington May 1973	National SO	LP: Decca SXL 6627 LP: London CS 6841 CD: Decca 443 0032/443 0392

Hamlet, overture from the incidental music

London September 1937	LPO	78: HMV C 3176 78: Electrola EH 1119/EB 158 78: Victor 13760

Marche slave

Minneapolis December 1958	Minneapolis SO	LP: Mercury MG 50201/SR 90201/ MMA 11112/AMS 16059 LP: Wing MGW 14076/SRW 18076/6747 050 LP: Philips GL 5837/SGL 5837/6736 002 CD: Mercury 434 3052
Detroit April 1978	Detroit SO	LP: Decca SXL 6895 LP: London CS 7118 CD: Decca 411 9542/414 4942/417 7422/ 425 0862/443 0032/443 0392

STEREO

TCHAIKOVSKY

FESTIVAL OVERTURE, Op. 49
(ORIGINAL SCORING)
CAPRICCIO ITALIEN

ANTAL DORATI
Minneapolis Symphony Orchestra
University of Minnesota BRASS BAND
BRONZE CANNON, Douay, France (1775)
COURTESY U.S. MILITARY ACADEMY, WEST POINT, NEW YORK
BELLS of the Laura Spelman Rockefeller Memorial Carillon, The Riverside Church

Romeo and Juliet

Chicago January 1954	Chicago SO	LP: Mercury MG 50037/MRL 2517 LP: Wing MGW 14018/SRW 18018/WL 1012
Watford June 1959	LSO	LP: Mercury MG 50209/SR 90209/ MMA 11166/AMS 16116 LP: Wing WL 1210 LP: Philips SDAL 503 CD: Mercury 416 4482/434 3532
Washington April 1974	National SO	LP: Decca SXL 6694/417 2771 LP: London CS 6891 CD: Decca 417 7422/443 0032/443 0392

Serenade for strings

Vienna June 1958	Philharmonia Hungarica	LP: Mercury MG 50200/MG 50344/SR 90200/ SR 90344/MMA 11091/AMS 16040 LP: Philips GL 5822/SGL 5822/6736 003 CD: Mercury 432 7502 <u>Waltz only</u> LP: Mercury MG 50395/SR 90395 LP: Wing WL 1209 LP: Philips SDAL 503/6747 247

The Tempest, symphonic fantasy

Washington April 1974	National SO	LP: Decca SXL 6694 LP: London CS 6891 CD: Decca 443 0032/443 0392

Voyevoda, symphonic ballad

Washington May 1973	National SO	LP: Decca SXL 6627 LP: London CS 6841 CD: Decca 443 0032/443 0392

MICHAEL TIPPETT (Born 1905)

Praeludium for brass, bells and percussion

London November 1962	BBC SO	Unpublished radio broadcast

GIUSEPPE VERDI (1813-1901)

La forza del destino, overture

Watford   LSO
July 1959

LP: Mercury MG 50156/SR 90156/
    MMA 11031/AMS 16058/SR2-9134
LP: Wing MGW 14053/SRW 18035/WL 1048
LP: Philips SFL 14075
LP: Pickwick S-4043
CD: Mercury 434 3452

Nabucco, overture

Watford   LSO
July 1959

LP: Mercury MG 50156/SR 90156/
    MMA 11031/AMS 16058
LP: Wing MGW 14053/SRW 18053/WL 1048
LP: Philips SFL 14075
LP: Pickeick S-4043
CD: Mercury 434 3452

Rigoletto, excerpt (Parmi veder)

New York   Victor SO
September   Tagliavini
1947

78: Victor VO 13/MO 1191
78: HMV DB 6586
45: Victor WDM 1191
45: HMV (France) 7RF 207
LP: Victor LM 20662

La traviata, Act 1 prelude

Watford   LSO
July 1959
45: Mercury XEP 9021
LP: Mercury MG 50156/SR 90156/
    MMA 11031/AMS 16058/SR2-9130
LP: Wing MGW 14053/SRW 18053/WL 1048
LP: Philips SFL 14075
LP: Pickwick S-4043
CD: Mercury 434 3452

La traviata, Act 3 prelude

Watford   LSO
July 1959
45: Mercury XEP 9021
LP: Mercury MG 50156/SR 90156/
    MMA 11031/AMS 16058
LP: Wing MGW 14053/SRW 14053/WL 1048
LP: Philips SFL 14075
LP: Pickwick S-4043
CD: Mercury 434 3452

I vespri siciliani, overture

Watford   LSO
July 1959
LP: Mercury MG 50156/SR 90156/
    MMA 11031/AMS 16058
LP: Wing MGW 14053/SRW 14053/WL 1048
LP: Philips SFL 14075
LP: Pickwick S-4043
CD: Mercury 434 3452

RICHARD WAGNER (1813-1883)

A Faust Overture

Amsterdam January 1982	Concertgebouw Orchestra	LP: Philips 6769 089/6514 219

Der fliegende Holländer

London August 1961	Covent Garden Orchestra & Chorus Rysanek, Elias, Liebl, London, Tozzi	LP: Victor LM 6156/LSC 6156/ RE 25035-25037/SER 4535-4537 LP: Decca 2BB 109-111/417 3191 CD: Decca 417 3192 <u>Excerpts</u> LP: Victor LM 2845/LSC 2845 LP: Decca SDD 439/414 1771 CD: Decca 417 3192

Götterdämmerung, Siegfried's Rhine journey

Washington April 1975	National SO	LP: Decca SXL 6743/VIV 48 LP: London CS 6970 CD: Decca 417 7752/444 3442

Götterdämmerung, Siegfried's Funeral march

Washington April 1975	National SO	LP: Decca SXL 6743/VIV 48 LP: London CS 6970 CD: Decca 417 7752/444 3442

Götterdämmerung, orchestral postlude after Brünnhilde's Immolation

Washington April 1975	National SO	LP: Decca SXL 6743 /VIV 48 LP: London CS 6970 CD: Decca 417 7752/444 3442

Lohengrin, prelude

Wembley June 1960	LSO	LP: Mercury MG 50287/SR 90287/ MMA 11176/AMS 16126 CD: Mercury 434 3422

Lohengrin, Act 3 prelude

Watford June 1959	LSO	45: Mercury XEP 9103/SEX 15042 LP: Mercury MG 50234/SR 90234/ MMA 11120/AMS 16067 LP: Philips SFL 14051 CD: Mercury 434 3422

Die Meistersinger von Nürnberg, overture

Wembley June 1960	LSO	LP: Mercury MG 50287/SR 90287/ MMA 11176/AMS 16126 LP: Philips GL 5821/SGL 5821/SFL 14051 CD: Mercury 434 3422

Parsifal, Good Friday music

Wembley June 1960	LSO	LP: Mercury MG 50287/SR 90287/ MMA 11176/AMS 16126 LP: Philips GL 5821/SGL 5821 CD: Mercury 434 3422

Das Rheingold, Prelude and Entry of the Gods

Washington April 1975	National SO	LP: Decca SXL 6743/VIV 48 LP: London CS 6970 CD: Decca 417 7752/444 3442

Siegfried, Forest murmurs

Washington April 1975	National SO	LP: Decca SXL 6743/VIV 48 LP: London CS 6970 CD: Decca 417 7752/444 3442

Tannhäuser, overture and Venusberg music

Watford June 1959	LSO	LP: Mercury MG 50234/SR 90234/ MMA 11120/AMS 16067 CD: Mercury 434 3422

Tristan und Isolde, Prelude and Liebestod

Watford June 1959	LSO	LP: Mercury MG 50234/SR 90234/ MMA 11120/AMS 16067 LP: Philips GL 5821/SGL 5821 CD: Mercury 434 3422 <u>Liebestod only</u> LP: Mercury MG 50532/SR 90532

Die Walküre, Ride of the Valkyries

Washington April 1975	National SO	LP: Decca SXL 6743/VIV 48 LP: London CS 6970 CD: Decca 417 7752/444 3442

Die Walküre, Wotan's Farewell and Magic Fire music

Washington April 1975	National SO	LP: Decca SXL 6743/VIV 48 LP: London CD 6970 CD: Decca 417 7752/444 3442

EMIL WALDTEUFEL (1837-1915)

Les patineurs, waltz

Vienna
June 1958
	Philharmonia
	Hungarica
		LP: Mercury MG 50190/MG 50289/MG 50444/
		    SR 90190/SR 90289/SR 90444/
		    MMA 11116/AMS 16063
		LP: Wing MGW 14087/SRW 18087/WL 1209
		CD: Mercury 434 3382
		<u>Wing issues incorrectly describe</u>
		<u>orchestra as Minneapolis SO</u>

CARL MARIA VON WEBER (1786-1826)

Euryanthe, overture

Amsterdam September 1959	Concertgebouw Orchestra	LP: Philips 835 062AY/GBL 5580/G05387R/ 6527 071/6530 020

Der Freischütz, overture

Amsterdam September 1959	Concertgebouw Orchestra	LP: Philips 835 062AY/GBL 5580/G05387R/ 6527 071/6530 020/6833 154

Oberon, overture

Amsterdam September 1959	Concertgebouw Orchestra	LP: Philips 835 062AY/GBL 5580/G05387R/ 6527 071/6530 020
Watford July 1962	LSO	LP: Mercury MG 50529/SR 90529/SR2-9134

Preciosa, overture

Amsterdam September 1959	Concertgebouw Orchestra	LP: Philips 835 062AY/GBL 5580/G05387R

ANTON WEBERN (1883-1945)

5 pieces for orchestra

Watford July 1962	LSO	LP: Mercury MG 50316/SR 90316 LP: Philips 838 409AY/AL 3539/SAL 3539 CD: Mercury 432 0062

LEO WEINER (1885-1960)

Suite on Hungarian folk tunes

Vienna June 1958	Philharmonia Hungarica	LP: Mercury MG 50132/SR 90132 LP: Philips CFL 1022/698 004CL

GRADUATION BALL
BAL DES CADETS
Johann Strauss-Dorati
VIENNA PHILHARMONIC · WIENER PHILHARMONIKER
ANTAL DORATI

The MUSIC of the BALLET

on
"His Master's Voice"

AURORA'S WEDDING
(*Tchaikovsky*)
The London Philharmonic Orchestra conducted by Efrem Kurtz.
C 2853–55 (4/- each)

LE BEAU DANUBE
(*J. Strauss, arr. Desormière*)
The London Philharmonic Orchestra conducted by Antal Dorati.
C 2869–71 (4/- each)

CHOREATIUM
(*Brahms—Symphony No. 4*)
The Saxon State Orchestra conducted by Karl Böhm.
DB 4684–88 (6/- each) and DBS 4689 (3/-)

LAC DE CYGNES
(*Tchaikovsky*)
The London Philharmonic Orchestra conducted by John Barbirolli.
C 2619–20 (4/- each)

PETROUCHKA
(*Stravinsky*)
The Philadelphia Orchestra conducted by Stokowski.
DB 3511–14 (6/- each)

THE SLEEPING PRINCESS
(*Tchaikovsky*)
Sadler's Wells Orchestra conducted by Constant Lambert.
C 3081–83 (4/- each)

SYLPHIDES
(*Chopin*)
The London Philharmonic Orchestra conducted by Malcolm Sargent.
C 2781–83 (4/- each)

SYMPHONIE FANTASTIQUE
(*Berlioz*)
Paris Conservatoire Orchestra conducted by Bruno Walter.
DB 3852–57 (6/- each)

FAÇADE (*Walton*)
The London Philharmonic Orchestra conducted by the Composer.
Suite No. 1—C 2336–37 (4/- each)
Suite No. 2—C 3042 (4/-)

PRÉSAGES
(*Tchaikovsky—Symphony No. 5*)
The Philadelphia Orchestra conducted by Stokowski.
DB 2548–53 (6/- each)
The London Philharmonic Orchestra conducted by Constant Lambert.
C 3088–92 (4/- each)

SCHEHERAZADE
(*Rimsky-Korsakov*)
The Philadelphia Orchestra conducted by Stokowski.
DB 2522–27 (6/- each)
The London Philharmonic Orchestra conducted by Antal Dorati.
C 2968–72 (4/- each)

THE GRAMOPHONE COMPANY LIMITED, HAYES, MIDDLESEX

IN MEMORIAM

Antal Doráti

It is with the deepest regret that we learned of the death of Maestro Antal Doráti. I knew him since the 1960s, when I was the in-house technician for his orchestra, the Stockholm Philharmonic, but it was only in his last year that we really started to work together. We discovered a deep empathy during the recording sessions for his Second Symphony, "Quereia Pacis", a record to which he was so much looking forward, but missed by two weeks. It was also Doráti who insisted that his recording of Ludwig van Beethoven's *Missa Solemnis*, in Berlin in July should be made by BIS. It was to be followed by a complete Brahms cycle with the Stockholm Philharmonic.

BIS has lost a great artist, and I a personal friend. Rest in peace, Tóni Bátyám.

Robert von Bahr
President, BIS Records

CD 406/7 (2 CD)

CD 408 *(To be released next month)*

Antal Dorati: a postscript

My first recollection of Antal Dorati came from an EMI newsletter about 1960, describing him as "the world's finest orchestral trainer" and as having made more gramophone records than any other conductor - statements which, more than 35 years later, still seem to be quite near the mark.

Beginning his musical training at the Liszt Academy in his native Budapest at the tender age of 14, Dorati counted among his teachers both Kodaly and Weiner. It has often been stated that Bartok was also his teacher, but this is not strictly true: Bartok was a friend of the Dorati family and a frequent visitor to their house, and no doubt wielded his influence as such. Dorati did become a life-long champion of Bartok and one of his finest interpreters.

On completing his studies he was offered a position of repetiteur at the Budapest Opera, and spent several years learning his craft in this time-honoured manner. He loved opera to the end of his life but never, except for some early years in Dresden and Münster, held permanent positions at a major house.

After leaving Germany in 1933, Dorati was offered a position as conductor for the Ballets Russes de Monte Carlo, with whom his very first engagement was not in Paris or London but in Bournemouth, the orchestra used being the local Municipal Orchestra, today's Bournemouth Symphony Orchestra.

The association with ballet led to a certain type-casting in that all the recordings which Dorati was offered during this period by HMV and Columbia were of music written or adapted for the ballet. The orchestra was Beecham's marvellous new London Philharmonic, and those records already display many of the features of the conductor's later and better-known performances: crisp and volatile precision, some hair-raisingly fast speeds (in music by Dargomitzky, Bizet and Rimsky-Korsakov) as well as many refreshingly idiosyncratic, old-world turns of phrase - which may surprise listeners who think of him as strict and inflexible. Re-issues of these 1930s shellacs (Dutton has published a single item on CD) would throw a fascinating light on Dorati's pre-war conducting style and put his later work in a new perspective.

In 1945 Antal Dorati was invited to lead the Dallas Symphony Orchestra. This was a break-through in more senses than one, for upon arriving and finding that virtually no orchestra existed, he proceeded, with great energy, to create one from scratch. Within a short time he doubled the concert schedule, introduced broadcasts and tours, giving premieres of works by Hindemith, William Schuman and others. Some recordings were made for Victor, including the Liszt First Concerto with Rubinstein and the very first version of Bartok's Second Violin Concerto with the young Menuhin.

The pattern of the work in Dallas, with Dorati appearing on the scene when musicians' morale was at a low point and going on to raise standards and self-confidence, would repeat itself many times later in other American and European centres - usually with a few sparks flying, as Dorati himself confesses in his autobiography "Notes of Seven Decades"!

Dallas was followed by the appointment to Minneapolis and the 10-year period which may be regarded as the highest point of the career. After some initial recordings for Victor, orchestra and conductor moved over to the smaller but ambitious Mercury label, where they chalked up around a 100 recordings. Many of these are being rediscovered as they emerge on CD, and a personal choice might include the Tchaikovsky and Stravinsky ballets, Bartok's Concerto for orchestra and Strauss' Heldenleben and concertos by Rachmaninov and Beethoven, among others.

Other early recordings included sessions with the Chicago Symphony and Concertgebouw Orchestras, followed by intensive work with the London Symphony Orchestra (still documented on Mercury). Dorati galvanised the London orchestra, also after a period spent in the doldrums, into a new era of brilliance and virtuosity . LPs of Borodin, Rimsky-Korsakov and Handel spring to mind, but more than anything a record of Smetana's "Moldau": I was struck by an unexpected gentleness and slow hypnotic flow of the river, with radiant strings in the moonlight episode - surely one of the steadiest and most satisfying versions of the ever-popular piece. My first encounter with Dorati in the concert hall was at an LSO concert around 1960, when the programme of orchestral showpieces culminated in a Tchaikovsky Fourth Symphony which had us on the edge of our seats!

The association with the LSO (and the resulting 50 Mercury LPs) was not Dorati's sole British connection. Work with the BBC Symphony Orchestra eventually led to his appointment as their chief conductor, and then, in the mid 1970s, to a similar position with the Royal Philharmonic - although I must confess to finding the recordings of this late period lacking in the fire of former days (exceptions can be found in records of Respighi with the RPO, Ravel with the Stockholm Philharmonic and Wagner with the National Symphony Orchestra of Washington DC).

The monumental set of complete Haydn Symphonies with the Philharmonia Hungarica will remain as one of Dorati's finest gramophone achievements, but ultimately it must be his work for the Mercury label (Minneapolis and LSO), in 20th century and Slav repertoire, that will stand the greatest test of time. The formidable orchestral "trainer" is less profound than Toscanini or Furtwängler when it comes to German symphonic repertoire, although he has a fine sensibility for the Strauss dynasty. His only recording with the Vienna Philharmonic Orchestra, enshrining Dorati's compilation of the ballet Graduation Ball, still awaits re-issue.

Richard Chlupaty   1997

George Szell
1897-1970

Discography compiled
by John Hunt

HENDRIK ANDRIESSEN (1892-1981)

Ricerare

Amsterdam 1965-1966	Concertgebouw Orchestra	LP: Dutch Radio RN 109225

DANIEL FRANCOIS AUBER (1782-1871)

Fra Diavolo, overture

Berlin 1926-1927	Staatskapelle	78: Parlophone E 10687/A 4022 78: Odeon O-7507 <u>Orchestra described as Grosses</u> <u>Sinfonie-Orchester</u>
Cleveland November 1957	CO	LP: Epic LC 3506

JOHANN SEBASTIAN BACH (1685-1750)

Suite No 3

Cleveland December 1954	CO	LP: Musical Appreciation Society MAR 26B <u>Orchestra described as Musical</u> <u>Appreciation Symphony Orchestra</u>

Violin Concerto in E

Cleveland January 1953	CO Francescatti	LP: Columbia (USA) ML 4648

Violin Concerto in G

New York January 1954	CO Szigeti	LP: Columbia (USA) ML 4891 LP: Philips ABL 3058/A01140L <u>Orchestra described as Columbia SO</u>

HENK BADINGS (1907-1987)

Symphonic Prologue

Amsterdam 1955	Concertgebouw Orchestra	LP: Dutch Radio RN 109240

SAMUEL BARBER (1910-1981)

Piano Concerto

Cleveland January 1964	CO Browning	LP: Columbia(USA) ML 6038/MS 6638 LP: Columbia 33CX 1937/SAX 2575 LP: CBS 61621 Excerpt published on an unnumbered LP entitled Introduction to Columbia Musical Treasures

BELA BARTOK (1881-1945)

Concerto for orchestra

Cleveland January 1965	CO	LP: Columbia (USA) ML 6215/MS 6815 LP: Columbia CX 5263/SAX 5263 CD: Sony MPK 45681 Excerpt LP: Columbia (USA) SOG 5

Piano Concerto No 1

New York April 1962	Columbia SO Serkin	LP: Columbia (USA) ML 5805/MS 6405 LP: CBS BRG 72109/SBRG 72109

Violin Rhapsody No 1

New York 1943	NYPSO Szigeti	CD: Dante LYS 85

LUDWIG VAN BEETHOVEN (1770-1827)

Symphony No 1

| Cleveland October 1964 | CO | LP: Epic LC 3892/BC 1292/SC 6050/BSC 150 LP: Columbia (USA) M7X 30281 LP: Columbia 33CX 1924/SAX 2565 LP: CBS 61150 CD: Sony SB5K 48396/SBK 46532 |

Symphony No 2

| Cleveland October 1964 | CO | LP: Epic LC 3892/BC 1292/SC 6050/BSC 150 LP: Columbia (USA) M7X 30281 LP: Columbia 33CX 1924/SAX 2565 LP: CBS 61150 CD: Sony SB5K 48396/SBK 47651/SB3K 62773 |

Symphony No 3 "Eroica"

Cleveland CO
February 1957
LP: Epic LC 3385/BC 1001/SC 6050/BSC 150
LP: Columbia (USA) M7X 30281/Y 34622
LP: Philips CFL 1001/EFL 2512/699 500CL
    SCFL 100/876 500CY *697 300 EL*
LP: Columbia 33CX 1938/SAX 2577
LP: CBS 61151
CD: Sony SB5K 48396/SBK 46328/MBK 45639
Excerpts issued on an unnumbered promotional LP

Salzburg Czech PO CD: Sony SMK 68447
August 1964

Symphony No 4

Cleveland CO
April 1947
78: Columbia (USA) M 705
78: Columbia (Canada) D 203
78: Columbia (Brazil) 30-5475-5478
LP: Columbia (USA) ML 4008

Cleveland CO
April 1963
LP: Epic LC 3864/BC 1264/SC 6050/BSC 150
LP: Columbia (USA) M7X 30281/Y 34600
LP: CBS 61152
CD: Sony SB5K 48396/SBK 48158

Symphony No 5

Cleveland November 1955	CO	LP: Epic LC 3195 LP: Philips SBL 5209/S04611L Excerpts issued on a Columbia Special Products LP
Cleveland Date uncertain	CO	VHS Video: Teldec 4509 950386 Laserdisc: Teldec 4509 950383 Rehearsal extract filmed for the Bell Telephone Hour

Cleveland
October 1963
	CO	LP: Epic LC 3882/BC 1282/SC 6050/
		    SC 6063/BSC 150/BSC 163
		LP: Columbia (USA) M7X 30281/
		    MG 30371/Y 34600
		LP: Columbia 33CX 1912/SAX 2552
		LP: CBS 61152/4455/5455
		CD: Sony SB5K 48396/SBK 47651/SB3K 62773

Amsterdam November 1966	Concertgebouw Orchestra	LP: Philips SAL 3667/802 769LY/ 900-169/6833 102/6566 004 CD: Philips 420 7712/442 7272
Salzburg August 1969	VPO	LP: Rococo 2081

Symphony No 6 "Pastoral"

New York December 1955	NYPSO	LP: Columbia (USA) ML 5057/Y3 35231 LP: Philips SBL 5206/S04622L
Cleveland January 1962	CO	LP: Epic LC 3849/BC 1249/SC 6050/ SC 6063/BSC 150/BSC 163 LP: Columbia (USA) M7X 30281 LP: Columbia 33CX 1905/SAX 2547 LP: CBS 61153/4163 CD: Sony SB5K 48396/SBK 46532/MBK 44810

Symphony No 7

Cleveland   CO
October 1959

LP: Epic LC 3658/BC 1066/SC 6050/BSC 150
LP: Philips 697 303EL
LP: Columbia (USA) M7X 30281/Y 34624
LP: Columbia 33CX 1869/SAX 2510
LP: CBS 61154
CD: Sony SB5K 48396/SBK 48158
Excerpts
LP: Epic PLC 1/PBC 1/Szell 50th anniversary

Symphony No 8

Cleveland   CO
April 1961

LP: Epic LC 3854/BC 1254/SC 6041/
    SC 6050/BSC 112/BSC 150
LP: Columbia (USA) M7X 30281
LP: Columbia 33CX 1850/SAX 2493
LP: CBS 61155-61166
CD: Sony SB5K 48356/SBK 46328

Symphony No 9 "Choral"

Cleveland   CO
April 1961   CO Choir
                 Addison, Hobson,
                 Lewis, Bell

LP: Epic SC 6041/SC 6050/SC 6063/
    BSC 112/BSC 150/BSC 163
LP: Philips 697 305EL
LP: Columbia (USA) M7X 30287/Y 34625
LP: Columbia 33CX 1867-1868/
    SAX 2512-2513
LP: CBS 61155-61156
CD: Sony SB5K 48396/SBK 46533/MYK 42532

Piano Concerto No 1

Cleveland   CO
February 1961   Fleisher

LP: Epic LC 3788/BC 1136/SC 6051/BSC 151
LP: Columbia (USA) M4X 30052/YT 35928
LP: Columbia 33SX 1767/SCX 2567
LP: CBS 77371
CD: Sony M3K 42445/SB3K 48397/SBK 47658
    SBK 62774

Cleveland   CO
May 1968   Gilels

LP: Angel 3731/36027
LP: World Records SM 156-160
LP: Eurodisc XK 80176/MK 85641
LP: Melodiya D026595-026596
    S01795-01796
CD: EMI CZS 569 5062

Piano Concerto No 2

Cleveland April 1961	CO Fleisher	LP: Epic LC 3789/BC 1137/SC 6051/BSC 151 LP: Columbia (USA) M4X 30052/YT 35928 LP: Columbia 33SX 1685/SCX 3541 LP: CBS 77371/61046 CD: Sony M3K 42445/SB3K 48397/SBK 48165
Lucerne August 1962	Lucerne Festival Orchestra Fleisher	CD: Relief CR 1881 <u>Second and third movements only</u>
Cleveland April-May 1968	CO Gilels	LP: Angel 3731/36028 LP: World Records SM 156-160 LP: Eurodisc XK 80176/MK 85642 LP: Melodiya D-26597-026598/ S01797-01798 CD: EMI CZS 569 5062

Piano Concerto No 3

New York June 1945	NYPSO Schnabel	LP: Discocorp SID 721 LP: Melodram MEL 203 CD: Music and Arts CD 681
Cleveland March- April 1961	CO Fleisher	LP: Epic LC 3790/BC 1138/SC 6051/BSC 151 LP: Columbia (USA) M4X 30052/YT 35489 LP: Columbia 33SX 1772/SCX 3572 LP: CBS 77371 CD: Sony M3K 42445/SB3K 48397/SBK 47658 SBK 62774
Cleveland April 1968	CO Gilels	LP: Angel 3731/36029 LP: World Records SM 156-160 LP: Eurodisc XK 80176/MK 80974 LP: Melodiya D026599-026600/ S01799-01800 CD: EMI CZS 569 5062

Piano Concerto No 4

New York December 1952	NYPSO Novaes	Unpublished radio broadcast

Cleveland   CO
January 1959   Fleisher
- LP: Epic LC 3574/LC 3789/BC 1025/
  BC 1137/SC 6051/BSC 151
- LP: Columbia (USA) M4X 30052/YT 35490
- LP: Philips A699515L
- LP: Columbia 33SX 1685/SCX 3541
- LP: CBS 77371
- CD: Sony M3K 42445/SB3K 48397/
  SBK 48165/MYK 44832

Cleveland   CO
April 1968   Gilels
- LP: Angel 3731/36030
- LP: World Records SM 156-160
- LP: Eurodisc XK 80176/MK 80975
- LP: Melodiya D025395-025396/
  S01801-01802
- CD: EMI CZS 569 5092

Piano Concerto No 5 "Emperor"

London   LPO
October 1938   Moiseiwitsch
- 78: HMV C 3043-3047/C 7517-7521 auto
- 78: Victor M 761
- CD: Koch 370352

London   LPO
September   Curzon
1950
- 78: Decca AX 282-286
- 78: Decca (Switzerland) K 2281-2285
- 78: London LA 123
- LP: Decca LXT 2506
- LP: London LLP 114/LLC 17504
- LP: Telefunken 648.112

Cleveland   CO
March 1961   Fleisher
- LP: Epic LC 3791/BC 1139/SC 6051/BSC 151
- LP: Columbia (USA) M4X 30052/YT 35491
- LP: Columbia 33SX 1777/SCX 3574
- LP: CBS 77371/61005
- CD: Sony M3K 42445/MBK 44891/
  SB3K 48397/SBK 46549

Excerpt
- LP: Columbia (USA) MG 31270

Cleveland   CO
May 1968   Gilels
- LP: Angel 3731/36031
- LP: World Records SM 156-160
- LP: Eurodisc XK 80176/MK 80976
- LP: EMI SXLP 30223
- LP: Melodiya D024623-024624/
  S01803-01804
- CD: EMI CZS 569 5092

Violin Concerto

Vienna June 1934	VPO Huberman	78: Columbia LX 509-513/LX 8256-8260 auto LP: Columbia (USA) ML 4769 LP: Rococo 2033 LP: EMI 143 5341 CD: Preiser 90118 CD: Magic Talent CD 48023 CD: Signature APR 5506 CD: Arlecchino ARL 153-154

Violin Romance No 1

New York 1945	NYPSO Szigeti	LP: Discocorp BWS 741 CD: Dante LYS 84

Coriolan, overture

Cleveland October 1966	CO	LP: Columbia (USA) ML 6366/MS 6966

Egmont, incidental music

Vienna December 1969	VPO Lorengar, Wussow	LP: Decca SXL 6465 LP: London CS 6675 CD: Decca 421 0242/425 9722/448 5932 Overture LP: Decca SPA 324 421 0242 and 425 9722 did not include spoken dialogue

Egmont, overture

Salzburg August 1963	Czech PO	CD: Sony SMK 68447
Cleveland October 1966	CO	LP: Columbia (USA) ML 6366/MS 6966 LP: CBS 61580 CD: Sony SB5K 48396/SBK 46532

Fidelio, overture

London August 1967	CO	LP: Columbia (USA) ML 6468/MS 7068 LP: CBS 72689/61580 CD: Sony SB5K 48396/SBK 46533

Die Geschöpfe des Prometheus, overture

Chicago March 1968	CSO	CD: Chicago Symphony Orchestra CD 90

König Stephan, overture

Cleveland October 1966	CO	LP: Columbia (USA) ML 6366/MS 6966 LP: CBS 61580 CD: Sony SBK 48158/SB3K 48396 <u>Excerpt</u> LP: Columbia (USA) MPS 12

Leonore No 1, overture

London August 1967	CO	LP: Columbia (USA) ML 6468/MS 7068 LP: CBS 72689/61580

Leonore No 2, overture

Cleveland October 1966	CO	LP: Columbia (USA) ML 6966/ML 6468/ MS 6966/MS 7068 LP: CBS 72689/61580

Leonore No 3, overture

Berlin 1927	Staatskapelle	78: Parlophone E 10545-10546 78: Odeon O 7502-7503
Cleveland April 1963	CO	LP: Epic LC 3864/BC 1264 LP: Columbia (USA) ML 6468/MS 7068 LP: CBS 72689/61580/30039

Missa Solemnis

Cleveland 1967	CO CO Chorus Endich, Kopleff, Haefliger, Flagello	Unpublished radio broadcast

HECTOR BERLIOZ (1803-1869)

Le carnaval romain, overture

Cleveland March 1958	CO	LP: Epic LC 3506

Marche hongroise (La damnation de Faust)

Lugano May 1957	CO	CD: Ermitage ERM 106
Tokyo May 1970	CO	Unpublished radio broadcast

GEORGES BIZET (1838-1875)

L'Arlésienne, suite no 1 and Farandole (suite no 2)

Cleveland March 1966	CO	LP: Columbia (USA) ML 6277/MS 6877 LP: CBS 61303 <u>Excerpts</u> LP: Columbia (USA) CSS 568/CCS 1318/ MS 7435/M2X 787/SOG 3/SOG 5

Carmen, excerpt (La fleur que tu m'avais jetée)

Berlin November 1926	Staatskapelle Pattiera <u>Sung in Italian</u>	78: Odeon O-7526 78: Parlophone E 10526/P 9029 LP: Rococo 5256 LP: Preiser LV 281 CD: Preiser 89222

Carmen, excerpt (Votre toast!)

Berlin October 1926	Staatskapelle Bohnen <u>Sung in German</u>	78: Odeon O-8304/O-6804 78: Ultraphon F 455 LP: Electrola E 83383 LP: Discophilia DISKGB 4 LP: Preiser LV 192

ALEXANDER BORODIN (1833-1887)

Polovtsian Dances

Cleveland February- March 1958	CO	LP: Epic LC 3483/BC 1002 LP: Columbia (USA) M2X 787/Y 30044 LP: Columbia 33CX 1847/SAX 2490 LP: CBS 61213 CD: Sony MBK 44805 <u>Excerpts</u> LP: Epic PLC/PBC 1 <u>Excerpts also on a Columbia Special</u> <u>Products LP</u>

JOHANNES BRAHMS (1833-1897)

Symphony No 1

Cleveland March 1957	CO	LP: Epic LC 3379/BC 1010 LP: Philips CFL 1010/699 503CL <u>Excerpts on an unnumbered promotional LP</u>
Cleveland October 1966	CO	LP: Columbia (USA) D3L 358/D3L 758 LP: Columbia CX 5279/SAX 5279 LP: CBS 77356 CD: Sony SB3K 48398/SBK 46534

Symphony No 2

Berlin 1925	Staatskapelle	78: Parlophone E 10487-10490
Cleveland January 1967	CO	LP: Columbia (USA) D3L 358/D3L 758 LP: Columbia CX 5284/SAX 5284 LP: CBS 77356 CD: Sony SB3K 48398/SBK 47652
Cleveland January 1967	CO	Unpublished radio broadcast

Symphony No 3

Amsterdam September 1951	Concertgebouw Orchestra	LP: Decca LXT 2676/LXT 5367/ACL 103 LP: London LLP 487/B 19050/K4R-1 LP: Turnabout THS 65003 CD: Decca 425 9942
Cleveland October 1964	CO	LP: Columbia (USA) ML 6085/MS 6685/ D3L 358/D3S 758 LP: Columbia 33CX 1933/SAX 2572 LP: CBS 77356 CD: Sony SB3K 48398/SBK 47652/MYK 42531

Symphony No 4

Cleveland April 1966	CO	LP: Columbia (USA) D3L 358/D3S 758 LP: CBS 77356 CD: Sony SB3K 48398/SBK 46330/MBK 44959

Piano Concerto No 1

London January- December 1938	LPO Schnabel	78: HMV DB 3712-3717/DB 8614-8619 auto 78: Victor M 677 LP: Rococo 2022 LP: World Records SH 223 LP: EMI 1C 181 52348-52349M CD: Pearl GEMMCD 9376
Cleveland November 1952	CO Serkin	LP: Columbia (USA) ML 4829/4111 LP: Philips ABL 3028/A01124L CD: Sony SM3K 47269
Cleveland February 1958	CO Fleisher	LP: Epic LC 3484/BC 1003 LP: Columbia (USA) Y 31273 LP: Philips A876501L LP: Columbia 33CX 1882/SAX 2526 <u>Excerpt</u> LP: Epic BC 1
London May 1962	LSO Curzon	LP: Decca LXT 6023/SXL 6023 LP: London CM 9329/CS 6329 CD: Decca 417 6412/425 0822
Cleveland April 1968	CO Serkin	LP: Columbia (USA) MS 7143/MG 31421 LP: CBS 72718 CD: Sony MK 41161/MBK 45644/SBK 48166

Piano Concerto No 2

Cleveland October 1962	CO Fleisher	LP: Epic LC 3853/BC 1253 LP: Columbia (USA) Y 32222 LP: Columbia 33CX 1890/SAX 2534
Cleveland January 1966	CO Serkin	LP: Columbia (USA) ML 6367/MS 6967/ MG 31421/M 31848 LP: CBS BRG 72557/SBRG 72557 CD: Sony MK 42262/SM3K 47269/SBK 53262

Violin Concerto

New York 1951	NYPSO Heifetz	LP: Movimento musica 01.015 CD: Music and Arts CD 766
Cleveland May 1969	CO Oistrakh	LP: Angel 36033 LP: EMI SLS 786/ASD 2525 LP: Eurodisc MK 80184/XFK 27945/ XGK 86095/XPK 88665 LP: Melodiya SM01861-01862 Excerpt LP: Angel SPRO 4898

Double Concerto

Cleveland May 1969	CO Oistrakh, Rostropovich	LP: Angel 36032 LP: EMI SLS 786/ASD 3312/1C 063 02009 LP: Melodiya SM01861-01862 CD: EMI CDM 764 7442/CMS 565 7012 Excerpt LP: Angel SPRO 4898

Academic Festival Overture

Cleveland October 1955	CO	LP: Musical Appreciation Society MAR 573/MARS 5558 <u>Orchestra described as Symphony Orchestra</u>
Cleveland Date not confirmed	CO	VHS Video: Teldec 4509 950386 Laserdisc: Teldec 4509 950383 <u>Rehearsal extract</u>
Cleveland October 1966	CO	LP: Columbia (USA) ML 6365/MS 6965/ SOG 5/CSS 671 LP: CBS 77356 CD: Sony MBK 44959/SB3K 48398/SBK 46330 Excerpt LP: Columbia (USA) MPS 12

Ein deutsches Requiem

Cleveland	CO	CD: Melodram CDM 17503
April 1969	CO Chorus	
	Janowitz, Krause	

Haydn Variations

Cleveland   CO   LP: Musical Appreciation Society MAR 573
October 1955   <u>Orchestra described as Symphony Orchestra</u>

Cleveland   CO   LP: Columbia (USA) ML 6085/ML 6365/
October 1964   MS 6685/MS 6965
                                LP: Columbia 33CX 1933/SAX 2572
                                CD: Sony MK 42531/SB3K 48398/SBK 46534

Piano Quintet in F minor

New York   Budapest String   CD: Bridge 9062
1945-1946   Quartet
                 Szell, piano

Tragic Overture

Cleveland   CO   LP: Columbia (USA) ML 6365/MS 6965
October 1966   LP: Columbia CX 5284/SAX 5284
                              LP: CBS 77356
                              CD: Sony SB3K 48398/SBK 46330

ANTON BRUCKNER (1824-1896)

Symphony No 3

Salzburg August 1965	Dresden Staatskapelle	CD: Sony SMK 68448
Cleveland January 1966	CO	LP: Columbia (USA) ML 6297/MS 6897/BC 1362 LP: CBS 61072 CD: Sony MPK 45880/SB2K 53519 <u>Excerpt</u> LP: Columbia (USA) MPS 10/SOG 3

Symphony No 7

Salzburg August 1968	VPO	LP: Rococo 2081 CD: Sony SMK 47646

Symphony No 8

Cleveland October 1969	CO	LP: Columbia (USA) M2 30070 LP: CBS 77235 CD: Sony SB2K 53519
Cleveland Date not confirmed	CO	CD: Artists' Live Recordings FED 072

Te Deum

Cleveland Date not confirmed	Soloists CO and Chorus	CD: Documents LV 941

PETER CORNELIUS (1824-1874)

Der Barbier von Bagdad, overture

Berlin 1926-1927	Staatskapelle	78: Parlophone E 10613

Der Barbier von Bagdad, excerpt (Vor deinem Fenster)

Berlin December 1926	Staatskapelle Talén	78: Odeon O-6589 LP: Preiser LV 157 LP: BASF 98 221756

CLAUDE DEBUSSY (1862-1918)

La mer

Lugano May 1957	CO	CD: Ermitage ERM 106
Cleveland January 1963	CO	LP: Epic LC 3863/BC 1263 LP: Columbia (USA) Y 31298 LP: Columbia 33CX 1896/SAX 2532 LP: CBS 61075 CD: Sony MBK 44804

LEX VAN DELDEN (Born 1919)

Symphony No 3 "Facets"

Amsterdam 1957	Concertgebouw Orchestra	LP: Dutch Radio RN 441.2 CD: Etcetera KTC 1156

FREDERICK DELIUS (1862-1934)

Irmelin, prelude

Cleveland October 1966	CO	LP: Epic LC 3330

ANTONIN DVORAK (1841-1904)

Symphony No 7

Cleveland   CO
March 1960
LP: Epic LC 3748/BC 1111/SC 6038/
    SC 6055/BSC 109/BSC 155
LP: Columbia (USA) D3S 814
LP: Columbia 33CX 1856/SAX 2501
LP: CBS 78304/4441/5441
Excerpts
LP: Columbia (USA) MS 7524/XEM 50311

Symphony No 8

Amsterdam   Concertgebouw
September 1951 Orchestra
78: Decca K 23281-23285
LP: Decca LXT 2461/LXT 2641/ACL 46
LP: London LLP 488/B 19107/23245
LP: Turnabout TV 34525
CD: Decca 425 9942

Cleveland   CO
October-
November 1958
LP: Epic LC 3532/BC 1015/SC 6038/
    SC 6055/BSC 109/BSC 155
LP: Columbia (USA) D3S 814
LP: CBS 78304/4322/5048
Excerpt
LP: Columbia (USA) BC 1
Excerpt also on Szell 50th anniversary LP

Cleveland   CO
April 1970
LP: Angel 36043
LP: EMI ASD 3312/1C 063 02095
CD: EMI CDM 565 9192/CMS 565 9152/
    CZS 569 5092

Symphony No 9 "From the New World"

London April 1937	Czech PO	78: HMV C 2949-2953/JX 9-13 78: Victor M 469 CD: Dutton CDEA 5002
Cleveland January 1952	CO	45: Columbia (USA) A 1082 LP: Columbia (USA) ML 4541/4131 <u>Excerpt on an unnumbered Columbia</u> <u>promotional LP</u>
Cleveland March 1959	CO	LP: Epic LC 3575/BC 1026/SC 6038/ SC 6055/BSC 109/BSC 155 LP: Columbia (USA) D3S 814/MG 30371 LP: CBS 78304/4402/5124 CD: Sony MYK 42530 <u>Excerpts</u> LP: Epic PLC 1/PBC 1

Cello Concerto

London April 1937	Czech PO Casals	78: HMV DB 3288-3292/14941-14945 78: Victor M 458 45: Victor WCT 39 LP: Victor LCT 1026 LP: Electrola E 80614 LP: HMV COLH 30/HLM 7013 LP: Angel 60240 CD: MM 30428 CD: Pearl GEMMCD 9349/GEMMCDS 9935 CD: EMI CDH 763 4982 CD: Magic Talent CD 48023 CD: Dutton CDEA 5002
Berlin June 1961	BPO Fournier	LP: DG LPM 18 755/SLPM 138 755/2535 106 CD: DG 423 8812/429 1552/439 4842
Cleveland Date not confirmed	CO Rostropovich	CD: Documents LV 941

Piano Concerto

Cleveland April 1954	CO Firkusny	LP: Columbia (USA) ML 4967/Y 35210 LP: Philips ABR 4052/A01619R

Violin Concerto

Amsterdam November 1966	Concertgebouw Orchestra Krebbers	CD: Music and Arts CD 291

Carnival Overture

Cleveland January 1963	CO	LP: Epic LC 3868/BC 1268 LP: Columbia (USA) M2L 326/M2S 726/ Y 30049/Y2 33524 LP: Columbia 33CX 1889/SAX 2539 LP: CBS 78299 CD: Sony MBK 44958

Slavonic Dance No 1 in C

Cleveland April 1947	CO	78: Columbia (USA) M 756 78: Columbia LX 1411 LP: Columbia (USA) ML 2023/ML 4785/ 4170/P 12752
Cleveland December 1956	CO	LP: Epic LC 3322/SC 6015 LP: Philips EFL 2515/SBR 6232

Cleveland
January 1963
	CO	LP: Epic LC 3868/BC 1268
		LP: Columbia (USA) M2L 326/M2S 726/
		    MS 7208/Y 30049/Y2 33524/MS 7524/
		    CSS 568/CSS 1318/DJD 13/XSM 111049
		LP: Columbia 33CX 1889/SX 6053/
		    SAX 2539/SCX 6053
		LP: CBS 78299/61089/30012/5504
		CD: Sony MBK 44802/SBK 48161
		<u>MS 7208, 61089 and 5504 omit repeats</u>

Slavonic Dance No 2 in E

Cleveland December 1956	CO	LP: Epic LC 3322/SC 6015 LP: Philips SBR 6232/EFL 2515
Cleveland January 1965	CO	LP: Columbia (USA) M2L 326/M2S 726/ MS 7208/Y2 33524 LP: Columbia SX 6053/SCX 6053 LP: CBS 78299/61089/5504 CD: Sony MBK 44802/SBK 48161 <u>MS 7208, 61089 and 5504 omit repeats</u>

Slavonic Dance No 3 in A flat

Cleveland CO
April 1947
78: Columbia (USA) M 756
78: Columbia LX 1411
LP: Columbia (USA) ML 2023/ML 4785/
    4170/P 17252

Cleveland CO
December 1956
LP: Epic LC 3322/SC 6015
LP: Philips SBR 6232/EFL 2515
Also on an unnumbered Columbia Special Products LP

Cleveland CO
April 1963
LP: Epic LC 3868/BC 1268
LP: Columbia (USA) M2L 326/M2S 726/
    MS 7208/Y 30049/Y2 33524
LP: Columbia 33CX 1899/SX 6053/
    SAX 2539/SCX 6053
LP: CBS 78299/61089/5504
CD: Sony MBK 44802/SBK 48161
MS 7208, 61089 and 5504 omit repeats

Cleveland CO
April 1970
LP: Angel 36043
LP: EMI ASD 3312/1C 063 02095
CD: EMI CZS 569 5092

Slavonic Dance No 4 in F

Cleveland CO
December 1956
LP: Epic SC 6015
LP: Philips EFL 2515

Cleveland CO
January 1965
LP: Columbia (USA) M2L 326/M2S 726/
    MS 7208/Y2 33524
LP: Columbia SX 6053/SCX 6053
LP: CBS 78299/61089/5504
CD: Sony MBK 44802/SBK 48161
MS 7208, 61089 and 5504 omit repeats

Slavonic Dance No 5 in A

Cleveland CO
December 1956
LP: Epic LC 3322/SC 6015
LP: Philips EFL 2515

Cleveland CO
January 1965
LP: Columbia (USA) M2L 326/M2S 726/
    MS 7208/Y2 33524
LP: Columbia SX 6053/SCX 6053
LP: CBS 78299/61089/5504
CD: Sony MBK 44802/SBK 48161
MS 7208, 61089 and 5504 omit repeats

Slavonic Dance No 6 in D

Cleveland   CO
December 1956

LP: Epic SC 6015
LP: Philips EFL 2515

Cleveland   CO
October 1964

LP: Columbia (USA) M2L 326/M2S 726/
    MS 7208/Y2 33524
LP: Columbia SX 6053/SCX 6053
LP: CBS 77829/61089/5504
CD: Sony MBK 44802/SBK 48161
MS 7208, 61089 and 5504 omit repeats

Slavonic Dance No 7 in C

Cleveland   CO
December 1956

LP: Epic SC 6015
LP: Philips EFL 2515

Cleveland   CO
October 1964

LP: Columbia (USA) M2L 326/M2S 726/
    MS 7208/Y2 33524
LP: Columbia SX 6053/SCX 6053
LP: CBS 77829/61089/5504
CD: Sony MBK 44802/SBK 48161
MS 7208, 61089 and 5504 omit repeats

Slavonic Dance No 8 in G

Cleveland   CO
April 1947

78: Columbia (USA) M 756
78: Columbia LX 1537
LP: Columbia (USA) ML 2023/ML 4785/
    4170/P 12752

Cleveland   CO
December 1956

LP: Epic LC 3322/SC 6015
LP: Philips EFL 2515/SBR 6232

Cleveland   CO
October 1964

LP: Columbia (USA) M2L 326/M2S 726/
    MS 7208/Y2 33524/M2X 787/SOG 5/
    MS 7524/DJS 13/XSM 111049
LP: Columbia SX 6053/SCX 6053
LP: CBS 78299/61089/5504/30012
CD: Sony MBK 44802/SBK 48161
MS 7208, 61089 and 5504 omit repeats

Mendelssohn: "Italian" Symphony, etc. ★ Szell — mono

Mendelssohn: "Italian" Symphony
"The Hebrides" Overture / Weber: "Oberon" Overture
George Szell and The Cleveland Orchestra

Slavonic Dance No 9 in B

Cleveland December 1956	CO	LP: Epic LC 3322/SC 6015 LP: Philips EFL 2515/SBR 6232
Cleveland January 1965	CO	LP: Columbia (USA) M2L 326/M2S 726/ MS 7208/Y2 33524 LP: Columbia SX 6053/SCX 6053 LP: CBS 78299/61089/5504 CD: Sony MBK 44802/SBK 48161 <u>MS 7208, 61089 and 5504 omit repeats</u>

Slavonic Dance No 10 in E

Cleveland April 1947	CO	78: Columbia (USA) M 756 LP: Columbia (USA) ML 2023/ML 4785/4170
Cleveland March 1956	CO	LP: Epic LC 3322/SC 6015 LP: Philips EFL 2515/SBR 6232

Cleveland
January 1963
	CO	LP: Epic LC 3868/BC 1268
		LP: Columbia (USA) M2L 326/M2S 726/
		     MS 7208/Y 30049/Y2 33524
		LP: Columbia 33CX 1899/SX 6053/
		     SAX 2539/SCX 6053
		LP: CBS 78299/61089/5504
		CD: Sony MBK 44802/SBK 48161
		<u>MS 7208, 61089 and 5504 omit repeats</u>

Cleveland April 1970	CO	LP: Angel 36043 LP: EMI ASD 3312/1C 063 02095 CD: EMI CZS 569 5092

Slavonic Dance No 11 in F

Cleveland March 1956	CO	LP: Epic SC 6015 LP: Philips EFL 2515/SBR 6232
Cleveland January 1965	CO	LP: Columbia (USA) M2L 326/M2S 726/ MS 7208/Y2 33524 LP: Columbia SX 6053/SCX 6053 LP: CBS 78299/61089/5504 CD: Sony MBK 44802/SBK 48161 <u>MS 7208, 61089 and 5504 omit repeats</u>

Slavonic Dance No 12 in D flat

Cleveland   CO   LP: Epic LC 3322/SC 6015
March 1956

Cleveland   CO   LP: Columbia (USA) M2L 326/M2S 726/
January 1965   MS 7208/Y2 33524
                                  LP: Columbia SX 6053/SCX 6053
                                  LP: CBS 78299/61089/5504
                                  CD: Sony MBK 44802/SBK 48161
                                  MS 7208, 61089 and 5504 omit repeats

Slavonic Dance No 13 in B flat

Cleveland   CO   LP: Epic SC 6015
March 1956   LP: Philips EFL 2515

Cleveland   CO   LP: Columbia (USA) M2L 326/M2S 726/
February 1965   MS 7208/Y2 33524
                                  LP: Columbia SX 6053/SCX 6053
                                  LP: CBS 78299/61089/5504
                                  CD: Sony MBK 44802/SBK 48161
                                  MS 7208, 61089 and 5504 omit repeats

Slavonic Dance No 14 in B flat

Cleveland   CO   LP: Epic SC 6015
March 1956   LP: Philips EFL 2515

Cleveland   CO   LP: Columbia (USA) M2L 326/M2S 726/
January 1965   MS 7208/Y2 33524
                                  LP: Columbia SX 6053/SCX 6053
                                  LP: CBS 78299/61089/5504
                                  CD: Sony MBK 44802/SBK 48161
                                  MS 7208, 61089 and 5504 omit repeats

Slavonic Dance No 15 in C

Cleveland April 1947	CO	78: Columbia (USA) M 756/M 855 78: Columbia LX 1537 LP: Columbia (USA) ML 2023/ML 4785/ 4170/P 12752
Cleveland March 1956	CO	LP: Epic LC 3322/SC 6015 LP: Philips EFL 2515/SBR 6232

Cleveland
January 1963
	CO	LP: Epic LC 3868/BC 1268
		LP: Columbia (USA) M2L 326/M2S 726/
		    MS 7208/Y 30049/Y2 33524/
		    CSM 386/CSS 386
		LP: Columbia 33CX 1899/SX 6053/
		    SAX 2539/SCX 6053
		LP: CBS 78299/61089/5504
		CD: Sony MBK 44802/SBK 48161
		MS 7208, 61089 and 5504 omit repeats

Slavonic Dance No 16 in A flat

Cleveland March 1956	CO	LP: Epic LC 3322/SC 6015
Cleveland January 1965	CO	LP: Columbia (USA) M2L 326/M2S 726/ MS 7208/Y2 33524 LP: Columbia SX 6053/SCX 6053 LP: CBS 78299/61089/5504 CD: Sony MBK 44802/SBK 48161 MS 7208, 61089 and 5504 omit repeats

CESAR FRANCK (1822-1890)

Variations symphoniques pour piano et orchestre

Cleveland October 1956	CO	Fleisher	LP: Epic LC 3330

CHARLES GOUNOD (1818-1893)

Faust, excerpt (Le veau d'or)

Berlin	Staatskapelle	78: Odeon O-8304/O-6804
October 1926	Bohnen	LP: Preiser LV 192
	Sung in German	LP: ELP 460
		LP: Electrola E 83383

EDVARD GRIEG (1843-1907)

Piano Concerto

Cleveland	CO	LP: Epic LC 3689/BC 1080
January 1960	Fleisher	LP: Columbia (USA) Y 30668
		LP: Philips EFM 2509/697 302
		LP: CBS 77342
		CD: Sony MPK 44849
		Excerpt
		LP: Columbia (USA) XEM 50311

Peer Gynt, suite no 1 and Solveig's Song (suite no 2)

Cleveland	CO	LP: Columbia (USA) ML 6277/MS 6877/
January 1966		MS 7505/MG 30074
		LP: CBS 61303/30004
		Excerpts
		LP: Columbia (USA) M2X 787/YO 27024/
		C 10017/CSS 568/CSS 1318

JACQUES HALEVY (1799-1862)

La juive, excerpt (Si la rigueur)

Berlin	Staatskapelle	78: Odeon O-8309/O-6808
October 1926	Bohnen	78: Decca (USA) 25810
	Sung in German	LP: Preiser LV 192
		LP: Electrola E 83383

GEORGE FRIDERIC HANDEL (1685-1759)

Music for the Royal Fireworks, suite arranged by Harty

London May 1962	LSO	LP: Decca LXT 5666/SXL 2302/SPA 120 LP: London CM 9035/CS 6236 LP: Telefunken ND 654 LP: Deram 8012 CD: Decca 417 6942/450 0012

Water Music, suite arranged by Harty and Szell

London May 1962	LSO	45: Decca CEP 5504/SEC 5504 LP: Decca LXT 5666/SXL 2302/SPA 120 LP: London CM 9035/CS 6236 LP: Telefunken ND 654 LP: Deram 8012 CD: Decca 417 6942/450 0012

Minuet (The Faithful Shepherd), arranged by Beecham

London May 1962	LSO	LP: Decca LXT 5666/SXL 2302/SPA 120 LP: London CM 9035/CS 6236 LP: Telefunken ND 654 LP: Deram 8012 CD: Decca 417 6942/450 0012

Largo (Serse), arranged by Reinhard

London May 1962	LSO	LP: Decca LXT 5666/SXL 6236/SPA 120 LP: London CM 9035/CS 6236 LP: Telefunken ND 654 LP: Deram 8012 CD: Decca 417 6942/450 0012

FRANZ JOSEF HAYDN (1732-1809)

Symphony No 88

Berlin 1924-1925	Staatskapelle	78: Odeon/Parlophone
Cleveland April 1954	CO	LP: Epic LC 3196 LP: Columbia (USA) Y 34636

Symphony No 92 "Oxford"

Cleveland April 1949	CO	78: Columbia (USA) M 880 LP: Columbia (USA) ML 4268 LP: Columbia 33CX 1028 LP: Columbia (Italy) QCX 10006 LP: Columbia (Austria) VCX 518 LP: Philips GBL 5521
Salzburg August 1959	Orchestre National	CD: Sony SMK 68446
Cleveland October 1961	CO	LP: Epic LC 3828/BC 1156 LP: Columbia 33CX 1885/SAX 2529 CD: Sony SBK 46332

Symphony No 93

Vienna 1954	VSO	CD: Orfeo C230 901A/C226 905R
Cleveland April 1968	CO	LP: Columbia (USA) ML 6406/MS 7006/ D3M 32321 LP: CBS 61052 CD: Sony MYK 42596/M2YK 45673/SBK 67175

Symphony No 94 "Surprise"

Cleveland May 1967	CO	LP: Columbia (USA) ML 6406/MS 7006/ D3M 32321 LP: CBS 61052 CD: Sony MYK 42596/M2YK 45673/SBK 46332

Symphony No 95

Cleveland January 1969	CO	LP: Columbia (USA) M 30366/D3M 32321 LP: CBS 61246 CD: Sony M2YK 45673/SBK 67175

Symphony No 96 "Miracle"

Cleveland October 1968	CO	LP: Columbia (USA) M 30366/D3M 32321 LP: CBS 61246 CD: Sony M2YK 45673/SBK 46332

Symphony No 97

Cleveland October 1957	CO	LP: Epic LC 3455
Cleveland October 1969	CO	LP: Columbia (USA) M 30646/D3M 32321 LP: CBS 61291 CD: Sony M2YK 45673/SBK 67175

Symphony No 98

Cleveland October 1969	CO	LP: Columbia (USA) M 30646/D3M 32321 LP: CBS 61291 CD: Sony M2YK 45673

Symphony No 99

Cleveland October 1957	CO	LP: Epic LC 3455

Symphony No 104 "London"

Cleveland April 1954	CO	LP: Epic LC 3196

HANS HENKEMANS (Born 1913)

Barcarola fantastica

Amsterdam Date not confirmed	Concertgebouw Orchestra	LP: Dutch Radio RN 109519

FERDINAND HEROLD (1791-1833)

Zampa, overture

Berlin 1926-1927	Staatskapelle	78: Parlophone E 10623 78: Odeon O-7505 78: Decca (USA) 25172 <u>Orchestra described as Grosses Sinfonie-Orchester</u>

PAUL HINDEMITH (1895-1963)

Symphonic Metamorphoses on themes of Carl Maria von Weber

Cleveland November 1947	CO	78: Columbia (USA) M 855 LP: Columbia (USA) ML 4177 LP: Philips ABL 3390
Cleveland October 1964	CO	LP: Columbia (USA) MS 7166 LP: Columbia 33CX 1935/SAX 2576 LP: CBS 61367 CD: Sony SBK 53258 <u>Excerpt</u> LP: Columbia (USA) CSS 1318

ENGELBERT HUMPERDINCK (1854-1921)

Dream Pantomime (Hänsel und Gretel)

Cleveland May 1967	CO	CD: Sony awaiting publication

LEOS JANACEK (1854-1928)

Sinfonietta

Cleveland CO
October 1965

LP: Columbia (USA) ML 6215/MS 6815/MS 7166
LP: Columbia CX 5263/SAX 5263
LP: CBS 61367
Excerpt
LP: Columbia (USA) SOG 5

ZOLTAN KODALY (1882-1967)

Hary Janos, suite

Cleveland CO
January 1969

LP: Columbia (USA) MS 7408
LP: CBS 61193
CD: Sony MYK 44831/SBK 48162
Excerpts
LP: Columbia (USA) C 10017/MS 7435/
    YO 27024

ERICH WOLFGANG KORNGOLD (1897-1957)

Die tote Stadt, excerpt (Glück, das mir verblieb)

Berlin April 1924	Staatskapelle Lehmann, Tauber	78: Parlophone R 20258 78: Decca (USA) 29012 45: Odeon O-20479 LP: Odeon OBL 1072 LP: Scala (USA) 837/1435 LP: Eterna (USA) 494 LP: EMI 1C 147 29116-29117M CD: Preiser 89219 CD: Claremont CDGSE 78-50-64 <u>Later dubbings of the 78s substituted an electrically recorded accompaniment not conducted by Szell</u>

Die tote Stadt, excerpt (Der Erste, der Lieb' mich gelehrt)

Berlin April 1924	Staatskapelle Lehmann	78: Odeon LXX 80945 LP: Rococo 5356 LP: Angel 6105 LP: Preiser LV 94 LP: EMI 1C 137 30704-30705M CD: EMI CDH 761 0422

Die tote Stadt, excerpt (Ich werde sie nicht wiedersehen)

Berlin April 1924	Staatskapelle Tauber	78: Parlophone R 20258 78: Decca (USA) 29012 45: Odeon O-20479 LP: Scala (USA) 837 LP: Pearl GEMM 214 CD: Preiser 89219 CD: Claremont CDGSE 78-50-64 <u>Later dubbings of the 78s substituted an electrically recorded accompaniment not conducted by Szell</u>

EDOUARD LALO (1823-1892)

Symphonie espagnole

Vienna June 1934	VPO Huberman	78: Columbia LX 347-349 78: Columbia (France) LFX 370-372 78: Columbia (USA) M 214 LP: Rococo 2002 LP: EMI 1C 053 01419M CD: Preiser 90118 CD: Signature APR 5506

TOEN DE LEEUW (Born 1926)

Retrograde Movements

Amsterdam December 1960	Concertgebouw Orchestra	LP: Dutch Radio RN 109226 CD: Donemus CVCD 10/BFOA 6

ANATOL LIADOV (1855-1914)

The Enchanted Lake

Cleveland October 1963	CO	LP: Epic LC 3873/BC 1272

ROLF LIEBERMANN (Born 1910)

Penelope

Salzburg August 1954	VPO Vienna Opera Chorus Goltz, Rothenberger, Schock, Klein, Dönch, Berry	CD: Orfeo C328 931I

Die Schule der Frauen

Salzburg August 1957	VPO Rothenberger, C.Ludwig, Gedda, Berry, Böhme	CD: Orfeo C429 962I

FRANZ LISZT (1811-1886)

Piano Concerto No 2

Cleveland January 1952	CO Casadesus	LP: Columbia (USA) ML 4588/Y 35216 LP: Philips ABR 4049/A01624R CD: Sony MYK 45508

CARL LOEWE (1796-1869)

Der Erlkönig

Berlin October 1926	Bohnen Szell, piano	78: Odeon O-6818/O-8301 78: Decca (USA) 25756 LP: Preiser LV 192

Prinz Eugen

Berlin October 1926	Bohnen Szell, piano	78: Odeon O-6818/O-8301 78: Decca (USA) 25756 LP: Preiser LV 192 LP: Electrola E 83383

GUSTAV MAHLER (1860-1911)

Symphony No 4

Cleveland	CO	LP: Columbia (USA) ML 6233/MS 6833/BC 1357
October 1965	Raskin	LP: Columbia CX 5283/SAX 5283
		LP: CBS 61056
		CD: Sony MYK 44713/MK 42416/SBK 46535

Symphony No 6

Cleveland	CO	LP: Columbia (USA) M2 31313
October 1967		CD: Sony SBK 47654

Symphony No 9

Cleveland	CO	CD: Documents LV 963
1968		CD: Memories HR 4180-4181
		CD: Stradivarius STR 10012

Symphony No 10, Adagio and Purgatorio

Cleveland	CO	LP: Epic LC 3568/BC 1024
November 1958		LP: Columbia (USA) M2 31313
		LP: Philips CFL 1071/SCFL 107
		LP: Columbia 33CX 1845/SAX 2488
		Excerpts on Szell 50th anniversary LP
		Adagio
		CD: Sony SBK 53259

Das Lied von der Erde

Berlin	CO	CD: Hunt CDGI 745
April 1967	Forrester,	
	Lewis	
Cleveland	CO	CD: Cleveland Orchestra TCO93-75
February 1970	Baker, Lewis	

Des Knaben Wunderhorn

London	LSO	LP: EMI SAN 218/ASD 143 4424/
March 1968	Schwarzkopf,	1C 065 00098
	Fischer-Dieskau	LP: Angel 36547
		CD: EMI CDC 747 2772

FELIX MENDELSSOHN-BARTHOLDY (1809-1847)

Symphony No 4 "Italian"

Cleveland November 1947	CO	78: Columbia (USA) M 733 LP: Columbia (USA) ML 4127/ML 4498
Cleveland October 1962	CO	LP: Epic LC 3859/BC 1259 LP: Columbia (USA) ML 6375/MS 6975 LP: Columbia 33CX 1880/SAX 2524 LP: CBS 61019 CD: Sony MYK 42547/SBK 46536 Excerpt LP: Columbia (USA) SOG 5

Violin Concerto

Cleveland December 1961	CO Francescatti	LP: Columbia (USA) ML 6158/ML 5751/ MS 6758/MS 6351 LP: CBS BRG 72044/SBRG 72044/61061 CD: Sony MPK 45700 Excerpt LP: Columbia (USA) MPS 12 ML 5751 and MS 6351 were labelled Columbia Symphony Orchestra

The Hebrides, overture

Cleveland October 1962	CO	LP: Epic LC 3859/BC 1259/SPM 1/SPS 1 LP: Columbia 33CX 1880/SAX 2524 LP: CBS 61019 CD: Sony SBK 46536

A Midsummer Night's Dream, incidental music: Overture, Scherzo, Intermezzo, Nocturne and Wedding March

New York January 1951	NYPSO	LP: Columbia (USA) ML 4498/Y3 35231 Rehearsal extracts of Overture and Wedding March on Columbia promotional LP; Scherzo on BM 13 (NYPSO 125th anniversary LP)
Amsterdam February 1957	Concertgebouw Orchestra	45: Philips A400 858E LP: Philips ABL 3238/A00475L/GBL 5677/ G05324R/835 006AY/SFM 23006/6580 027 LP: Epic LC 3433/BC 1023/839 511 LP: Fontana (Holland) ZKY 894044 CD: Philips 432 2282/442 7272 This performance omits Intermezzo; A400 858E contains only Scherzo, Nocturne and Wedding March
Cleveland January 1967	CO	LP: Columbia (USA) ML 6402/MS 7002 LP: CBS 61076 CD: Sony MYK 42547/SBK 48264 Excerpts LP: Columbia (USA) MS 7435/M2X 787

A Midsummer Night's Dream, overture

Stockhom August 1963	Stockholm RO	LP: Bis BISLP 331-333

MODEST MUSSORGSKY (1839-1881)

Boris Godunov

New York February 1943	Metropolitan Opera Orchestra & Chorus Thorborg, Maison, Kipnis, Moscona, Warren <u>Kipnis sings in Russian, rest of cast in Italian</u>	CD: Walhall WHL 12 Excerpts LP: Ed Smith EJS 550 CD: Music and Arts CD 867
New York December 1943	Metropolitan Opera Orchestra & Chorus Thorborg, Tokatyan, Pinza, Moscona, Warren <u>Sung in Italian</u>	LP: Ed Smith UORC 258 Excerpts LP: Ed Smith EJS 561

Khovantschina, prelude

Cleveland March 1958	CO	LP: Epic LC 3483/BC 1002 LP: Columbia (USA) Y 30044 LP: Columbia 33CX 1847/SAX 2490 LP: CBS 61213/30050

Pictures from an exhibition, arranged by Ravel

Cleveland October 1963	CO	LP: Epic LC 3872/LC 3890/BC 1272/BC 1290 LP: Columbia (USA) Y 32223 LP: Columbia 33CX 1916/SAX 2556 LP: CBS 4462/5462 CD: Sony MBK 44805/SBK 48162

WOLFGANG AMADEUS MOZART (1756-1791)

Symphony No 28

Cleveland CO
October 1965
- LP: Columbia (USA) ML 6258/MS 6858
- LP: Columbia CX 5280/SAX 5280
- LP: CBS 61197
- CD: Sony SM3K 46515

Symphony No 33

Cleveland CO
October 1962
- LP: Epic LC 3873/BC 1273
- LP: Columbia (USA) ML 6258/MS 6858
- LP: Columbia 33CX 1913/SAX 2553
- LP: CBS 61197
- CD: Sony SM3K 46515

Excerpt
- LP: Columbia (USA) MPS 9

Symphony No 34

Amsterdam   Concertgebouw
November 1966 Orchestra
- LP: Philips SAL 3667/802 769LY/900 169
- CD: Philips 438 5242/442 7272

Amsterdam   Concertgebouw
November 1966 Orchestra
- CD: Music and Arts CD 291

Symphony No 35 "Haffner"

Salzburg   Orchestre
August 1959   National
- CD: Sony SMK 68446

Cleveland CO
January-
March 1960
- LP: Epic LC 3740/BC 1106
- LP: Columbia (USA) ML 6258/MS 6858/ MG 30368
- LP: Columbia 33CX 1885/SAX 2529
- LP: CBS 61023
- CD: Sony MBK 45640/SBK 46333/ SB3K 62773/SM3K 46515

Excerpt
- LP: Columbia (USA) MPS 12
- Excerpt also on Szell 50th anniversary LP

Symphony No 38 "Prague"

Cleveland October 1965	CO	Columbia (USA) unpublished <u>First movement only recorded</u>

Symphony No 39

Cleveland April 1947	CO	78: Columbia (USA) M 801 LP: Columbia (USA) ML 4109
Cleveland October 1955	CO	LP: Musical Appreciation Society MAR 6225 <u>Performers described as George Szell and his orchestra</u>
Cleveland March 1960	CO	LP: Epic LC 3740/BC 1106 LP: Columbia (USA) MG 30368 LP: CBS 61023 CD: Sony MBK 45640/SM3K 46515
Cleveland Octover 1965	CO	Unpublished radio broadcast

Symphony No 40

Cleveland November 1955	CO	LP: Epic LC 3287
London August 1967	CO	LP: Columbia (USA) MG 30368 LP: CBS 61228 CD: Sony MYK 42538/SBK 46333/ SB3K 62773/SM3K 46515
Tokyo May 1970	CO	Unpublished radio broadcast

Symphony No 41 "Jupiter"

Cleveland November 1955	CO	LP: Epic LC 3287
Salzburg August 1958	Concertgebouw Orchestra	CD: Sony SMK 68445

Cleveland
October 1963
	CO	LP: Epic LC 3883/BC 1282
		LP: Columbia (USA) ML 6369/MS 6969/
		   MG 30368/MG 30841
		LP: Columbia 33CX 1912/SAX 2552
		LP: CBS 61228
		CD: Sony MYK 42538/SBK 46333/
		   SB3K 62773/SM3K 46515

Cleveland October 1965	CO	Unpublished radio broadcast
Blossom July 1968	CO	Unpublished radio broadcast

Clarinet Concerto

Cleveland October 1961	CO Marcellus	LP: Epic LC 3841/BC 1241 LP: Columbia (USA) ML 6368/MS 6968 LP: Columbia 33CX 1892/SAX 2536 LP: CBS 61195/D3M 33261 CD: Sony MYK 42598/SBK 62424/SBT 62424

Concerto for 2 pianos

Cleveland December 1955	CO R.& G.Casadesus	LP: Columbia (USA) ML 5151/Y2 34641 <u>Orchestra described as Columbia SO</u>

Piano Concerto No 9

Salzburg August 1958	Concertgebouw Orchestra Firkusny	CD: Sony SMK 68445

Piano Concerto No 12

Cleveland December 1955	CO Casadesus	LP: Columbia (USA) ML 5151/Y2 34641 <u>Orchestra described as Columbia SO</u>

Piano Concerto No 15

Cleveland	CO	LP: Columbia (USA) MS 7245
October 1968	Casadesus	LP: CBS 61348
		CD: Sony MPK 46736

Piano Concerto No 17

Cleveland	CO	LP: Columbia (USA) ML 5169/Y3 34642
November 1955	Serkin	LP: Philips CFL 1016
		LP: CBS 77431/M3P 39655
		CD: Sony SM3K 47207/SM3K 47269
		<u>Orchestra described as Columbia SO</u>

Cleveland	CO	LP: Columbia (USA) MS 7245
October 1968	Casadesus	LP: CBS 61348

Piano Concerto No 18

Cleveland	CO	LP: Columbia (USA) ML 5276/Y3 34641
November 1956	Casadesus	LP: Philips GBL 5510
		LP: CBS 4237
		<u>Orchestra described as Columbia SO</u>

Piano Concerto No 19

New York	Columbia SO	LP: Columbia (USA) ML 5934/MS 6534
April 1961	Serkin	LP: CBS BRG 72178/SBRG 72178/61136
		CD: Sony SM3K 47207

Piano Concerto No 20

New York	NYPSO	LP: MJA 1971
December 1944	Schnabel	LP: Discocorp BWS 723
		CD: Music and Arts CD 750

Cleveland	CO	LP: Columbia (USA) ML 5276/Y2 34641
November 1956	Casadesus	LP: Philips GBL 5510
		LP: CBS 4237
		<u>Orchestra described as Columbia SO</u>

New York	Columbia SO	LP: Columbia (USA) ML 5934/MS 6534
April 1961	Serkin	LP: CBS BRG 72178/SBRG 72178/61136
		CD: Sony SM3K 47207

276 Szell

Piano Concerto No 21

Cleveland November 1961	CO Casadesus	LP: Columbia (USA) ML 6095/MS 6695 LP: CBS BRG 72234/SBRG 72234/MG 30841/ 　　M 31814/D3M 32796/61578 CD: Sony MYK 42594/SBK 45980/SBK 67178/ 　　SB5K 45977/SM3K 46519 Excerpt LP: Columbia (USA) MS 7507/MG 31267

Piano Concerto No 22

New York November 1959	Columbia SO Casadesus	LP: Columbia (USA) ML 5594/MS 6194 LP: CBS D3M 32796/61021 CD: Sony SM3K 46519
Cleveland January 1967	CO Frankl	Unpublished radio broadcast

Piano Concerto No 23

New York November 1959	Columbia SO Casadesus	LP: Columbia (USA) ML 5594/MS 6194 LP: CBS D3M 32796/61021 CD: Sony MPK 45884/SM3K 46519
Vienna December 1964	VPO Curzon	Decca unpublished

Piano Concerto No 24

Cleveland January 1954	CO Casadesus	LP: Columbia (USA) ML 4901 LP: Philips ABL 3060/A01142L LP: CBS 4074 Orchestra described as Columbia SO
Cleveland November 1961	CO Casadesus	LP: Columbia (USA) ML 6095/MS 6695 LP: CBS BRG 72234/SBRG 72234/M 31814/ 　　D3M 32796/61578 CD: Sony MYK 42594/SM3K 46519

Piano Concerto No 25

Cleveland November 1955	CO Serkin	LP: Columbia (USA) ML 5169/Y3 34642 LP: Philips CFL 1016 LP: CBS M3P 39655/77431 CD: Sony SM3K 47269 Orchestra described as Columbia SO
Cleveland January 1959	CO Fleisher	LP: Epic LC 3574/BC 1025 LP: Philips A699 515L LP: CBS D3M 33261 CD: Sony MYK 44832/M3K 42445

Piano Concerto No 26

Cleveland January 1954	CO Casadesus	LP: Columbia (USA) ML 4901 LP: Philips ABL 3060/A01142L LP: CBS 4074 Orchestra described as Columbia SO
New York November 1962	Columbia SO Casadesus	LP: Columbia (USA) ML 5803/MS 6403 LP: CBS BRG 72107/SBRG 72107/ D3M 32796/61597 CD: Sony MPK 45884/SBK 67178/SM3K 46519

Piano Concerto No 27

New York November 1962	Columbia SO Casadesus	LP: Columbia (USA) ML 5803/MS 6403 LP: CBS BRG 72107/SBRG 72107/ D3M 32796/61597
Vienna December 1964	VPO Curzon	Decca unpublished

Violin Concerto No 1

New York January 1961	Columbia SO Stern	LP: Columbia (USA) ML 5927/MS 6557 LP: CBS BRG 72179/SBRG 72179/4383/5109 CD: Sony M2YK 45614/SM3K 46523/SM3K 66475

Violin Concerto No 3

New York December 1955	NYPSO Szigeti	Unpublished radio broadcast
New York January 1961	Columbia SO Stern	LP: Columbia (USA) ML 6462/MS 7062 LP: CBS 72662 CD: Sony M2YK 45614/SM3K 66475

GEORGE SZELL

BEETHOVEN
Symphony No. 8

BEETHOVEN
Symphony No. 9

Heather Harper   Ronald Dowd
Janet Baker   Franz Crass

NEW PHILHARMONIA CHORUS
Chorus Master Wilhelm Pitz

NEW PHILHARMONIA ORCHESTRA
Leader Carlos Villa

Royal Festival Hall (General Manager John Denison CBE)
Tuesday 12 November and
Thursday 14 November, 1968 at 8
Programme Two shillings and sixpence

CONCERTGEBOUW - AMSTERDAM

WOENSDAG 23 NOVEMBER / DONDERDAG 24 NOVEMBER 1960 - 8.15 UUR

ABONNEMENTSCONCERT - SERIE B Nr. 7

HET CONCERTGEBOUWORKEST

Dirigent **George Szell**
Solist **Leon Fleisher**, piano

PROGRAMMA

ROBERT SCHUMANN
1810-1856

Ouverture „Manfred", op. 115 (1848)

JOSEPH HAYDN
1732-1809

Symfonie G gr. t., nr. 92 (1788), „Oxford-symfonie"

Adagio - Allegro spiritoso
Adagio
Menuetto: Allegretto
Presto

Pauze

JOHANNES BRAHMS
1833-1897

Tweede concert, Bes gr. t., op. 83 (1881)
VOOR PIANO EN ORKEST
Allegro non troppo
Allegro appassionato
Andante
Allegretto grazioso

STEINWAY & SONS' CONCERTVLEUGEL

Violin Concerto No 5

Salzburg August 1959	Orchestre National Morini	CD: Sony SMK 68446
New York April 1963	Columbia SO Stern	LP: Columbia (USA) ML 5927/MS 6557 LP: CBS BRG 72179/SBRG 72179/ MG 30841/4383/5109 CD: Sony M2YK 45614/SM3K 46523

Sinfonia concertante for violin and viola

Cleveland December 1963	CO Druian, Skernick	LP: Epic LC 3881/BC 1281/BC 1352 LP: Columbia (USA) ML 6025/MS 6625 LP: Columbia CX 5280/SAX 5280 LP: CBS 72662/MG 30841/D3M 33266/61195 CD: Sony MYK 42598/SBK 45980/ SBK 67177/SB5K 45977

Divertimento No 2 K131

Cleveland April 1963	CO	LP: Epic LC 3873/BC 1273 LP: Columbia (USA) ML 6368/MS 6968 LP: Columbia 33CX 1913/SAX 2553 LP: CBS D3M 33261 Excerpt LP: Columbia (USA) SOG 5

Serenade No 9 "Posthorn"

Cleveland January 1969	CO	LP: Columbia (USA) MS 7273 LP: CBS 72772/D3M 33261/61585 CD: Sony MYK 45509/SBK 48266/SM3K 46515

Serenade No 13 "Eine kleine Nachtmusik"

Cleveland October 1968	CO	LP: Columbia (USA) MS 7273 LP: CBS 72772/D3M 33261/MG 30841 CD: Sony MBK 44811/SBK 48266/SM3K 46515

Requiem

Cleveland	CO	CD: Cleveland Orchestra TC093-75
May 1968	CO Chorus	CD: Stradivarius STR 10006
	Raskin, Kopleff,	
	Haefliger, Paul	

Exsultate jubilate

		LP: Epic BC 1352
Cleveland	CO	LP: Columbia (USA) ML 6025/MS 6625
May 1964	Raskin	CD: Sony MK 42416/MYK 45509/SBK 45982/
		SB5K 45977/SM3K 46515

Alma grande e nobil core, concert aria

London	LSO	LP: EMI ASD 2493/1C 065 01959
March 1968	Schwarzkopf	LP: Angel 36643
		CD: EMI CDC 747 9502/CDH 763 7022

Ch'io mi scordi di te?, concert aria

London	LSO	LP: EMI ASD 2493/1C 063 01959
March 1968	Schwarzkopf,	LP: Angel 36643
	Brendel	CD: EMI CDC 747 9502/CDH 763 7022

Così fan tutte, excerpt (L'amore è un ladroncello)

Blossom	CO	LP: Rococo 5374
July 1968	Schwarzkopf	CD: Hunt CDGPI 745

Don Giovanni

New York	Metropolitan Opera	Unpublished Met broadcast
December 1944	Orchestra & Chorus	
	Kirk, Steber,	
	Sayao, Kullmann,	
	Pinza, Baccaloni,	
	Moscona	

Don Giovanni, excerpt (Mi tradi)

Blossom July 1968	CO Schwarzkopf	LP: Rococo 5374 CD: Hunt CDGI 745

Nehmt meinen Dank, concert aria

London March 1968	LSO Schwarzkopf	LP: EMI ASD 2493/1C 063 01959 LP: Angel 36643 CD: EMI CDC 747 9502/CDH 763 7022

Le nozze di Figaro, overture

Cleveland October 1957	CO	LP: Epic LC 3506 LP: Columbia (USA) MS 6858/MS 7507/ MS 7435/SOG 5/CSS 568/CSS 864/ CSS 1318 LP: Columbia CX 5280/SAX 5280 LP: CBS MG 30841/MG 31267/MG 35188/ D3M 33261 CD: Sony SM3K 46515
Cleveland May 1969	CO	Unpublished radio broadcast

Le nozze di Figaro, excerpt (Deh vieni non tardar)

Blossom July 1968	CO Schwarzkopf	LP: Rococo 5374 CD: Hunt CDGI 745

Der Schauspieldirektor, overture

Cleveland January 1966	CO	LP: CBS M2X 787/MG 30841

Vado ma dove?, concert aria

London March 1968	LSO Schwarzkopf	LP: EMI ASD 2493/1C 063 01959 LP: Angel 36643 CD: EMI CDC 747 9502/CDH 763 7022

Die Zauberflöte

Salzburg	VPO	LP: Penzance PR 38
July 1959	Vienna Opera Chorus	LP: Melodram MEL 007
	Della Casa, Sciutti,	CD: Melodram CDM 27505
	Köth, Simoneau,	<u>Excerpts</u>
	Berry, Böhme,	CD: Melodram CDM 26526
	Hotter	

Die Zauberflöte, excerpt (Dies Bildnis ist bezaubernd schön)

Berlin	Staatskapelle	78: Odeon O-6589
December 1926	Talén	LP: Preiser LV 157

Piano Quartet No 1

New York	Members of the	78: Columbia (USA) M 773
August 1946	Budapest Quartet	LP: Columbia (USA) ML 4080/3216 0139
	Szell, piano	CD: Sony MPK 47685

Piano Quartet No 2

New York	Members of the	78: Columbia (USA) M 669
August 1946	Budapest Quartet	LP: Columbia (USA) ML 4080/3216 0139
	Szell, piano	CD: Sony MPK 47685

Violin Sonata No 17 K296

Cleveland	Druian	LP: Columbia (USA) ML 6464/MS 7064
August 1967	Szell, piano	LP: CBS 61055
		CD: Sony MPK 47685

Violin Sonata No 18 K301

Cleveland	Druian	LP: Columbia (USA) ML 6464/MS 7064
August 1967	Szell, piano	LP: CBS 61055
		CD: Sony MPK 47685

Violin Sonata No 21 K304

Cleveland	Druian	LP: Columbia (USA) ML 6464/MS 7064
August 1967	Szell, piano	LP: CBS 61055
		CD: Sony SBK 45981/SB5K 45977

Violin Sonata No 24 K376

Cleveland	Druian	LP: Columbia (USA) ML 6464/MS 7064
August 1967	Szell, piano	LP: CBS 61055

Violin Sonata No 32 K454

Details	Druian	LP: Columbia (USA) ML 5005
not confirmed	Szell, piano	LP: Vanguard S 265/7

Violin Sonata No 33 K481

Details	Druian	LP: Columbia (USA) ML 5005
not confirmed	Szell, piano	LP: Vanguard S 265/7

OTTO NICOLAI (1810-1849)

Die lustigen Weiber von Windsor, overture

Berlin	Staatskapelle	78: Odeon O-7504
1924		78: Parlophone E 10588
		78: Decca (USA) 25142

SERGEI PROKOFIEV (1891-1953)

Symphony No 1 "Classical"

Cleveland October 1968	CO	CD: Cleveland Orchestra TC093-75

Symphony No 5

Vienna 1954	VSO	CD: Orfeo C230 901A/C226 905R
Cleveland October 1959	CO	LP: Epic LC 3688/BC 1079 LP: Philips CFL 1072/SCFL 108 Excerpts LP: Epic PLC 1/PBC 1/XEM 50311 <u>Excerpt also on Szell 50th anniversary LP</u>

Piano Concerto No 1

Cleveland March 1966	CO Graffman	LP: Columbia (USA) ML 6325/MS 6295 LP: CBS BRG 72506/SBRG 72506

Piano Concerto No 3

Cleveland March 1966	CO Graffman	LP: Columbia (USA) ML 6325/MS 6295 LP: CBS BRG 72506/SBRG 72506

Violin Concerto No 1

New York 1945	NYPSO Szigeti	LP: Discocorp BWS 741 CD: Dante LYS 85

Lieutenant Kije, suite

Cleveland January 1969	CO	LP: Columbia (USA) MS 7408 LP: CBS 61193 CD: Sony MYK 44831/SBK 48162 Excerpts LP: Columbia (USA) C 10017/MS 7435/ YO 27024

GIACOMO PUCCINI (1858-1924)

La Bohème, excerpt (Che gelida manina)

Berlin	Staatskapelle	78: Odeon O-7526
November 1926	Pattiera	78: Parlophone E 10526/P 9029
		LP: Rococo 5256
		LP: Preiser LV 281
		CD: Preiser 89222

Tosca, excerpt (Recondita armonia)

Berlin	Staatskapelle	78: Odeon O-7533
November 1926	Kiepura	78: Parlophone R 20008
		78: Columbia (USA) 17310D
		LP: EMI 1C 147 29135-29136M

Tosca, excerpt (E lucevan le stelle)

Berlin	Staatskapelle	78: Odeon O-7533
November 1926	Kiepura	78: Parlophone R 20008
		78: Columbia (USA) 17310D
		LP: EMI 1C 147 29135-29136M

Turandot, excerpt (Nessun dorma)

Berlin	Staatskapelle	78: Parlophone P 9623/P 9821
November 1926	Oehmann	LP: Preiser LV 181
	Sung in German	

SERGEI RACHMANINOV (1873-1943)

Rhapsody on a theme of Paganini

Cleveland	CO	LP: Epic LC 3330
October 1956	Fleisher	Excerpt
		45: Epic 5-9310

MAURICE RAVEL (1875-1937)

Daphnis et Chloé, second suite

Cleveland   CO
November 1963

LP: Epic LC 3863/BC 1263
LP: Columbia (USA) Y 31928
LP: Columbia 33CX 1896/SAX 2532
LP: CBS 61075
CD: Sony MBK 44804/SBK 47664

Pavane pour une infante défunte

Cleveland   CO
January 1963

LP: Epic LC 3863/LC 3891/BC 1263/
    BC 1291/BC 24146
LP: Columbia (USA) M2X 787/Y 31928
LP: Columbia 33CX 1896/SAX 2532
LP: CBS 61075
CD: Sony MBK 44805

Le tombeau de Couperin

Cleveland   CO
September
1965

CD: Cleveland Orchestra TC093-75

NIKOLAI RIMSKY-KORSAKOV (1844-1908)

Capriccio espagnol

Cleveland   CO
February-
March 1958

45: Philips 496 503CE
LP: Epic LC 3483/LC 3891/BC 1002/
    BC 1291/BC 24146
LP: Columbia (USA) Y 30044
LP: Columbia 33CX 1847/SAX 2490
LP: CBS 61213
CD: Sony MBK 44805
Excerpt
LP: Epic BC 1

GIOACHINO ROSSINI (1792-1868)

La gazza ladra, overture

Cleveland March 1958	CO	LP: Epic LC 3506
Cleveland May 1967	CO	LP: Columbia (USA) ML 6431/MS 7031/ MS 7435/M2X 787/M 30305/MG 35187 LP: CBS 61215

L'italiana in Algeri, overture

Cleveland May 1967	CO	LP: Columbia ML 6431/MS 7031/MG 35187 LP: CBS 61215

La scala di seta, overture

Cleveland May 1967	CO	LP: Columbia (USA) ML 6431/MS 7031/ MG 35187/CSS 1318 LP: CBS 61215

Il turco in Italia, overture

Cleveland May 1967	CO	LP: Columbia (USA) ML 6431/MS 7031/ MG 35187 LP: CBS 61215

Il viaggio a Reims, overture

Cleveland May 1967	CO	LP: Columbia (USA) ML 6431/MS 7031/ MG 35187 LP: CBS 61215

FRANZ SCHUBERT (1797-1828)

Symphony No 8 "Unfinished"

Cleveland November 1955	CO	LP: Epic LC 3195 LP: Philips SBL 5209/S04611L
Cleveland March 1960	CO	LP: Epic LC 3828/BC 1156 LP: Columbia (USA) ML 6375/MS 6975/ MG 30371 LP: Columbia 33CX 1850/SAX 2493 LP: CBS 4455/5455 CD: Sony MK 42415/SBK 48268
Cleveland February 1970	CO	Unpublished radio broadcast

Symphony No 9 "Great"

Cleveland November 1957	CO	LP: Epic LC 3431/BC 1009 LP: Columbia (USA) Y 30669 LP: Philips A699 506L LP: Columbia 33CX 1873/SAX 2517 LP: World Records T 627/ST 627 CD: Sony MK 42415/SBK 48268 <u>Excerpt</u> LP: Epic PLC 1/PBC 1
Cleveland April 1970	CO	LP: Angel 36044 LP: EMI 1C 063 02094 CD: Laserlight 16224 CD: EMI CZS 569 3642
San Francisco Date not confirmed	San Francisco SO	CD: Archive Documents ADCD 200-201 <u>Rehearsal extract only</u>

Rosamunde, overture

Berlin 1926-1928	Staatskapelle	78: Odeon O 7500-7501 78: Parlophone E 10510-10511
Amsterdam December 1957	Concertgebouw Orchestra	LP: Philips ABL 3238/A00475L/ G05331R/SFM 23006 LP: Epic LC 3433/BC 1023 LP: Fontana (Holland) ZKY 894 069 CD: Philips 432 2282/442 7272
Cleveland January 1967	CO	LP: Columbia (USA) ML 6402/MS 7002 LP: CBS 61076
Cleveland January 1967	CO	Unpublished radio broadcast

Rosamunde, Entr'acte in B minor

Amsterdam December 1957	Concertgebouw Orchestra	LP: Philips ABL 3238/A00475L/ G05331R/SFM 23006 LP: Epic LC 3433/BC 1023 LP: Fontana (Holland) ZKY 894 069 CD: Philips 432 2282/442 7272

Rosamunde, Entr'acte in B flat

Berlin 1926-1928	Staatskapelle	78: Odeon O 7501
Amsterdam December 1957	Concertgebouw Orchestra	45: Philips A400 059E LP: Philips ABL 3238/A00475L/ G05331R/SFM 23006 LP: Epic LC 3433/BC 1023 LP: Fontana (Holland) ZKY 894 069 CD: Philips 432 2282/442 7272
Cleveland January 1967	CO	LP: Columbia (USA) ML 6402/MS 7002 LP: CBS 61076

Rosamunde, Ballet music no 2 in G

Amsterdam December 1957	Concertgebouw Orchestra	45: Philips A400 059E LP: Philips ABL 3238/A00475L/ 　　G05331R/SFM 23006 LP: Epic LC 3433/BC 1023 LP: Fontana (Holland) ZKY 894 069 CD: Philips 432 2282
Cleveland January 1967	CO	LP: Columbia (USA) ML 6402/MS 7002/ 　　MS 7526/C 10017/YO 27024 LP: CBS 61076

Piano Quintet in A "Trout"

New York 1945-1946	Members of the Budapest Quartet Moleux, Szell, piano	CD: Bridge 9062

WILLIAM SCHUMAN (1910-1992)

Song of Orpheus

Cleveland January 1964	CO Rose	LP: Columbia (USA) ML 6038/MS 6638 LP: Columbia 33CX 1937/SAX 2575

ROBERT SCHUMANN (1810-1856)

Symphony No 1 "Spring"

Cleveland October 1958	CO	LP: Epic LC 3612/BC 1039/SC 6039/BSC 110 LP: Columbia (USA) Y3 30844 LP: Columbia 33CX 1831/SAX 2475 LP: CBS 77344/61595 CD: Sony MH2K 62349

Symphony No 2

Cleveland November 1952	CO	LP: Columbia (USA) ML 4817 LP: Philips NBR 6033/A01616R
Lugano May 1957	CO	CD: Ermitage ERM 106
Cleveland October 1960	CO	LP: Epic LC 3832/BC 1159/SC 6039/BSC 110 LP: Columbia (USA) Y3 30844 LP: Columbia 33CX 1853/SAX 2496 LP: CBS 77344 CD: Sony MH2K 62349 Excerpt CD: Sony Masterworks Heritage Sampler SSK 6368

Symphony No 3 "Rhenish"

Cleveland October 1960	CO	LP: Epic LC 3774/BC 1130/SC 6039/BSC 110 LP: Columbia (USA) Y3 30844 LP: Columbia 33CX 1861/SAX 2506 LP: CBS 77344/61595 CD: Sony MH2K 62349 Excerpt on Szell 50th anniversary LP
Amsterdam November 1966	Concertgebouw Orchestra	CD: Music and Arts CD 291

Symphony No 4

Cleveland November 1947	CO	78: Columbia (USA) M 821 LP: Columbia (USA) ML 2040/ML 4794 LP: Philips A01603R
Cleveland October 1955	CO	LP: Musical Appreciation Society MAR 579/MARS 5558 <u>Orchestra described as Symphony Orchestra</u>
Cleveland March 1960	CO	LP: Epic LC 3854/BC 1254/SC 6039/BSC 110 LP: Columbia (USA) Y3 30844 LP: Philips S04602L LP: Columbia 33CX 1831/SAX 2475 LP: CBS 77344 CD: Sony MH2K 62349

Piano Concerto

Cleveland January 1960	CO Fleisher	LP: Epic LC 3689/BC 1080/SC 6039/BSC 110 LP: Columbia (USA) Y 30668 LP: Philips EFL 2509/697 302EL LP: CBS 77344 CD: Sony MPK 44849

Introduction and allegro appassionato

Cleveland March 1959	CO Serkin	CD: Cleveland Orchestra TC093-75

Manfred, overture

Cleveland January 1958	CO	LP: Epic LC 3612/BC 1039/SC 6039/BSC 110 LP: CBS 77344 CD: Sony MH2K 62349

JEAN SIBELIUS (1865-1957)

Symphony No 2

Amsterdam November- December 1966	Concertgebouw Orchestra	LP: Philips AL 3515/SAL 3515/835 306/ AO2436L/PHM 500-092/PHS 900-092 CD: Philips 420 7712/442 7272
Tokyo May 1970	CO	CD: Cleveland Orchestra TC093-75 <u>One of Szell's last public appearances;</u> <u>also unpublished video recording</u>

Symphony No 3

Cleveland December 1946	CO	CD: Cleveland Orchestra TC093-75

BEDRICH SMETANA (1824-1884)

The Moldau (Ma Vlast)

New York January 1951	NYPSO	78: Columbia (USA) M 1004 LP: Columbia (USA) ML 2177/ML 4785/ Y3 35231 LP: Columbia 33C 1019 LP: Quintessence QC 5019 LP: CBS 4170
Cleveland December 1954	CO	LP: Musical Appreciation Society MAR 610 <u>Orchestra described as Musical</u> <u>Appreciation SO</u>

Cleveland
January 1963
	CO	LP: Epic LC 3868/BC 1268
		LP: Columbia (USA) MS 7435/M2X 787/
		  Y 30049
		LP: Columbia 33CX 1899/SX 6053/
		  SAX 2539/SCX 6053
		CD: Sony MBK 44958/MYK 42530/SBK 48264

From Bohemia's Woods and Fields (Ma Vlast)

New York   NYPSO   78: Columbia (USA) M 1004
January 1951   LP: Columbia (USA) ML 2177/ML 4785/
                                    Y3 35231
                                LP: Columbia 33C 1019
                                LP: Quintessence QC 5019
                                LP: CBS 4170
                                Excerpt on Columbia promotional LP

String Quartet No 1 "From my Life", arranged for orchestra by Szell

Cleveland   CO   78: Columbia (USA) M 887
April 1949   LP: Columbia (USA) ML 2095
                                LP: Epic SC 6015

San Francisco   San Francisco SO   CD: Archive Documents ADCD 200-201
Date not   Rehearsal extract only
confirmed

The Bartered Bride, overture

Cleveland   CO   LP: Epic LC 3506
March 1958   Also on an unnumbered Columbia Special
                                Products LP

The Bartered Bride, excerpts: Polka, Furiant and Dance of the Comedians

Cleveland   CO   LP: Epic LC 3868/LC 3891/BC 1268/
January 1963   BC 1291/BC 24146
                                LP: Columbia (USA) Y 30049/M2X 787
                                LP: Columbia 33CX 1899/SX 6053/
                                    SAX 2539/SCX 6053
                                CD: Sony MBK 44958/SBK 48279

The Bartered Bride, excerpt (The man who's madly in love)

Berlin   Staatskapelle   78: Odeon O-8309/O-6808
October 1926   Bohnen   78: Decca (USA) 25810
                Sung in German LP: Preiser LV 192
                                LP: Electrola E 83383

JOHANN STRAUSS (1825-1899)

An der schönen blauen Donau, waltz

Vienna June 1934	VPO	78: HMV C 1686/S 10460/FKX 26 78: Victor M 805 45: Victor WBC 1008 LP: Victor LBC 1008 CD: DG 435 3352 CD: Preiser 90090/90115/90118
Cleveland January 1962	CO	LP: Epic LC 3858/LC 3891/BC 1258/ BC 1291/BC 24146 LP: Columbia (USA) MS 7435/M2X 787/ Y 30053 LP: Columbia 33SX 1618/SCX 3514 LP: CBS 61212

Die Fledermaus, overture

Cleveland March 1956	CO	LP: Epic LC 3506 LP: Columbia (USA) GB 12/GS 12 LP: Telarc CLO 20-789 Also on an unnumbered Columbia Special Products LP

Frühlingsstimmen, waltz

Vienna June 1934	VPO	78: HMV C 2687 78: Victor 13597 45: Victor WBC 1008 LP: Victor LBC 1008 CD: EMI CDH 764 2992/CHS 764 2942 CD: Preiser 90115/90118/90139
Cleveland January 1962	CO	LP: Epic LC 3858/BC 1258 LP: Columbia (USA) Y 30053/YO 27024/C10017 LP: Columbia 33SX 1618/SCX 3574 LP: CBS 61212

Perpetuum mobile

Cleveland   CO   LP: Epic LC 3858/BC 1258
January 1962   LP: Columbia (USA) Y 30053/M2X 787/
                                SPM 1/SPS 1/CSS 568
                            LP: Columbia 33SX 1618/SCX 3514
                            LP: CBS 61212
                            Also on unnumbered Sound of Genius LP

Tritsch-Tratsch, polka

Vienna   VPO   78: HMV C 2687
June 1934   45: Victor WBC 1008
                            LP: Victor LBC 1008
                            CD: EMI CDH 764 2992/CHS 764 2942
                            CD: Preiser 90115/90139

JOSEF STRAUSS (1827-1870)

Delirien, waltz

Cleveland   CO   LP: Epic LC 3858/BC 1258
January 1962   LP: Columbia (USA) Y 30053
                            LP: Columbia 33SX 1618/SCX 3514
                            LP: CBS 61212

Dorfschwalben aus Oesterreich, waltz

Cleveland   CO   LP: Epic LC 3858/BC 1258
January 1962   LP: Columbia (USA) Y 30053
                            LP: Columbia 33SX 1618/SCX 3514
                            LP: CBS 61212

JOHANN & JOSEF STRAUSS

Pizzicato polka

Vienna June 1934	VPO	78: HMV C 2687 45: Victor WBC 1008 LP: Victor LBC 1008 CD: Preiser 90115
Cleveland January 1962	CO	LP: Epic LC 3858/BC 1258 LP: Columbia (USA) Y 30053 LP: Columbia 33SX 1618/SCX 3514 LP: CBS 61212

RICHARD STRAUSS (1864-1949)

Das Bächlein

London March 1968	LSO Schwarzkopf	LP: EMI ASD 2493/1C 063 01959 LP: Angel 36643 CD: EMI CDC 747 2762

Der Bürger als Edelmann, excerpts from the suite

Cleveland October 1968	CO	CD: Cleveland Orchestra TCO93-75

Don Juan

Cleveland March 1957	CO	LP: Epic LC 3439/BC 1011 LP: Columbia (USA) Y 30313/SPM 1/SPS 1 LP: Philips A699505L LP: Columbia 33CX 1852/SAX 2495 LP: CBS 61216/5059 CD: Sony SBK 48272 <u>Excerpt</u> LP: Epic BC 1

Don Quixote

Cleveland October 1960	CO Fournier	LP: Epic LC 3786/BC 1135 LP: Columbia (USA) Y 32224 LP: Columbia 33CX 1852/SAX 2495 LP: CBS 61110/4332/5054 <u>Issued on CD by Sony in Japan; excerpt on Szell 50th anniversary LP</u>
Amsterdam 1964	Concertgebouw Orchestra Fournier	CD: Music and Arts CD 291

Freundliche Vision

Berlin September 1965	Berlin RO Schwarzkopf	LP: EMI CX 5258/SAX 5258/ASD 2888/ 1C 063 00608 LP: Angel 36347 CD: EMI CDC 747 2762

Die heiligen 3 Könige aus Morgenland

Berlin September 1965	Berlin RO Schwarzkopf	LP: EMI CX 5258/SAX 5258/ASD 2888/ 1C 063 00608 LP: Angel 36347 CD: EMI CDC 747 2762

Horn Concerto No 1

Cleveland October 1961	CO Bloom	LP: Epic LC 3841/BC 1241 LP: Columbia 33CX 1892/SAX 2536 LP: CBS 61355

NO. 1 IN A SERIES OF OLD CARNEGIE HALL PROGRAM COVERS
PUBLISHERS: S. D. SCOTT PRINTING CO., INC., 161 GRAND STREET, NEW YORK 13, N. Y.

Columbia Artists Management Inc.
PRESENTS

TOWN HALL
FRIDAY EVENING, FEB. 5, 1960 at 8:30

NICANOR ZABALETA
HARPIST

Counterpoint, Decca and Period Records

TOWN HALL
SUNDAY AFT., FEB. 7, 1960 at 5:30

DALE MOORE   ERNST WOLFF
BARITONE   PIANIST

In a Recital of Songs by Hugo Wolf

Steinway Piano

TOWN HALL
SUNDAY EVENING, FEB. 7, 1960 at 8:30

DOROTHY SCHMIDT
MEZZO-CONTRALTO
Paul Sargent at the Steinway

TOWN HALL
SATURDAY AFT., FEB. 13, 1960 at 5:30
Arnold EIDUS, Violin — David MANKOVITZ, Viola
George RICCI, Cello

STRADIVARI STRING QUARTET

TOWN HALL
Sunday Aft., Feb. 14, 1960 at 5:30 P.M.

HELEN KETTNER
PIANIST
Steinway Piano

CARNEGIE HALL   Saturday Afternoons, February 6 and 27, 1960 at 2:40

CLAUDIO ARRAU
PIANIST

BALDWIN PIANO   ANGEL, COLUMBIA and DECCA RECORDS

CARNEGIE HALL   Monday, Feb. 8 and Monday, Feb. 15, 1960 at 8:30
Two Concerts by

THE CLEVELAND ORCHESTRA
George Szell, Conductor

February 8, **HENRY SZERYNG**, Violinist   February 15, **LEON FLEISHER**, Pianist
Single tickets on sale

CARNEGIE HALL   FRIDAY EVENING, FEB. 12, 1960 at 8:30

NICOLAI GEDDA
SWEDISH-RUSSIAN TENOR

assisted by
THE CAPPELLA RUSSIAN MALE CHORUS   NICHOLAS AFONSKY, Conductor
Werner Singer at the Baldwin

CARNEGIE HALL   SUNDAY EVENING, FEB. 14, 1960 at 8:30

THE MINNEAPOLIS SYMPHONY ORCHESTRA
Antal Dorati, Conductor

BERLIOZ   SESSIONS   SCHULLER   BRAHMS
            (1st N. Y. Performance)   (1st N. Y. Performance)

BALDWIN PIANO   MERCURY RECORDS

4 letzte Lieder

Amsterdam June 1964	Concertgebouw Orchestra Schwarzkopf	Unpublished radio broadcast <u>Im Abendrot</u> LP: Dutch Radio RN 109479L
Berlin September 1965	Berlin RO Schwarzkopf	LP: EMI CX 5258/SAX 5258/ASD 2888/ 1C 063 00608 LP: Angel 36347 CD: EMI CDC 747 2762
Blossom July 1968	CO Schwarzkopf	Unpublished radio broadcast <u>Im Abendrot</u> LP: Telarc TSP 4008

Meinem Kinde

London March 1968	LSO Schwarzkopf	LP: EMI ASD 2493/1C 063 01959 LP: Angel 36643/3754 CD: EMI CDC 747 2762

Morgen

London March 1968	LSO Schwarzkopf Peinemann, violin	LP: EMI ASD 2493/1C 063 01959 LP: Angel 36643 CD: EMI CDC 747 2762

Muttertändelei

Berlin September 1965	Berlin RO Schwarzkopf	LP: EMI CX 5258/SAX 5258/ASD 2888/ 1C 063 00608 LP: Angel 36347 CD: EMI CDC 747 2762

Das Rosenband

London March 1968	LSO Schwarzkopf	LP: EMI ASD 2493/1C 063 01959 LP: Angel 36643 CD: EMI CDC 747 2762

Der Rosenkavalier

New York February 1944	Metropolitan Opera Orchestra & Chorus Jessner, Conner, Novotna, Baum, List, Olitzki	Unpublished Met broadcast
Salzburg August 1949	VPO Vienna Opera Chorus Reining, Güden, Novotna, Rosvaenge, Prohaska, Hann	LP: Cetra LO 69 CD: Arlecchino ARL 46-48

Ruhe meine Seele

London March 1968	LSO Schwarzkopf	LP: EMI ASD 2493/1C 063 01959 LP: Angel 36643 CD: EMI CDC 747 2762

Sinfonia domestica

Cleveland January 1964	CO	LP: Columbia (USA) ML 6027/MS 6627 LP: Columbia 33CX 1904/SAX 2545 LP: CBS 61355 CD: Sony SBK 53511 Excerpt LP: Columbia (USA) MPS 3 Excerpt also on an unnumbered Sound of Genius LP

Till Eulenspiegels lustige Streiche

Cleveland April 1949	CO	78: Columbia (USA) MX 327 LP: Columbia (USA) ML 2079/ML 4800
Cleveland December 1954	CO	LP: Musical Appreciation Society MAR 610 Orchestra described as Musical Appreciation SO
Cleveland March 1957	CO	LP: Epic LC 3439/BC 1011 LP: Columbia (USA) Y 30313 LP: Philips A699 505L LP: Columbia 33CX 1856/SAX 2501 LP: CBS 61216/5059 CD: Sony SBK 48272

Tod und Verklärung

Cleveland March 1957	CO	LP: Epic LC 3439/BC 1011 LP: Columbia (USA) Y 30313 LP: Philips A699 505L LP: Columbia 33CX 1845/SAX 2488 LP: CBS 61216/5059 CD: Sony SBK 53511
Blossom July 1968	CO	Unpublished radio broadcast

Waldesligkeit

Berlin September 1965	Berlin RO Schwarzkopf	LP: EMI CX 5258/SAX 5258/ASD 2888/ 1C 063 00608 LP: Angel 36347 CD: EMI CDC 747 2762

Wiegenlied

London March 1968	LSO Schwarzkopf	LP: EMI ASD 2493/1C 063 01959 LP: Angel 36643 CD: EMI CDC 747 2762

Winterweihe

London March 1968	LSO Schwarzkopf	LP: EMI ASD 2493/1C 063 01959 LP: Angel 36643 CD: EMI CDC 747 2762

Zueignung

Berlin September 1965	Berlin RO Schwarzkopf	LP: EMI CX 5258/SAX 5258/ASD 2888/ 1C 063 00608 LP: Angel 36347 CD: EMI CDC 747 2762

IGOR STRAVINSKY (1882-1971)

L'oiseau de feu, suite (1919 version)

Cleveland October 1955	CO	LP: Musical Appreciation Society MAR 5611/MARS 5558 <u>Orchestra described as Symphony Orchestra</u>
Cleveland February- March 1961	CO	LP: Epic LC 3812/LC 3890/BC 1149/BC 1290 LP: Columbia 33CX 1916/SAX 2556 LP: CBS 4462/5462 CD: Sony SBK 47664 <u>Excerpt</u> LP: Columbia (USA) SPM 1/SPS 1 <u>Excerpt also on Szell 50th anniversary LP</u>

GIUSEPPE TARTINI (1692-1770)

Violin Concerto in D

Cleveland January 1954	CO Szigeti	LP: Columbia (USA) ML 4891 LP: Philips ABL 3058/A01140L <u>Orchestra described as Columbia SO</u>

PIOTR TCHAIKOVSKY (1840-1893)

Symphony No 4

Walthamstow September 1962	LSO	LP: Decca SPA 206 LP: London 6987 CD: Decca 425 9722
Cleveland 1968	CO	CD: Memories HR 4180-4181

Symphony No 5

Cleveland October 1959	CO	LP: Epic LC 3647/BC 1064 LP: Columbia (USA) Y 30670 LP: CBS 61289 Excerpt LP: Epic PLC 1/PBC 1

Piano Concerto No 1

London September 1950	New SO Curzon	78: Decca X 53059-53062 LP: Decca LXT 2559 LP: London LLC 17505 LP: Telefunken 648.112
New York May 1952	NYPSO Horowitz	LP: Penzance PR 17/P 100B LP: Movimento musica 01.008 CD: Movimento musica 011.007
Cleveland January- March 1969	CO Graffman	LP: Columbia (USA) MS 7339/MG 30838 LP: CBS 61174/5500/M 31832 CD: Sony MYK 44772/M2YK 46460

Rococo Variations

New York 1955	NYPSO Rose	LP: Columbia (USA) GB 1/Y 35210

Capriccio italien

Cleveland February 1958	CO	LP: Epic LC 3483/BC 1002 LP: Columbia (USA) Y 30044/ M2X 787/SPM 1/SPS 1 LP: Columbia 33CX 1847/SAX 2490 LP: CBS 61213 Excerpt LP: Epic BC 1

GIUSEPPE VERDI (1813-1901)

La forza del destino, overture

Cleveland 1968	CO	CD: Memories HR 4180-4181

Otello

New York February 1946	Metropolitan Opera Orchestra & Chorus Roman, Lipton, Ralf, Warren	Unpublished Met broadcast

Rigoletto, excerpt (Questo e quella)

Berlin November 1926	Staatskapelle Kiepura	78: Odeon O-7532/O-9601 78: Parlophone R 20016 LP: EMI 1C 142 29135-29136M

Berlin May 1927	Staatskapelle Tauber	78: Odeon O-4950/J 2937 LP: Odeon O 60686/E 80959/ORX 124 LP: Eterna (USA) 701 LP: EMI HQM 1111 LP: Angel 60086 LP: Pearl GEMM 153 CD: Pearl GEMMCD 9327

Rigoletto, excerpt (La donna è mobile)

Berlin November 1926	Staatskapelle Kiepura	78: Odeon O-7532/O-9601 78: Parlophone R 20016

Berlin May 1927	Staatskapelle Tauber	78: Odeon O-4950/J 2937/188581 LP: Odeon O 60686/E 80959/ORX 124 LP: Eterna (USA) 701 LP: EMI HQM 1111 LP: Angel 60086 LP: Pearl GEMM 153

JOHAN WAGENAAR (1862-1941)

The Taming of the Shrew, overture

Date not confirmed	Concertgebouw Orchestra	LP: Philips 114 026L Recorded for the series Five Centuries of Dutch Music

RICHARD WAGNER (1813-1883)

A Faust Overture

Cleveland December 1965	CO	LP: Columbia (USA) ML 6284/MS 6884/ D3M 32317 LP: CBS 61263 CD: Sony M2YK 46466
Amsterdam November 1966	Concertgebouw Orchestra	CD: Music and Arts CD 291

Der fliegende Holländer, overture

New York January 1954	NYPSO	LP: Columbia (USA) ML 4918/AL 55/ Y3 35231
Cleveland December 1965	CO	LP: Columbia (USA) ML 6284/MS 6884/ D3M 32317 LP: Columbia CX 5277/SAX 5277 LP: CBS 61263 CD: Sony MYK 42597/M2YK 46466 Also issued on an unnumbered promotional LP

Götterdämmerung, Dawn and Siegfried's Rhine Journey

Cleveland November 1956	CO	LP: Epic LC 3321
Cleveland October 1968	CO	LP: Columbia (USA) MS 7291/D3M 32317 LP: CBS 61114 CD: Sony MYK 44769/M2YK 46466/SBK 48175

Götterdämmerung, Siegfried's Funeral March

Cleveland November 1956	CO	LP: Epic LC 3321
Cleveland October 1968	CO	LP: Columbia (USA) MS 7291/D3M 32317 LP: CBS 61114 CD: Sony MYK 44769/M2YK 46466/SBK 48175

Lohengrin, prelude

Cleveland December 1965	CO	LP: Columbia (USA) ML 6284/MS 6884/ D3M 32317 LP: Columbia CX 5277/SAX 5277 LP: CBS 61263 CD: Sony M2YK 46466

Lohengrin, excerpt (In fernem Land)

Berlin December 1926	Staatskapelle Talén	78: Odeon O-6576 LP: Preiser LV 157

Die Meistersinger von Nürnberg

New York February 1945	Metropolitan Opera Orchestra & Chorus Steber, Thorborg, Kullmann, Garris, Janssen, List, Pechner	Unpublished Met broadcast
New York December 1945	Metropolitan Opera Orchestra & Chorus Steber, Thorborg, Kullmann, Garris, Gynrod, List, Pechner	Unpublished Met broadcast

Die Meistersinger von Nürnberg, overture

London October 1938	LPO	78: HMV C 2809
New York January 1954	NYPSO	LP: Columbia (USA) AL 55/ML 4918/ Y3 35231
Cleveland January 1962	CO	LP: Epic LC 3845/BC 1245 LP: Columbia (USA) ML 6371/MS 6971/ MS 7511/SOG 5/MGP 13/D3M 32317 LP: Columbia 33CX 1867-1868/CX 5277/ SAX 2512-2513/SAX 5277 LP: CBS 61263/30008 CD: Sony MLK 39438/MYK 42597/ M2YK 46466/SBK 48175

Die Meistersinger von Nürnberg, excerpt (Am stillen Herd)

Berlin November 1926	Staatskapelle Oehmann	78: Odeon O-7530/O-8702 78: Parlophone P 9030/E 10552 LP: Preiser LV 181
Berlin December 1926	Staatskapelle Talén	78: Odeon O-6576 LP: Preiser LV 157

Die Meistersinger von Nürnberg, excerpt (Morgenlich leuchtend)

Berlin November 1926	Staatskapelle Oehmann	78: Odeon O-7530 78: Parlophone E 10552/P 9030 LP: Preiser LV 181

Das Rheingold, Entry of the Gods

Cleveland October 1968	CO	LP: Columbia (USA) MS 7291/D3M 32317 LP: CBS 61114 CD: Sony MYK 44769/M2YK 46466/SBK 48175

Rienzi, overture

New York January 1954	NYPSO	LP: Columbia (USA) AL 54/ML 4918/ Y3 35231
Cleveland December 1965	CO	LP: Columbia (USA) ML 6284/MS 6884/ D3M 32317 LP: Columbia CX 5277/SAX 5277 LP: CBS 61263 CD: Sony M2YK 46466 <u>Excerpt</u> LP: Columbia (USA) SOG 4

Siegfried, Forest murmurs

Cleveland November 1956	CO	LP: Epic LC 3321
Cleveland October 1968	CO	LP: Columbia (USA) MS 7291/D3M 32317 LP: CBS 61114 CD: Sony MYK 44769/M2YK 46466/SBK 48175

Siegfried Idyll

Cleveland September 1969	CO	CD: Cleveland Orchestra TCO93-75

Tannhäuser

New York December 1942	Metropolitan Opera Orchestra & Chorus Traubel, Thorborg, Melchior, Garris, Janssen, Kipnis	LP: Raritas OPR 400 LP: Melodram MEL 306 CD: Music and Arts CD 664 CD: As-Disc AS 1101-1103 CD: Radio Years RY 26-28 <u>Excerpts from Acts 2 and 3</u> LP: Ed Smith EJS 544
New York January 1954	Metropolitan Opera Orchestra & Chorus Harshaw, Varnay, Vinay, Sullivan, London, Hines	Unpublished Met broadcast

Tannhäuser, overture (Dresden version)

New York January 1954	NYPSO	45: Philips ABE 10197 LP: Columbia (USA) AL 55/ML 4918/Y3 35231
Cleveland January 1962	CO	LP: Epic LC 3845/BC 1245 LP: Columbia (USA) ML 6371/MS 6971/ D3M 32317 LP: Columbia 33CX 1689/SAX 2510 CD: Sony MYK 42597/M2YK 46466

Tristan und Isolde, Prelude and Liebestod

Cleveland
January 1962
	CO	LP: Epic LC 3845/BC 1245
		LP: Columbia (USA) ML 6371/MS 6971/
		     D3M 32317
		LP: Columbia 33CX 1867-1868/
		     SAX 2512-2513
		LP: CBS 77235
		CD: Sony MYK 42597/M2YK 46466/SBK 48175
		<u>Liebestod only</u>
		LP: Columbia (USA) SPM 1/SPS 1

Die Walküre

New York December 1944	Metropolitan Opera Orchestra Traubel, Bampton, Thorborg, Melchior, Janssen, Kipnis	Unpublished Met broadcast

Die Walküre, Ride of the Valkyries

Cleveland November 1956	CO	LP: Epic LC 3321
Cleveland October 1968	CO	LP: Columbia (USA) MS 7291/MS 7353/ D3M 32317 LP: CBS 61114 CD: Sony MYK 44769/M2YK 46466/SBK 48175

Die Walküre, Magic Fire music

Cleveland November 1956	CO	LP: Epic LC 3321
Cleveland October 1968	CO	LP: Columbia (USA) MS 7291/D3M 32317 LP: CBS 61114 CD: Sony MYK 44769/M2YK 46466

WILLIAM WALTON (1902-1983)

Symphony No 2

Cleveland March 1961	CO	LP: Epic LC 3812/BC 1149 LP: Columbia ML 6136/MS 6736/Y 33519 LP: Columbia 33CX 1816/SAX 2459 LP: CBS 61087 CD: Sony MPK 46732/SBK 62753

Variations on a theme by Hindemith

Cleveland October 1964	CO	LP: Columbia (USA) ML 6136/MS 6736/ Y 33519 LP: Columbia 33CX 1935/SAX 2576 LP: CBS 61087 CD: Sony MPK 46732/SBK 53258/SBK 62753

Partita for orchestra

Cleveland January 1959	CO	LP: Epic LC 3568/BC 1024 LP: Columbia 33CX 1816/SAX 2459 LP: CBS 61264 CD: Sony MPK 46732/SBK 62753 <u>Excerpt</u> LP: Epic BC 1/PLC 1/PBC 1

CARL MARIA VON WEBER (1786-1826)

Konzertstück for piano and orchestra

Cleveland January 1952	CO Casadesus	LP: Columbia ML 4588/Y 35216 LP: Philips ABR 4049/A01624R CD: Sony MYK 45508 Excerpt on an unnumbered Columbia promotional LP

Der Freischütz, overture

New York January 1952	NYPSO	45: Columbia (USA) AL 19 45: Philips CFE 15057 LP: Columbia (USA) GB 1/Y3 35231
Blossom August 1969	CO	LP: Telarc TSP 4008

Oberon, overture

Berlin 1927	Staatskapelle	78: Homochord 4-9010 Orchestra described as Berlin SO
London 1935-1936	LPO	78: HMV C 2826 78: HMV (France) L 1007
New York January 1952	NYPSO	45: Philips CFE 15057 LP: Columbia (USA) AAL 19/GB 1/Y3 35231
Cleveland January 1963	CO	LP: Epic LC 3859/BC 1259 LP: Columbia 33CX 1880/SAX 2524 LP: CBS 61019
Tokyo May 1970	CO	Unpublished radio broadcast One of Szell's last public appearances

MISCELLANEOUS & TRADITIONAL

Deck the Halls with Boughs of Holly

Cleveland   CO   LP: Columbia (USA) MS 7322/CSS 547/C10967
May 1966   LP: CBS 30046
                                     CD: Sony MK 39093

Joy to the World

Cleveland   CO   LP: Columbia (USA) MS 7322
May 1966   LP: CBS 30046
                                     CD: Sony MK 39093

Patapan

Cleveland   CO   LP: Columbia (USA) CSS 547
May 1966

Discographies

Teachers and pupils
Schwarzkopf / Ivogün / Cebotari /
Seinemeyer / Welitsch / Streich / Berger
7 separate discographies, 400 pages

The post-war German tradition
Kempe / Keilberth / Sawallisch / Kubelik /
Cluytens
5 separate discographies, 300 pages

**Mid-century conductors
and More Viennese singers**
Böhm / De Sabata / Knappertsbusch / Serafin /
Krauss / Dermota / Rysanek / Wächter /
Reining / Kunz
10 separate discographies, 420 pages

Leopold Stokowski
Discography and concert register, 300 pages

Tenors in a lyric tradition
Fritz Wunderlich / Walther Ludwig /
Peter Anders
3 separate discographies, 350 pages

Makers of the Philharmonia
Galliera / Susskind / Kletzki / Malko / Matacic /
Dobrowen / Kurtz / Fistoulari
8 separate discographies, 300 pages

A notable quartet
Janowitz / Ludwig / Gedda / Fischer-Dieskau
4 separate discographies, 600 pages

Hungarians in exile
Reiner / Dorati / Szell
3 separate discographies, 300 pages

The art of the diva
Muzio / Callas / Olivero
3 separate discographies, 225 pages

The lyric baritone
Reinmar / Hüsch / Metternich / Uhde /
Wächter
5 separate discographies, 225 pages

Price £22 per volume (£28 outside UK)
*Special offer any 3 volumes for
£55 (£75 outside UK)*
Postage included
Order from: John Hunt, Flat 6,
37 Chester Way, London SE11 4UR

Credits

Valuable help with the supply of
information or illustration material
for these discographies came from:

John Ardoin, Dallas
Mike Ashman, Ware
Ray Burford, Sony Classical London
Richard Chlupaty, London
Clifford Elkin, Glasgow
Bill Flowers, London
Michael Gray, Alexandria VA
Syd Gray, Hove
Paul Gunther, Minnesota Orchestra
Bill Holland, Polygram London
Ken Jagger, EMI Classics London
Roderick Krüsemann, Amsterdam
Luis Luna, Berlin
Alan Newcombe, DG Hamburg
John Raymon, London
Phil Rees, Pewsey
Malcolm Walker, Harrow

Music and Books published by Travis & Emery Music Bookshop:

Mellers, Wilfrid: Caliban Reborn - Renewal in Twentieth Century Music
Mellers, Wilfrid: François Couperin and the French Classical Tradition
Mellers, Wilfrid: Harmonious Meeting
Mellers, Wilfrid: Le Jardin Retrouvé, The Music of Frederic Mompou
Mellers, Wilfrid: Music and Society, England and the European Tradition
Mellers, Wilfrid: Music in a New Found Land: ... ... American Music
Mellers, Wilfrid: Romanticism and the Twentieth Century (from 1800)
Mellers, Wilfrid: The Masks of Orpheus: ...... the Story of European Music.
Mellers, Wilfrid: The Sonata Principle (from c. 1750)
Mellers, Wilfrid: Vaughan Williams and the Vision of Albion
Panchianio, Cattuffio: Rutzvanscad Il Giovine
Pearce, Charles: Sims Reeves, Fifty Years of Music in England.
Playford, John: An Introduction to the Skill of Musick.
Purcell, Henry et al: Harmonia Sacra ... The First Book, (1726)
Purcell, Henry et al: Harmonia Sacra ... Book II (1726)
Quantz, Johann: Versuch einer Anweisung die Flöte traversiere zu spielen.
Rameau, Jean-Philippe: Code de Musique Pratique, ou Methodes.
Rastall, Richard: The Notation of Western Music.
Rimbault, Edward: The Pianoforte, Its Origins, Progress, and Construction.
Rousseau, Jean Jacques: Dictionnaire de Musique
Rubinstein, Anton : Guide to the proper use of the Pianoforte Pedals.
Sainsbury, John S.: Dictionary of Musicians. Vol. 1. (1825). 2 vols.
Simpson, Christopher: A Compendium of Practical Musick in Five Parts
Spohr, Louis: Autobiography
Spohr, Louis: Grand Violin School
Tans'ur, William: A New Musical Grammar; or The Harmonical Spectator
Terry, Charles Sanford: Four-Part Chorals of J.S. Bach. (German & English)
Terry, Charles Sanford: Joh. Seb. Bach, Cantata Texts, Sacred and Secular.
Terry, Charles Sanford: The Origins of the Family of Bach Musicians.
Tosi, Pierfrancesco: Opinioni de' Cantori Antichi, e Moderni
Van der Straeten, Edmund: History of the Violoncello, The Viol da Gamba ...
Van der Straeten, Edmund: History of the Violin, Its Ancestors... (2 vols.)
Walther, J. G.: Musicalisches Lexikon ober Musicalische Bibliothec

Travis & Emery Music Bookshop
17 Cecil Court, London, WC2N 4EZ, United Kingdom.
Tel. (+44) 20 7240 2129

© Travis & Emery 2009

Music and Books published by Travis & Emery Music Bookshop:
Anon.: Hymnarium Sarisburiense, cum Rubricis et Notis Musicis.
Agricola, Johann Friedrich from Tosi: Anleitung zur Singkunst.
Bach, C.P.E.: edited W. Emery: Nekrolog or Obituary Notice of J.S. Bach.
Bateson, Naomi Judith: Alcock of Salisbury
Bathe, William: A Briefe Introduction to the Skill of Song
Bax, Arnold: Symphony #5, Arranged for Piano Four Hands by Walter Emery
Burney, Charles: The Present State of Music in France and Italy
Burney, Charles: The Present State of Music in Germany, The Netherlands ...
Burney, Charles: An Account of the Musical Performances ... Handel
Burney, Karl: Nachricht von Georg Friedrich Handel's Lebensumstanden.
Cobbett, W.W.: Cobbett's Cyclopedic Survey of Chamber Music. (2 vols.)
Corrette, Michel: Le Maitre de Clavecin
Crimp, Bryan: Dear Mr. Rosenthal ... Dear Mr. Gaisberg ...
Crimp, Bryan: Solo: The Biography of Solomon
d'Indy, Vincent: Beethoven: Biographie Critique
d'Indy, Vincent: Beethoven: A Critical Biography
d'Indy, Vincent: César Franck (in French)
Frescobaldi, Girolamo: D'Arie Musicali per Cantarsi. Primo & Secondo Libro.
Geminiani, Francesco: The Art of Playing the Violin.
Handel; Purcell; Boyce; Geene et al: Calliope or English Harmony: Volume First.
Hawkins, John: A General History of the Science and Practice of Music (5 vols.)
Herbert-Caesari, Edgar: The Science and Sensations of Vocal Tone
Herbert-Caesari, Edgar: Vocal Truth
Hopkins and Rimboult: The Organ. Its History and Construction.
Hunt, John: Adam to Webern: the recordings of von Karajan
Isaacs, Lewis: Hänsel and Gretel. A Guide to Humperdinck's Opera.
Isaacs, Lewis: Königskinder (Royal Children) A Guide to Humperdinck's Opera.
Lacassagne, M. l'Abbé Joseph : Traité Général des élémens du Chant.
Lascelles (née Catley), Anne: The Life of Miss Anne Catley.
Mainwaring, John: Memoirs of the Life of the Late George Frederic Handel
Malcolm, Alexander: A Treaty of Music: Speculative, Practical and Historical
Marx, Adolph Bernhard: Die Kunst des Gesanges, Theoretisch-Practisch
May, Florence: The Life of Brahms
Mellers, Wilfrid: Angels of the Night: Popular Female Singers of Our Time
Mellers, Wilfrid: Bach and the Dance of God
Mellers, Wilfrid: Beethoven and the Voice of God

Travis & Emery Music Bookshop
17 Cecil Court, London, WC2N 4EZ, United Kingdom.
Tel. (+44) 20 7240 2129

1999: 978-1-901395-97-6: The Furtwaengler Sound Sixth Edition: Discography and Concert Listing.
1999: 978-1-901395-98-3: The Great Dictators: 3 Discographies: Evgeny Mravinsky, Artur Rodzinski, Sergiu Celibidache.
1999: 978-1-901395-99-0: Sviatoslav Richter: Pianist of the Century: Discography.
2000: 978-1-901395-04-4: Philharmonic Autocrat 1: Discography of: Herbert Von Karajan [Third Edition].
2000: 978-1-901395-05-1: Wiener Philharmoniker 1 - Vienna Philharmonic and Vienna State Opera Orchestras: Discography Part 1 1905-1954.
2000: 978-1-901395-06-8: Wiener Philharmoniker 2 - Vienna Philharmonic and Vienna State Opera Orchestras: Discography Part 2 1954-1989.
2001; 978-1-901395-07-5: Gramophone Stalwarts: 3 Separate Discographies: Bruno Walter, Erich Leinsdorf, Georg Solti.
2001: 978-1-901395-08-2: Singers of the Third Reich: 5 Discographies: Helge Roswaenge, Tiana Lemnitz, Franz Voelker, Maria Mueller, Max Lorenz.
2001: 978-1-901395-09-9: Philharmonic Autocrat 2: Concert Register of Herbert Von Karajan Second Edition.
2002: 978-1-901395-10-5: Sächsische Staatskapelle Dresden: Complete Discography.
2002: 978-1-901395-11-2: Carlo Maria Giulini: Discography and Concert Register.
2002: 978-1-901395-12-9: Pianists For The Connoisseur: 6 Discographies: Arturo Benedetti Michelangeli, Alfred Cortot, Alexis Weissenberg, Clifford Curzon, Solomon, Elly Ney.
2003: 978-1-901395-14-3: Singers on the Yellow Label: 7 Discographies: Maria Stader, Elfriede Troetschel, Annelies Kupper, Wolfgang Windgassen, Ernst Haefliger, Josef Greindl, Kim Borg.
2003: 978-1-901395-15-0: A Gallic Trio: 3 Discographies: Charles Muench, Paul Paray, Pierre Monteux.
2004: 978-1-901395-16-7: Antal Dorati 1906-1988: Discography and Concert Register.
2004: 978-1-901395-17-4: Columbia 33CX Label Discography.
2004: 978-1-901395-18-1: Great Violinists: 3 Discographies: David Oistrakh, Wolfgang Schneiderhan, Arthur Grumiaux.
2006: 978-1-901395-19-8: Leopold Stokowski: Second Edition of the Discography.
2006: 978-1-901395-20-4: Wagner Im Festspielhaus: Discography of the Bayreuth Festival.
2006: 978-1-901395-21-1: Her Master's Voice: Concert Register and Discography of Dame Elisabeth Schwarzkopf [Third Edition].
2007: 978-1-901395-22-8: Hans Knappertsbusch: Kna: Concert Register and Discography of Hans Knappertsbusch, 1888-1965. Second Edition.
2008: 978-1-901395-23-5: Philips Minigroove: Second Extended Version of the European Discography.
2009: 978-1-901395--24-2: American Classics: The Discographies of Leonard Bernstein and Eugene Ormandy.

Discography by Stephen J. Pettitt, edited by John Hunt:
1987: 978-1-906857-16-5: Philharmonia Orchestra: Complete Discography 1945-1987

Available from: Travis & Emery at 17 Cecil Court, London, UK.
(+44) 20 7 240 2129. email on sales@travis-and-emery.com .

© Travis & Emery 2009

Discographies by Travis & Emery:

Discographies by John Hunt.

1987: 978-1-906857-14-1: From Adam to Webern: the Recordings of von Karajan.
1991: 978-0-951026-83-0: 3 Italian Conductors and 7 Viennese Sopranos: 10 Discographies: Arturo Toscanini, Guido Cantelli, Carlo Maria Giulini, Elisabeth Schwarzkopf, Irmgard Seefried, Elisabeth Gruemmer, Sena Jurinac, Hilde Gueden, Lisa Della Casa, Rita Streich.
1992: 978-0-951026-85-4: Mid-Century Conductors and More Viennese Singers: 10 Discographies: Karl Boehm, Victor De Sabata, Hans Knappertsbusch, Tullio Serafin, Clemens Krauss, Anton Dermota, Leonie Rysanek, Eberhard Waechter, Maria Reining, Erich Kunz.
1993: 978-0-951026-87-8: More 20th Century Conductors: 7 Discographies: Eugen Jochum, Ferenc Fricsay, Carl Schuricht, Felix Weingartner, Josef Krips, Otto Klemperer, Erich Kleiber.
1994: 978-0-951026-88-5: Giants of the Keyboard: 6 Discographies: Wilhelm Kempff, Walter Gieseking, Edwin Fischer, Clara Haskil, Wilhelm Backhaus, Artur Schnabel.
1994: 978-0-951026-89-2: Six Wagnerian Sopranos: 6 Discographies: Frieda Leider, Kirsten Flagstad, Astrid Varnay, Martha Moedl, Birgit Nilsson, Gwyneth Jones.
1995: 978-0-952582-70-0: Musical Knights: 6 Discographies: Henry Wood, Thomas Beecham, Adrian Boult, John Barbirolli, Reginald Goodall, Malcolm Sargent.
1995: 978-0-952582-71-7: A Notable Quartet: 4 Discographies: Gundula Janowitz, Christa Ludwig, Nicolai Gedda, Dietrich Fischer-Dieskau.
1996: 978-0-952582-72-4: The Post-War German Tradition: 5 Discographies: Rudolf Kempe, Joseph Keilberth, Wolfgang Sawallisch, Rafael Kubelik, Andre Cluytens.
1996: 978-0-952582-73-1: Teachers and Pupils: 7 Discographies: Elisabeth Schwarzkopf, Maria Ivoguen, Maria Cebotari, Meta Seinemeyer, Ljuba Welitsch, Rita Streich, Erna Berger.
1996: 978-0-952582-77-9: Tenors in a Lyric Tradition: 3 Discographies: Peter Anders, Walther Ludwig, Fritz Wunderlich.
1997: 978-0-952582-78-6: The Lyric Baritone: 5 Discographies: Hans Reinmar, Gerhard Huesch, Josef Metternich, Hermann Uhde, Eberhard Waechter.
1997: 978-0-952582-79-3: Hungarians in Exile: 3 Discographies: Fritz Reiner, Antal Dorati, George Szell.
1997: 978-1-901395-00-6: The Art of the Diva: 3 Discographies: Claudia Muzio, Maria Callas, Magda Olivero.
1997: 978-1-901395-01-3: Metropolitan Sopranos: 4 Discographies: Rosa Ponselle, Eleanor Steber, Zinka Milanov, Leontyne Price.
1997: 978-1-901395-02-0: Back From The Shadows: 4 Discographies: Willem Mengelberg, Dimitri Mitropoulos, Hermann Abendroth, Eduard Van Beinum.
1997: 978-1-901395-03-7: More Musical Knights: 4 Discographies: Hamilton Harty, Charles Mackerras, Simon Rattle, John Pritchard.
1998: 978-1-901395-94-5: Conductors On The Yellow Label: 8 Discographies: Fritz Lehmann, Ferdinand Leitner, Ferenc Fricsay, Eugen Jochum, Leopold Ludwig, Artur Rother, Franz Konwitschny, Igor Markevitch.
1998: 978-1-901395-95-2: More Giants of the Keyboard: 5 Discographies: Claudio Arrau, Gyorgy Cziffra, Vladimir Horowitz, Dinu Lipatti, Artur Rubinstein.
1998: 978-1-901395-96-9: Mezzo and Contraltos: 5 Discographies: Janet Baker, Margarete Klose, Kathleen Ferrier, Giulietta Simionato, Elisabeth Hoengen.

www.ingramcontent.com/pod-product-compliance
Lightning Source LLC
Chambersburg PA
CBHW070936230426
43666CB00011B/2456